MARIA FYFE was the only female Labour MF
elected in 1987. She was an MP for 14 yea
time, she campaigned for poverty-stricken ar
stepping down in 2001. She has always bee
paigning for the equal representation of wo

*The book she has written is a gem. It zips along on a skilful mix of
genuinely funny anecdotes, telling vignettes and perceptive political
analysis. It serves future historians well too, for it will serve as a
necessary counterbalance to the leadership-centric books and
diaries which have followed the Tony Blair-Peter Mandelson years.
But it has a more immediate attraction than that. The Nats gets a
good pre-referendum kicking from Oor Maria. Recalling that the
Nats used to call the Scots Labour MPs 'the feeble fifty,' she points
out the SNP were nowhere to be seen the night a last ditch Tory
filibuster failed to halt the Minimum Wage Bill.*
Alasdair Buchan, TRIBUNE

*A feisty, irrepressible, red flag idealist... the only woman
Scottish MP in a gang of fifty. She could not be bullied,
bamboozled or bribed. She did not fit comfortably into
the Procrustean bed of a biddable Blair babe.*
Paul Flynn, THE HOUSE MAGAZINE

A Problem Like Maria

A woman's eye view of life as an MP

MARIA FYFE

Luath Press Limited
EDINBURGH
www.luath.co.uk

First published 2014

ISBN: 978-1-910021-04-0

The publishers acknowledge the support of

ALBA | CHRUTHACHAIL

towards the publication of this volume.

The paper used in this book is recyclable. It is made from
low chlorine pulps produced in a low energy, low emissions manner
from renewable forests.

Printed and bound by
Bell & Bain Ltd., Glasgow

Typeset in 11 point Sabon
by 3btype.com

For my sons, Stephen and Chris

Acknowledgements

My thanks to Michael Palmer and David Hendry, and the staff at Gartnavel Hospital, without whom I would not have been around to write this book.

Also Janet Andrews, Tom Brown, Catriona Burness, Malcolm Burns, Jim Cassidy, Anna Dyer, Liz Kristiansen, Jim Mearns and my brother, Joe O'Neill, for their useful comments, suggestions and encouragement.

I have tried my utmost to avoid errors: if any are present, they are mine and mine alone, and none the fault of those mentioned above. Any factual corrections will be welcomed, especially since a significant aim of writing this book was to set the record straight on that period in our UK Parliament.

Another aim was to encourage interest in a political life when widespread cynicism discourages good people from thinking about it. My third and final aim was to reveal the funny side of a Parliamentary career. Every walk of life has its jokes at its own expense and its absurdities, and Parliament could often be the best show in town.

Contents

Chronology

1987   General Election. Share of votes in Scotland: Labour 42.38 per cent, Conservative 24.03, Alliance 19.2 per cent, SNP 14.04 per cent, Others 0.3 per cent. First female MP in Glasgow Maryhill. 7,861 out of work in Maryhill, fifth highest in the country.
Poll Tax for England and Wales debated in Commons.

1988   January: Fight Alton Bill rally in Glasgow.
March: four months after start of Intifada against Israeli occupation, delegation sent to West Bank and Gaza.
Nigel Lawson's budget reducing corporation tax for small businesses introduced.
April: Bill against Blacklisting introduced.
May: Glasgow May Day Rally.
24 May: Section 28 enacted.
May: visit to Nicaragua, invited by Sandinista women.
July: Campaign for a Scottish Assembly publishes 'Claim of Right for Scotland'.
September: Tribune Rally at Labour Party Conference in Blackpool.
Conference votes to have a woman on every parliamentary shortlist.
10 November: Glasgow Govan by-election. Jim Sillars overturns 19,500 Labour majority.
21 November: Committees of 100 against Poll Tax launched.
24 November: first meeting of the Anti-Blacklisting Campaign.

1989   3 March: Scottish Constitutional Convention meets for first time. Canon Kenyon Wright makes famous 'We say Yes' speech.
Numerous calls for gender balance in future Scottish Assembly.
14 April: SCC working group on women's issues set up.
7 June: John Smith, Shadow Chancellor of Exchequer, sings theme from *Neighbours*, mocking Thatcher/Lawson disagreement on Exchange Rate Mechanism.
9 June: Nigel Lawson, Chancellor of Exchequer, resigns.
18 June: Women's Claim of Right published.

September: appointed front bench spokesperson on women by Neil Kinnock.

December: STUC Women's Committee publish 'Equal Voice for Women'. Call for 50:50 from Day One of Scottish Assembly.

1990   10 February: British-Irish Parliamentary Body founded.

March: riot in London against Poll Tax.

March: Labour Scottish Conference at Dunoon supports equal male/female outcome for seats in Scottish Assembly.

April: Human Fertilisation and Embryology Bill.

August: Saddam Hussein invades Kuwait.

22 November: Margaret Thatcher stands down.

1991   15 January: vote in Commons to support war in Iraq (Maria resigns from front bench).

17 January: Allied commanders launch military offensive.

21 January: John Cryer tables amendment calling for peaceful settlement, but is not selected by the Speaker.

9 February: Labour Party Scottish Executive calls for a ceasefire.

15 February: Iraqi Revolutionary Council sues for peace, Britain and America reject proposals.

Harry Ewing, MP for Falkirk East, co-chairs with Maria new organisation, 'Scottish Labour Against War in the Gulf.'

March: Labour Party Scottish Conference welcomes end of hostilities and liberation of Kuwait, calls for democracy in Kuwait, regrets action before sanctions exhausted.

September, Paul Foot in Mirror tells about Economic League's blacklisting.

Elected convener of Scottish Group of Labour MPs.

1992   April: Poll Tax abolished by John Major's Government, Council Tax substituted.

April: General Election. Results in Scotland: Labour 39 per cent, Conservative 25.6 per cent, Liberal Democrat 13.1 per cent, SNP 21.5 per cent, Others 0.8 per cent.

SNP says its top political priority is destruction of Labour Party. Wins three seats.

27 April: Betty Boothroyd elected Speaker – first woman.

July: John Smith elected Labour leader with 91 per cent support.

10 July: 'away day' meeting of Scottish Group of Labour MPs discusses way forward.

Scotland United makes common cause with SNP.

July: appointed to Scottish front bench.

16 September: Black Wednesday. Britain forced to withdraw Sterling from European Exchange Rate Mechanism.

Interest rates up to 13 per cent.

November: Tory Government abolishes Wages Councils.

December: NHS Trusts to run Scottish hospitals announced to media but not Parliament.

Only three GPs in Glasgow choose to be fund-holding.

1993   Government announces plans to privatise water. Ten thousand at Labour/STUC rally.

August: White Paper for Children's Bill (Scotland) published, 25 years since last legislation for children.

September: Labour Conference decides 50 per cent of selection conferences for new candidates in safe and marginal seats will have women-only shortlists. Still only three Labour women MPs in Scotland out of 49.

Scottish Homes survey reveals 95,000 houses below tolerable standard. Glasgow Director of Public Health reports half of households with children have dampness and condensation.

1994   *Tribune* proclaims end of the Economic League.

March: Strathclyde Regional Council holds referendum on water privatisation. 70 per cent turnout, 97 per cent against. Government abandons plan.

12 May: John Smith dies.

October: Tony Blair makes his Clause 4 speech at Labour Conference. Jim Mearns, Maryhill delegate, calls for card vote.

November: given Scottish Education brief.

1995   March, Scottish Labour Conference approves Report, 'A Parliament for Scotland', calls for equal representation of men and women.

April: Government admits Poll Tax in Scotland cost £1.5 billion.

29 April: Special Conference of Labour Party on Clause 4.

October, resigned from front bench.

November: formal contract between Liberal Democrats and Labour on achieving gender equality in Scottish Parliament.
30 November: Scottish Constitutional Convention publishes 'Scotland's Parliament: Scotland's Right'.

1996   February: William Duff, dentist, struck off. Later pleads guilty to fraud.
13 March: Dunblane massacre. Gunman kills 16 children and their class teacher.
September: TUC Conference. Stephen Byers says Labour planning to dump Unions. Neither Cabinet nor National Policy Forum has discussed it.
Kim Howells calls for humanely getting rid of word 'Socialism'.
November: elected chair of Labour delegation to Council of Europe.
Elected chair of Scottish all-party group on children.

1997   May: New Labour wins General Election with over 13,500,000 votes and 179 seat majority. 418 Labour MPs, of which 101 are women. There are now eight Labour women MPs in Scotland.
In Maryhill, Labour wins 19,301 votes, SNP second with 5,037.
Scottish parties' support: Labour 45.6 per cent, Liberal Democrat 13.0 per cent, SNP 22.1 per cent, Conservative 17.5 per cent, Others 2.0 per cent.
Donald Dewar becomes Secretary of State for Scotland.
25 June: Tony Blair proposes two questions on Scottish Parliament, the second one on tax varying powers.
July: White Paper on Scotland's Parliament published.
Backbench Labour committee on International Development created, self as convener.
8 July: debate on Glasgow housing – result £26 million to refurbish city housing.
Gordon Brown pays off £900 million Glasgow housing debt. Glasgow Housing Association formed.
11 September: Referendum on Scottish Parliament. Both questions win handsomely.
11 December: Lone Parent Benefit cut. Forty-seven Labour MPs vote against, 100 abstain.
17 December: Scotland Bill presented to House of Commons.

1998 Scotland Act: first line, 'There shall be a Scottish Parliament'.
January: Labour women's caucus set up in Commons and Lords.
National Minimum Wage Act passed.
October: Augusto Pinochet in London Clinic.
24 November: Queen's Speech: Bill to remove right of hereditary peers to sit and Vote in House of Lords.

1999 25 January: vote on equal age of consent defeated.
30 March: Labour Government Employment Relations Bill makes blacklisting illegal.
April: Child Benefit for first child up 20 per cent.
12 April: Friends of Ireland, Friends of Good Friday Agreement launched.
Agreed Ireland Forum, elected Secretary.
First elections to Scottish Parliament. Labour 28 men, 28 women. Only party to deliver on 50:50. Women form 37.2 per cent of total elected.
12 May: Scottish Parliament meets for first time.
2 December: Good Friday Agreement came into force.

2000 Mike Tyson boxing match in Glasgow.
Clare Short publishes White Paper on World Poverty.
11 October: Donald Dewar dies.
23 October: Betty Boothroyd resigns as MP, Michael Martin elected Speaker.
21 December: Maryhill man, Ian Gordon, cleared of murder conviction following five-year campaign.

2001 January: after long campaign, VAT on feminine hygiene reduced from 17.5 per cent to five per cent.
March: International Development Bill, establishes in legislation reduction of poverty as aim of UK development assistance.
Unemployment in Scotland lowest since 1976, highest employment since 1960. Long-term unemployment down by 60 per cent since 1997.
May: General Election. Scottish results: Labour 43.9 per cent, SNP 20.1 per cent, Liberal Democrat 16.4 per cent, Conservative 15.6 per cent, Scottish Socialists 3.1 per cent.
11 September: Twin Towers attacked.
7 October: Afghan War declared.

2003   15 February: Marches against war in Iraq.
        26 February: 122 Labour backbenchers vote against support for
        USA again in Iraq.
        17 March: Robin Cook resigns.
        April: Tax Credits introduced.

2007   May: SNP form minority Government with Conservative support
        in Scottish Parliament.
        30 June: attack on Glasgow Airport foiled by John Smeaton and
        others.

2008   Global economic crisis. National debt less than inherited from
        John Major in 1997.

2010   Regulations on blacklisting added by Gordon Brown Govern-
        ment.

2011   SNP forms majority Government in Scottish Parliament. Women
        MSPs now down to 34.8 per cent.
        July onwards: hacking scandal begins to be exposed.
        December: Johann Lamont elected first Leader of Labour Party in
        Scotland.

2013   April: 'Bedroom Tax' hits.
        8 April: Margaret Thatcher dies.

CHAPTER ONE

I Could Have Danced All Night

1987

IN THE 1987 GENERAL ELECTION only one female Labour MP was elected in Scotland. Me. It seems hard to believe now, but back then female MPs were rare creatures indeed. Of course everyone knew there was a Queen Bee at Westminster, frequently spotted in her Downing Street habitat. If there were precious few other women in Parliament, that didn't matter a jot – to many, across all political parties. *Women belonged in the home, not the House. Let the best man win.* This opinion was widely held by the frequent fliers to Westminster, where they gathered together and drank at their watering holes. How could their favourite son succeed them if uppity women could have a go?

Now here I was, newly elected for Glasgow Maryhill, one of Labour's safest seats.

That day, Britain elected a record number of women MPs, a 78 per cent increase over the previous General Election in 1983. That meant a total of 41, compared to 23 at the previous election. The 41 consisted of 21 Labour, 17 Conservative, two Liberal-SDP Alliance and one Scottish Nationalist. Despite that upswing, women still only accounted for 6.3 per cent of total MPs. Scotland was even worse, with only 4.16 per cent. That amounted to three women out of a total 72 MPs: Margaret Ewing for the Scottish Nationalists, Ray Michie for the Alliance and myself. I knew before the election was even called I would be the only Labour woman in Scotland, because the few other female party members who had been selected to fight a seat were doing so in constituencies they were highly unlikely to win. I vowed I would do everything in my power to get more Labour women into Westminster.

In the run up to the election, *The Scotsman* ran brief commentaries on all the seats. For my own constituency it said:

> Glasgow Maryhill has returned a Labour MP in every General Election since the Second World War, and it would probably need a comparable cataclysm to unsettle political allegiance to any significant degree in this Socialist citadel.

Amen to that. So why couldn't my sisters enjoy their share when it came to winning similarly committed constituencies? I will never forget the tiny old lady, who looked about 90 but had a firm step, approaching me outside a polling station in 1987 to tell me what a great pleasure it was to be able to vote for a woman for the first time in her life.

For the first time in *my* life I had found myself under attack in the press. Previous media attention had, if anything, been complimentary about my activities as a councillor. Now the *News of the World* was claiming that I opposed the expulsion of Militant Tendency supporters from the Labour Party, when in fact I was entirely hostile to their activities and aims. They were using the Labour Party for their own ends, and fellow left wingers who defended them were profoundly mistaken. This was not a point of view I had been shy to express, especially in my years as a Glasgow councillor, fighting Tory cuts as well as seeing off the Trots.

Not that the Murdoch press had it in for me alone. Similar claims were made against Clare Short and Neil Kinnock, of all people – remember his attack on Derek Hatton for the mess he made of Liverpool? – as well as many others. The *Sunday Times* ran a headline, 'Kinnock's Hard Left Nightmare', and listed me along with Tommy McAvoy, who went on to be a senior Labour whip and member of the House of Lords. Scottish Secretary Malcolm Rifkind, not to be outdone by Rupert Murdoch's distortions, disgraced himself when he named eight Scottish Labour candidates, including myself, as 'infected with the same left wing virus as the "Loony Left" in London, and well to the left of those retiring'. I was indeed to the left of my own predecessor, but the excesses of some in the Party in a few of the London boroughs were not for me (although I must put it on record that many of the stories told about them were exaggerated or simply not true).

Going by their future careers, if Tommy, Adam Ingram (Defence Minister), John McFall (Treasury Select Committee Chair), Henry McLeish (First Minister in the Scottish Parliament), and John Reid (arch Blairite and holder of several posts at Secretary of State level) were indeed hard left, how would they describe the rest of us? Another edition had several of us listed as 'Kinnock's 101 Damnations'. Beneath an unflattering picture of each candidate was a description of our views that upset the *Sunday Times*. This went down well with Maryhill Constituency Labour Party. Other Labour candidates jokingly claimed that they were jealous, wondering why they too had not been attacked. Why, they demanded, were they being denied this useful dose of street cred?

While some in the leadership were concerned about such attacks, my own view was that I would start to worry the day the Murdoch press praised me. I have kept a copy of my election address as a keepsake, and I see that I questioned 'why financial skulduggery should earn more than a lifetime's honest work'. Can't have left wing stuff like that, can we?

Though I was the Labour candidate for super-safe Maryhill, I was nervous of letting down the Party in any way. Considering the treatment I had been receiving from Murdoch's minions, I felt anxious when a reporter from *The Sun* phoned to ask me for an interview. I lay awake worrying about what this portended. Was he running some anti-Labour story? Was some scandal about to unfold? I was confident my sons were neither drug addicts nor pushers, neither drink drivers nor hooligans, or advocates of any ultra-left idiocy, so could it be something to do with the local Labour Party? I had no reason to think so... Helen Liddell, now a member of the House of Lords, at that time secretary of the Labour Party in Scotland, had told all of the new candidates to phone her if we had any problems. So I did, and she advised me not to worry.

'Put on your best dress and have some flowers around the house. Hide away your more left wing books in case he notices them. Oh, and have something baking in the oven.'

'But', I protested, 'no-one bakes wearing their best dress. They'll think I'm an idiot.'

'Not at all', said Helen. 'They're men. They won't know any better.'

Nevertheless, I was nervous enough that I asked the reporter to meet me at my campaign rooms, rather than my house. That way my agent, John Gray, would be a witness if I needed one. John himself was a much respected and well known councillor. When the reporter showed up he was all joviality, but I still did not feel reassured. Just at that point, a woman with a problem she wanted me to look into turned up on the doorstep, so John took her into the back room for a cup of tea until I could make myself available. That was my attempt at precaution fallen apart.

I turned reluctantly to the reporter. What he wanted to do, he explained, was a piece contrasting me with Anna McCurley, the well known Tory MP seeking re-election in Renfrewshire. So, what issues did he have in mind, I asked.

'No,' he replied, 'nothing as heavy as that. It's because she's a blonde and you're a brunette.' Ye Gods! My late husband Jim, a reporter himself, had a way with that kind of thing. He once submitted a piece which described the local Fire Master as blonde and petite. When the editor said, 'You can't write that!' Jim replied that the paper described women like that all the time, even when her height and colour of hair had absolutely nothing to do with the story.

The man from *The Sun* took down some personal details while the photographer readied himself. When he pulled a long-stemmed red rose out of a bag and asked me to put it between my teeth, I politely declined. I wasn't about to burst into Carmen's 'Habanera'.

'Then how about in your hair? No?'

'No. Definitely not.'

At least these guys are drawing the line at asking me to do a Page Three, I thought. They seemed to mean well, even if they were reducing politics to a level of triviality I had never before encountered. I suggested cutting the stem and fastening it to my dress, to which they reluctantly agreed. The subsequent piece did neither Anna nor me any harm, but Anna lost her seat to Tommy Graham in that year when Labour won 50 seats in Scotland.

Maryhill Labour Party was not the first to publish a leaflet addressed to women voters – all the parties had done that during the inter-war years, just after the franchise was extended – but it had never been done, as far as I know, in my own years of involvement in politics. In it, I took up issues such as equal pay, elimination of low pay, and much greater provision of nurseries for the under-fives in their own localities. *Cosmopolitan* did something unusual for a woman's magazine until then: it asked readers to identify the three issues that were of most concern to them, then asked all candidates, male and female, where they stood on such matters. I was happy to support married women being taxed as individuals, sufficient money for a national programme of screening for cervical and breast cancer, and better services provided for those least able to look after themselves, thus creating more help for carers. Eventually the first two were won, but carers are still without the level of help they need. We hear of elderly and infirm people who have no-one living with them to help with their daily needs, getting no more than 15 minutes of a paid worker's time. There is no time for conversation, as she hurries on, unpaid for the travelling time between jobs. This is a national scandal, and nothing to boast about.

That year, at the behest of Jo Richardson, our Shadow Minister for Women, Labour promoted a Charter for Women and Work, and undertook to create a Minister for Women in a future Labour Government. The Tories scoffed at such notions. They evidently could not foresee the day when David Cameron would appoint his own Women's Minister, and now national screening for breast cancer is so taken for granted that I doubt that any Chancellor, however cutbacks crazy he is, would dare to end it.

And so, as the weeks went on in the run up to polling day, I went around Maryhill, knocking on as many doors as possible, morning, noon and night. One afternoon, having sent party workers away to help in a marginal seat, I decided to go on my own to The Botany, an area of Maryhill since transformed, but at that time very run down and its tenement flats far from *des res*. It was called The Botany because back when even the theft of a loaf for your starving family could have you deported to Botany Bay, you would start your journey on board a vessel moored nearby on the Forth and Clyde canal. Then you would sail to where the canal met the River Clyde, and transfer to an ocean-going ship bound for Australia.

I rang a doorbell and was invited in. The man who answered went on to tell me how difficult it was finding a job: not an unusual problem in Maryhill at that time. I asked him sympathetically if he was getting interviews. He said, 'Not even that. As soon as they read I've been in prison that's the end of it.' So I asked him what his sentence had been for. 'Arson', he replied. 'I don't even know why I did it.' I retreated step by step towards the door and made my exit. Back in the campaign rooms, I told John Gray about it. 'You stupid besom,' he scolded me. 'Don't you ever go out knocking doors on your own again – and for God's sake don't go into anyone's house when there's nobody around to see where you've got to.' And so he went on to put his foot down and protect me from myself for the next 14 years.

I plodded on without further mishap until, at last, the day of the General Election arrived. More than two thirds of the Maryhill electorate voted. That was a typical turnout of the time, but it has been falling since. The highest results, other candidates having a few hundred or less, were:

Elspeth Attwooll, Lib/SDP Alliance	4,118
Maria Fyfe, Labour	23,482
Simon Kirk, Conservative	3,307
Gavin Roberts, SNP	3,895
David Spaven, Scottish Greens	529

Labour's share of the vote was 64.6 per cent. Elspeth Attwooll came second, but her percentage share of the vote was halved from 22.1 per cent in 1983 to 11.7 per cent. The SNP came third with 11.0 per cent, the Tories fourth with 9.4 per cent, and the Greens took 1.5 per cent. The SNP were still suffering from having brought down the Callaghan Government and let in Margaret Thatcher, and the Tories always did very poorly in a seat like Maryhill.

So Labour's majority in Maryhill was a thumping, joyful, unbelievable and glorious 19,364 – about 8,000 more than our previous result. All over the city, similar results for Labour candidates were announced. Many a previous majority, including my own constituency, had been doubled. But then, not many copies of the *Sunday Times* are sold in Maryhill. I felt a sense of awe that all those people voted Labour, and few had even heard of me before I became the candidate. They had trusted Labour again and again, and I told myself I must never let them down.

The Glasgow *Evening Times* wrote:

> Throughout a night of high drama, the picture was constantly repeated. In Scotland and the North, Labour increased majorities, snatched seats, the Alliance was smashed, and the Tories were lucky to scrape home in some seats they have held for generations.

The SNP didn't warrant a mention. The share of votes in Scotland was:

Conservative 24 per cent
Labour 43.3 per cent
Alliance 18.4 per cent
SNP 14 per cent
Others 0.3 per cent

I felt a joy on election night that was unique amongst the successful Scottish Labour candidates. As I stood on the platform with my sons, Stephen and Chris, nearby, I reflected that I had just become Labour's tenth ever woman to be elected in a Scottish constituency.

But I didn't want to settle for being a Queen Bee amongst all the men. My task now was to make things better for women. At the following year's Scottish party conference, I made a comment that seems to have stuck in a lot of minds, as I have had it repeated back to me many times: 'Labour likes having women MPs, but it likes them one at a time.'

* * *

You have probably noticed, when watching Parliament on television, jugs of water and glasses sitting on the table close to the despatch box. They are meant for the use of frontbenchers. On the night I was to make my maiden speech, I was so nervous that my throat had gone completely dry. Some kindly soul handed me up a glass, and I drank it down hurriedly in case I were called by the Speaker, nearly giving myself hiccups in my haste. But then I thought to myself, the people of Maryhill sent me here to speak up for them, and I'm going to do that to the best of my ability.

I began by commenting on Labour's huge success in my home city, saying Glasgow was the city that had everything – except a Tory MP. I went on to attack the Government on the continuing high levels of unemployment in Maryhill: 29 per cent of adult males, and in Woodlands ward, where I lived, 34.4 per cent. Half the youths in that ward were unemployed.

I drew attention to something I learned while studying for my Economic History degree: when the Forth and Clyde canal which runs through Maryhill was completed in 1784, it was made possible by a cash grant of £50,000 (£25 million at 1987 prices) from William Pitt's Tory Government. The private company that had started up work on the canal had become 'a lame duck' in the Conservative parlance of Margaret Thatcher's day. It had run out of money and could not raise enough cash on its own. Back then, all those years ago, the Government did not shrug their shoulders and let it fail. They had the wisdom and foresight to put serious money into the scheme, and in doing so created jobs all the way along the canal. Maryhill prospered. Mining, glass-making, chemical, engineering and other industries flourished, but by now were mostly gone. Would that present-day Conservatives, I went on to say, had anything like as much sense as their predecessors of some 200 years before.

The Speaker, Jack Weatherill, was thoughtful enough to send me a 'well done' note, but the kind man probably did likewise with everyone. When walking down the Ways and Means corridor later that night, I was stopped by a Tory backbencher I had never met before, but came to know as a decent bloke. He said I sounded as if I hated the Conservatives. Considering what they were doing to my city, to working people's rights, and the massive unemployment they had deliberately created as a means to weaken the trade unions, it would be surprising if I did not hate them, and I told him so. He was quite taken aback because the parliamentary convention up to that time was that maiden speeches should be uncontroversial, and be received politely with no heckling or abusive behaviour.

smartest suit I had. The ladies, I was told, were expected to wear skirts or dresses. I told anyone who made this comment that no-one since I was a schoolgirl had ever told me what to wear, and now that I was middle aged, they weren't going to start now. Today we can see women members wearing smart trousers, and it is taken for granted. Progress creeps along. But the Commons still has the pink ribbons attached to the coat hangers in the Members' cloakroom, where you can hang your sword in safe keeping because you will not be permitted to take it into the Chamber. Well, debates there have been known to get heated. So why, in the name of all logic, do they still have the red lines going the length of the green carpet, two sword lengths apart? One of my colleagues thought it would be a good laugh to buy a sword, hang it on his ribbon, and claim whatever it cost on expenses, as obviously the Parliamentary authorities must think each of us needed one, or they would not supply a ribbon on every coat hanger to hold it. In light of recent events, I am glad for him that he desisted. It must be the better part of two centuries since men last went about ready to draw sword, except of course for those younger ones in some of our big cities, whose favourite pastime is gang warfare. Regardless of such realities, some love this kind of tradition. I find it merely irritating. Besides which, it gives the impression that nearly a hundred years on since female emancipation, the institution has not yet caught up with the entry of female members. Apart from Boudicca and Britannia, one would be hard-pressed to think of any sword-wielding women.

So we had ribbons for non-existent swords, but no waste paper bins. When I started to attend meetings of numerous committees I found it surprising that members tossed papers they were finished with on the floor – and we got through a great deal of paper. Thinking, 'Why is it all these men have not a notion of how annoying it is for others to have to pick up after them?', I asked the chairman if he would get some bins supplied. He explained to me that doing so would be against the traditions of the House. Therefore the cleaners had to waste effort, bending up and down along all the rows of seats in 16 committee rooms? He had an answer to that too. 'Surely you, a Labour member, wouldn't want to throw them out of work?' Maybe they could do some more useful work, I thought, but I was beginning to see what I was up against.

Nor had we new boys and girls known about the daily ritual of Prayers before business in the Chamber began. Members would turn round and stand facing the wall, because you could not be properly reverential if you were facing your opponents. And you were not allowed to clap. The day we opened for business, all the new Labour members began clapping when Neil Kinnock walked into the Chamber. A senior member turned round and told us we must not clap. That was not proper Parliamentary conduct. We should say 'Hear, hear' or tap the bench in front of us. Five minutes later he was yelling abuse across the Chamber.

I was only in the place a month when I got into a row over the dining habits of some of the members. I had received an invitation to enjoy a free bottle of champagne at Lockets Restaurant, near the House of Commons. I had not realised until then that some restaurants, including Lockets, had division bells, calling Members to the House for a vote, so a nightly scene in them would feature MPs bolting for the door. Lockets, their invitation said, prided themselves on keeping their meals warm, or if an MP was delayed, replacing it. I was miffed because I remembered only too well the night I was sitting up in the Gallery, hearing the division bell ring, and seeing Tory MPs in their dinner jackets pouring hurriedly into what had been an empty Chamber to vote to cut Glasgow's money. I had not known until then that MPs could and did vote following a debate they had not even heard. It was that very night that I decided I would like to be a Labour MP and stand up for Glasgow.

I was accused of being hair-shirted. But if we started earlier in the day, and finished at a sensible time, everyone could spend as long as they wanted in restaurants, with no division bell to make them bolt their food down.

Scottish MPs, male and female, would be heckled with what some Tory idiots obviously thought was wit: 'Speak English, will you', they would shout in public school accents, either genuine or cultivated. When someone did that to me, in a debate not long after I entered Parliament, I countered, 'If the honourable gentleman doesn't understand my accent, that is the least important thing about Scotland that he doesn't understand.' None of my colleagues were in the Chamber at the time to back me up, but the SNP's Alex Salmond, elected for the first time that year like me, complained about the insult. It was a gift to the SNP, and he wasn't going to miss the chance. To my surprise, the incident was reported in a Canadian newspaper, which I only heard of because someone in Ontario sent me the cutting, with an approving comment on my riposte in the editorial. But what makes these MPs behave in such a crass way? If I could understand Cockney and Scouse and Zummerset, and would never dream of pretending I could not, what was wrong with their ears? We would sarcastically advise them to watch *Taggart* or *Rab C. Nesbitt* until they got the hang of it. One guy, who did watch *Taggart* regularly, asked me in all seriousness how a woman had come to be the MP for a tough place like Maryhill. I informed him that this series was fiction, not a documentary. We did not have all these murders every week, just some, occasionally. John Smith once remarked to me that they could not place us socially, because their ears were not attuned to the variety of Scottish accents, and that bothered them.

The boorish behaviour was even continued in the dining rooms, where some Tory members would bray so loudly that people seated at neighbouring tables could hardly hear each other speak.

When my brother Jim, dining with me one night in the Strangers' Dining Room, heard this for the first time, he dealt with it in a way that never would have occurred to me. He began by loudly declaiming: 'Bray, bray, bray, bray, bray.' Then, putting incredulity into his voice, he asked, 'Bray???' Answering himself, he nodded gravely, and cried 'Bray!'

They got the message.

New members, back then, found themselves in a place of work where there was not even the smallest of offices to accommodate all of them. I was allocated a desk in The Cloisters, a gloomy quadrangle of ancient grey stonework with a patch of grass in the middle, where so little sunlight reached that I could hardly read my papers. The electric lighting, such as it was, barely competed with church candles. Down each side of the square there were placed a number of ancient moquette sofas. They never seemed to be vacuumed, and if you hit the seat clouds of dust would rise. That summer, when hotel rooms were hard to find, particularly during Wimbledon, Tommy Graham, newly elected for Renfrewshire West, occasionally ended up sleeping on the sofa nearest his desk. Well, it was better than a park bench, where he had also slept on a few warm summer nights. With his shirt buttons popping open over his ample stomach, he lay snoring when the rest of us arrived in the morning: it was not a pretty sight. It was so hard to find accommodation that, one night, after one fruitless phone call after another, I ended up in a suspiciously cheap hotel in Victoria. Neil Carmichael, an old chum and former MP for Glasgow Kelvingrove who was now in the Lords, had suggested I try it, although he himself had not been there for many years. My fears were more than vindicated. When I arrived late at night after the final vote, I noticed that the carpet in the foyer had chewing gum trodden into it in several places.

The walls were brown with years of tobacco smoke. The lock on my bedroom door was broken, so I had to push a chest of drawers up against the door, in case I was disturbed by any of the drunken Australians rampaging up and down the corridor. I left first thing next morning, without risking breakfast.

In the Quad individual desks were placed behind one another all the way around its four sides. Tommy, who suffered industrial deafness, spoke so loudly on the phone three desks back that I could hear every word he said. Keith Vaz, immediately behind me, would be on the phone almost daily, scolding the editor of his local paper, something that had never once crossed my mind to do. I might write a complaint, but who except Keith would talk to him as if he were a naughty boy, and threaten to put him over his knees and spank him. It was small consolation that, immediately at my side, there was a tiny room of historic importance: it was here that the warrant for the execution of Charles I had been signed. If I didn't get out of this place soon, I mutinously thought, I'd be signing someone else's death warrant. Even 20 years ago, as a young secretary with the Scottish Gas Board, I had better office space than this. I discovered others were succeeding in moving out to better accommodation. The Whips, who organised these matters, were already identifying their favourites. Even worse, I gathered that some members curried favour by giving presents of flowers and chocolates to the wives of certain whips. And lo and behold! Suddenly a room could be found for them. So I marched to the office of Derek Foster, Labour's Chief Whip, and told him that if I didn't soon have a desk somewhere in peace, I would be offering a sarcastic poem about the working conditions of a new MP to *Tribune*, the mainstream Labour left weekly, widely read by party members. I got my office, albeit shared with two others, but it was close to the committee corridor and therefore highly convenient. Others had to run back and forth in the rain from outer offices when the division bell rang.

Nowadays there are splendid offices across the road in Portcullis House, reached by a conveniently sheltered underground walkway, allocated to new Members immediately they enter Parliament. That office block, by the way, cost far more to build than the Scottish Parliament, but I have never seen a word of complaint about that in the media, although they droned on endlessly about Holyrood's spiralling costs.

In the old building the carpets on some of the staircases were so worn they were a danger. I grumbled about this one day to John Smith as we walked down a staircase together, saying that with all the money wasted in this place on, for one example, ridiculously expensive wallpaper, you would think they could renew the carpets. He laughed to hear what he called a typical Scottish housewife's remark.

And then there were the mice. I was somewhat startled one day when, having a cuppa in the Members' Tearoom, I saw a mouse run across the floor. I was languidly told they were a permanent, if fairly infrequent feature, because the Houses of Parliament were so close to the Thames. Why not get a cat? I asked. The answer was that no-one wanted to take responsibility for it when the place was closed during the recesses. Here we were, running the country, but finding a cat too much to cope with. In recent times there have been three or four cats in Downing Street, but to the best of my knowledge the Commons has still not got around to that solution. They still, all these years later, have not found a way to deal with the mice.

However, in spite of all my frustrations at some of the baffling, outdated and frankly ludicrous attitudes and customs of Parliament, I loved being there. It was like nowhere else on earth. To me, becoming a Labour MP was a dream come true, and a privilege to be treasured.

CHAPTER TWO

This Old House

1987

AT THE FIRST SCOTTISH Question Time after the 1987 General Election, when the Tories had won UK-wide, but not in Scotland, the government benches in the Chamber were packed with Tory backbenchers from constituencies in England. At that time in Scotland, there were 62 Opposition, including 50 Labour Members, and only 10 Conservative MPs. Some of those ten had ministerial positions in other departments, so there were only a few Scottish Tories present. The Speaker took questions turnabout from side to side, like a metronome, as is done at all ministerial question times. It was difficult to get a chance to ask a question at all, because there were so many Labour MPs holding Scottish seats, and the Speaker would call equal numbers of Members from the other side of the Chamber. It did not matter that they came from the Tory shires and the posher parts of London, attending just to curry favour with their whips, or as a device to raise something concerning their own constituency. Indeed, sometimes Tories whose seats were outside Scotland were called twice in the one session, when many Labour MPs with constituencies in Scotland were not called at all for months on end. It was a bit of a giveaway when some of these Tories, pretending an interest in Scottish affairs, could not pronounce place names like Milngavie or Tighnabruaich. In effect, in those days before Parliament was televised, Labour's electoral success in Scotland was being hidden from radio listeners, and it would sound as if we were equal in numbers, when we had in fact beaten the Scottish Tories out of the park.

Televising parliamentary proceedings would have let viewers see that at least we were present and doing our best to be heard. Dennis Canavan, indignant that this was happening at the first Scottish Questions of the new Parliament, and to draw attention to it, shouted out 'I spy strangers!' This historic cry goes back centuries to when the Commons had to protect its autonomy. When such a call is made, a vote has to be taken to decide whether to clear the public gallery. I voted with him, thinking this was a good wheeze. Dennis pointed out he was not objecting to the tourists passing an hour in the gallery. They must have been wondering what on earth was going on, and why they were being evicted when they had done nothing wrong. His ire was directed at the Tory MPs from constituencies in England who had no real interest in Scotland. However, Donald Dewar told us he should not have done that. He disagreed with Dennis's argument that the Tories had no mandate to rule over Scottish affairs, having had such a humiliatingly low level of support at the recent General Election. Donald's view was that, nevertheless, the Tories had won a UK-wide general election. What would Dennis say if Labour had won in England and the Tories in Scotland? In my view you didn't need to support the 'no mandate' argument in order to draw attention to the fact that the run of questions gave the wrong impression of relative strengths when it came to Scottish affairs. And here we are now, with a Con-Dem Government, and only one Conservative MP in the whole of Scotland. Except now there is a huge change for the better. Nowadays we have a Scottish Parliament to deal with devolved issues, and no-one was more wholeheartedly in favour of achieving that than Donald himself. It still leaves us with the same nonsense, though, for Scottish Questions at Westminster.

1987 was the election that threw up what was called 'the democratic deficit', and the devolution debate came to life again. It was Jean McFadden, former Leader of Glasgow's Labour Council, who made a point to me that, until then, I had never considered: we really needed a Scottish Assembly, because when Whitehall ruled the roost, even when there was a Labour Government, the needs of Scottish councils could be ignored. It would be harder for a parliamentary body ruling Scottish domestic affairs to be so detached from the consequences of its actions. I think this is proving true. The Nationalist Government forced Scottish local authorities to accept a council tax freeze, on pain of getting a larger cut in their grant if they refused – and went on to cut the grant even further than promised, as well as imposing the freeze for several years. But knowledge of this kind of thing is nowadays much more widespread and commented on in the Scottish media. I don't think any of us anticipated that we would one day have a Scottish government that was as centralising as this one.

We continued to fight back against the Tories at every Scottish Questions session. Other members came in to enjoy the spectacle. Frank Dobson said he could sell tickets for it. I don't know why we were unlike other parts of Britain, but Scottish Labour members at that time seem to have gained a reputation for getting stuck in, for being forthright, for having no deference to any Minister, however exalted, and generally being as difficult as human ingenuity could devise.

George Foulkes, angrily getting in a reply to Douglas Hogg one day, called him 'an arrogant little shit'. When the Speaker indignantly rose to his feet and ordered him to withdraw that word immediately, George coolly asked him, 'Which word do you want me to withdraw, arrogant, little or shit?' Back home, people came up to George in the street and said, 'Good for you! Wish I could have been there to say that!'

I was particularly irritated by Philip Oppenheim, whose mother was also an MP at that time. A fairly young Tory, tall, blond-haired and born with a mouthful of silver spoons, he made a habit of attending Scottish Questions. There was always a disdainful sneer on his face when he spoke, looking across to the Labour scruff on the Opposition benches. So one day I called out that if he insisted on making that face, he would stay like that when he grew up. Some have said that was ageist of me. I think if an adult behaves like a brat, then he has only himself to blame if he is treated like one.

We thoroughly enjoyed these sessions, lambasting the Tories. Yet the Nationalists had the gall to dub us 'the feeble fifty'. That was some nerve, coming from a party that had won only three seats in Scotland in 1987. The voting public were continuing to make them pay for colluding with Margaret Thatcher eight years before in bringing down James Callaghan's Government, and landing us with all that Thatcher went on to do.

Getting called in debates, as well as questions for ministers, was a constant struggle. I thought, particularly as I was the only woman out of 50 Scottish Labour MPs, I should expect a right to my fair share of chances to speak, particularly when matters relating to women were being debated. Indeed, that was the ruling logic when Parliament was debating, for instance, agricultural affairs. They wouldn't have dreamed of having any such debate without calling MPs from the shires. And yet, when we had a debate in the Scottish Grand Committee on the running of Corntonvale, the only all-female prison in Scotland, I was finally called to speak for exactly one minute, after other speakers had taken their full ten minutes, and before the front benchers made their closing speeches in the debate. I had a particular point to make about the narrow curriculum of education and training offered to the women, when male prisoners were offered so much more that could help them find work on their release from prison. Yet – I am not making this up – the women spent their days sewing

And, of course, there was the Poll Tax. The *Glasgow Guardian*, our local weekly, ran the story on their front page with the banner headline, 'Maryhill MP Hits Out Over Poll Tax'. I had questioned in Parliament why the Government had come up with a scheme that was so monstrously unfair, and had been described by Local Government accountants as an administrative nightmare. I pointed out the average rates bill for a household in Glasgow was £514, but the Poll Tax would be £292 per head. So a two adult household would pay a huge amount more than before, and young family members over eighteen would have to fork out the same, despite being more likely to be on much lower wages than their elders.

I expected political points to be made through heckling. That was fair enough. I did it back to them, and relished doing so. What I had not expected was the kind of boorish behaviour that would draw a reprimand from any schoolteacher in the classroom, but went unremarked by the Speaker or his deputies until it got out of hand. I could not believe my eyes and ears when I began to notice what happened sometimes when women got up to speak; on the first occasion it was Clare Short. She was on her feet, deploring the demeaning of women in the *Sun* page three pictures. Some Tory backbenchers were loudly scoffing while they made cupping motions with their hands at chest level. I made up my mind then that if they ever did that to me, I would stop mid-sentence and say, 'Mr Speaker, I understand only Members are permitted to sit in this Chamber, but somehow some ill-mannered adolescents seem to have found their way in.' Shows how much I had to learn about the place. No Speaker likes to be told, in effect, he is not doing his job. When things get so unruly he cannot hear a Member speak, he has to shout, 'Order! Order!' and repeat himself five minutes later when disorder has broken out again.

I didn't see it at the time, but now, looking back, I see that kind of behaviour as a none-too-subtle attack on our very right to speak. A politician's main tool is her or his voice. If you are unable to be heard, you are quite literally silenced. There had been a miners' MP some years before me. He had been an effective union man, and so they sent him to Parliament. But he was so intimidated by the atmosphere in the Chamber that he gave up trying to speak, and never set foot there again to utter even a question.

Another extraordinary aspect of my new life was the feeling that I was travelling backwards in time. I had occasionally worn trouser suits to my work as a Further Education lecturer since the mid-'70s, but it was frowned upon when I turned up for Parliamentary work one day in the shrouds! Their learning opportunities amounted to a choice between hairdressing and beauty therapy, while the men were taught a variety of trades. I also felt that not enough attention was paid by the Government to the welfare of babies born to prisoners, or to the children in care while their mother was in prison, for a crime involving no violence. Defiantly, I ate into the front bench time. What did I care for this gentlemen's agreement?

It was the same in the Chamber. On one occasion, we were hearing a report from the EU on workplace issues. Not one female backbencher was called. I complained to the Speaker, Jack Weatherill. He told me that, firstly, it was unwise to criticise any decision of the Speaker or his deputies. Secondly, 'the ladies' did not usually take an interest in these matters, and those Members who had been called had some involvement and had spoken on the subject in the past. So, I asked him, would they have to die before anyone else could get a look-in? And why did he think I was standing up trying to be called, over and over again for hours, if I was not taking an interest? He just said he understood my point but he couldn't call everybody, and he tried to give everyone a fair crack over the weeks. He added with a smile, 'One day many years from now, you may complain about letting these whipper-snappers into the debate, and your knowledge and wisdom left unheard.' Yet I felt he was missing the point. There were so few women of any generation being heard, and we had perspectives on many issues that were not being paid attention.

I became so frustrated with this kind of casual sexism, especially where Scottish affairs were concerned, that I decided I would take it further. After all, the voters in Maryhill had sent me there. How were they supposed to know I was doing my damnedest to take part, and not shirking my responsibilities? So I gathered my evidence. I combed the columns in Hansard to prove how seldom I was called compared to my male colleagues. I told Donald Dewar that if matters did not improve, I would go public. Donald had no responsibility for any of this, but as leader of the Scottish group of Labour MPs, he had a lot of clout. I don't know what he did, or to whom he spoke, but things definitely did get better.

There were times, of course, when we were more than happy simply to play a supporting role, such as the night we debated the Felixstowe Bill, a Tory plan to expand the docks there at the behest of P&O, who had newly acquired them. Would the company be paying for this work? No, don't be daft. The taxpayers would. And why would the Government want to do their bidding? Maybe the fact that P&O contributed to Tory

Party funds helped. T&GWU Members in particular were keen to oppose it, as it would cost jobs at other docks around our coast. It was also a matter of exposing corruption and misuse of the democratic process.

At that time you could still get away with filibustering. And this one was a beauty. Peter Hardy, Labour MP for Wentworth, raised a point that had not until then been considered: the threat to bird life if this upheaval went ahead. He knew, as a keen twitcher himself, that a particular bird – I cannot now remember what it was – would most probably be hugely disturbed and no longer nest in that area. This enabled the rest of us to keep him going with questions posed to him. Would this affect herons? How about robins? What of ducks and seagulls? And on, and on, affecting concern for just about every damned bird anyone had ever heard of in these isles. In answering our anxious questions in the affirmative or in the negative, and at considerable length, he even gave impressions of the songs of different species. How the Hansard writers coped with this I never discovered. We kept this up right through the night to breakfast time, thereby wrecking the next day's timetable, while our colleague, maintaining a perfectly straight face, responded judicially and knowledgeably, until the Bill was talked out. The Tories were puce with rage. You can't get away with that now. More's the pity.

Then, later on, Parliament was televised. I voted enthusiastically for this reform, thinking the antics of some Members – sometimes so bad it would disgrace a primary one classroom – would have to stop if they knew their own constituents were observing how they behaved. Better still, the appallingly right wing views of some would be exposed. I had begun to realise that the parliamentary reporters, whether TV, radio, or nationals, were seldom interested in anything more than the front bench speeches that were handed to them in advance, so that all they had to do was check against delivery. The best a backbencher could usually hope for was a write-up in their local papers or an interview on local or regional radio and TV. Or you could grab attention by saying something way over the top. Then you got into the papers, no doubt about it, but your constituents thought you were off your head.

Little did I realise how easy it was to forget we were on camera. The viewing public would get the impression from watching Prime Minister's Questions that the place was just a bear garden. Ya-boos galore, but not that many witty heckles or counter-arguments, waving order papers to express delight, and behaving, when party leaders entered the Chamber, as if they were greeting gladiators about to tackle the lions. It was vital as a MP to be seen to be there, and who knows, once in a blue moon actually be called to ask the Prime Minister a question, but I hated those twice-weekly quarter hours. I wished the general public could see more of the serious work of Parliament, in select committees and standing committees on Bills.

The same people who behaved like overgrown schoolboys (if you think that is an exaggeration, I can recall once visiting the smoking room to find some of the younger and more agile Tories running around and leaping over armchairs) would make an inordinate fuss about what other Members were wearing in the Chamber. One hot and sticky summer day, when Jeremy Corbyn had turned up wearing a safari suit, a Tory member called upon the Speaker to express his view on the standard of dress to be expected. Speaker Weatherill (a tailor in his past life) ruled that while a Member could wear anything he liked, a suit was the normal dress code, and if Members did not show respect in the standard of their dress, they would risk not being called. Thereupon, another timewaster complained that none of the ladies were wearing suits, and were all in summer dresses – not businesslike attire. 'I think the ladies are always charmingly dressed', Weatherill replied. Then, thankfully, he added, 'And I want to hear no more on this subject.'

There were endearing oddities of life in the Westminster bubble. Once Donald Dewar was informed by one of the Palace of Westminster police-men that his office had been burgled. It hadn't. Nothing was missing. It was just in its usual chaotic state. Donald didn't file stuff. He found it by the archaeological method: the lower down the heap, the further back the date.

He shared a flat with Sam Galbraith and Lewis Moonie, across the landing from me in a block in Kennington. It was I who had found this newly refurbished block full of empty flats for sale. I told my colleagues who were still looking for accommodation the good news that here was a place only half an hour's walk from the House of Commons. That nearly resulted in me gazumping myself, when the developer told me he wanted more money than we had already agreed for the first floor flat I had chosen, because there was so much interest being expressed in them! It may be of interest that my monthly claim for accommodation was precisely £111.65 for the next 14 years, considerably less than hotel bills or rented digs would have been.

Anyway, Lewis asked me one day if I had ever seen Donald's bedroom.

Throwing open the door, he waved his arm to show a room like a monk's cell. A narrow bed, a bedside table and lamp, and a metal rail across a corner that held a number of hangers. That was all. I used to reprove Donald for running up and down between Scotland and London so much. He regularly left Parliament at night to board a sleeper to Glasgow or Edinburgh, take part in a meeting the next morning, then rush back to London for that day's votes. All these night journeys by sleeper, woken up by the train jolting out of stations, could not be good for him. Then John Maxton pointed out that the sleeper cabin was more comfortable than Donald's home in Glasgow.

Their flat in Kennington was a household to compare with *The Odd Couple*. There seemed to be some uncertainty about how to work the washing machine, only Lewis being confident about it. They spent fortunes in the local laundry, and were amazed that I actually washed and ironed my clothes. How did I find time, they wondered. Well, it's not difficult. You can compose questions or a speech in your head while doing the washing up or the ironing. But one other Glasgow seat member, who shall remain nameless, told them he had a better idea: 'You know these huge, super-sized stamped envelopes we get? I put my socks, pants and shirts in them and send them up to my wife, and they're ready for me when I go home at the weekend.'

David Blunkett's guide dog deserved its fame. A creature of remarkably good conduct, he/she (I can't remember) could be relied upon to sit quietly at his feet wherever he went. But one day there was a small puddle on the floor of the Members' Lobby, and some Tory MP suggested that the dog must be the culprit. David was outraged. How dare he? It was probably some drunken Tory, he fumed. When I once had a party of primary schoolchildren from Maryhill down to see Parliament at work, their teacher had them well trained. On their return they all dutifully wrote their thank you letters, and said what they liked best about their visit. By a clear majority, it was getting to pat David Blunkett's dog. They enjoyed my story of the Member for a Scottish seat who did one of the silliest things I had ever heard of when down there: wanting to send David a letter, he thoughtfully had it put into Braille. Then he faxed it. Mind you, this probably didn't do much for their respect for those who run the country.

I was told by the Labour Whips I had to find a 'pair'.[1] This wouldn't have been difficult, given that Tory MPs desperate to find a pair were constantly phoning me. I refused them all. Pairing meant that, on all except three-line whipped votes, if one of us was given leave of absence, the other had to abstain from voting if in the building, or just leave. I didn't like this at all. Suppose a vote came up that I cared about, and wanted a record of my support or rejection? Eventually I had to comply when the Labour Whips' Office obtained the agreement of the Parliamentary Labour Party to make it a rule. Even then, I got into trouble for occasionally forgetting I was supposed to be paired, and the Tory whips complained to our whips. I cannot even remember the name of my pair, but the poor man fell sick for a long time and the arrangement came to grief anyway. By that time, both sets of whips had enough pairs to satisfy them.

I was praised for my high attendance at parliamentary committees and my voting record, but it annoys me to this day that the record is distorted against hard working MPs whose responsibilities take them away from the House. If you are away elsewhere – and I don't mean junkets – to carry out parliamentary business or a task on behalf of your party, you cannot be in the voting lobby at the same time, but no account is taken of this when the voting records are revealed to the public.

Likewise, a decision to abstain cannot be distinguished from mere absence under the antiquated voting system. In other Parliaments, members can record For, Against or Abstention electronically while remaining in their seats, and this saves a lot of time too. Some argue that the benefit of trooping through the voting lobbies is that backbench Members can lie in wait for Ministers and get to talk with them immediately instead of making an appointment several days or weeks later, but this is a much exaggerated benefit. I don't recall ever managing to see a Minister that way without someone else butting in, usually without so much as an apology for their interruption. Parliamentary manners are peculiarly unlike anywhere else. In this respect they lack common courtesy, but there is also a touch of *toujours la politesse* in the custom of sending people appreciative notes for their contributions to debates. When Tony Blair announced he was changing the Prime Minister's Questions slot to one half-hour a week instead of the annoyingly time-wasting two quarter-hours, he was attacked for this by the Tories. I thought that was a good idea. A

---

1 If three heavy lines are drawn underneath a business item, it means you are under orders to be present and vote as your party wishes, and if you abstain or vote against, you can expect some displeasure to be expressed. Two lines means your party would like you to vote, but you can be paired. One line essentially means: don't even bother turning up if you have something better to do.

little time could be saved for each one of us doing it this way. Perhaps I should explain that it wasn't a case of two quarters equal a half, so what difference did it make? It was the time wasted having to get onto a green bench at least twenty minutes before it even began, so as to ensure a seat. And you couldn't just get on with some paperwork while waiting: the Speaker wouldn't allow that. When the Speaker called me at the tail-end of that day's PMQs, I dropped what I had been going to say, and supported this sensible change. To my surprise, I had a handwritten note from Tony later the same day to thank me. It has to be said, of course, that there were a number of occasions he would be doing nothing of the kind.

A good record of attendance and voting is important, not just because that is, after all, what you are basically paid to do. It is important if you are going to rebel on any issue, because the whips cannot claim you are simply lazy or disloyal. It is really quite hard for the whips to force people into line if they don't want a peerage or a knighthood, don't want time off for junkets, know they are unlikely to be promoted as punishment for past disobedience, and in short cannot be sweetened with anything they can offer.

On one occasion, I was all set to be supportive, having read all the items of business coming up, and seen nothing to worry me. I entered the Chamber and heard our shadow minister closing the debate on the subject. I was so much in disagreement with his argument that I couldn't in good conscience vote my support. The Whips were pretty annoyed, as I had failed to report my intended dissent in advance as we were required to do. Summoned to Tommy McAvoy's office, I explained that I didn't know I was against until I heard our front bencher speak. This didn't go down too well.

There was one splendid occasion many years later when Labour was in power, and one of my colleagues, Terry Rooney, was summoned to be ticked off by a whip for voting against the official line. This was despite the fact the issue was not even a matter of party policy, it was not set out in the manifesto, and had not been discussed in the Parliamentary Labour Party. As the meeting concluded, the whip said jovially, 'So you'll be voting Labour next time, will you?'

'I always do, even when the Government doesn't,' Terry replied.

The whips had another ploy. They would send a copy of a Member's voting record to their Constituency Labour Party, in the hope that the members in that locality would take them to task and even raise the threat of deselection. Didn't work in Maryhill, though. When these reports arrived, Councillor Bill Butler (who later became a member of the Scottish Parliament) was usually the one to propose a motion in my support, which was passed unanimously, and a copy sent to the Whips. Indeed, with tongue in cheek, on one occasion they passed a motion reproving me for not voting against the official line more often.

I was told by Anne McGuire, some years later when she became one of the Scottish Labour whips, that they made up little ditties about our occasionally recalcitrant Members. 'How Do You Solve a Problem Like Maria?' was their song for me. I tell this story because, in spite of our disagreements, there was no ill will. Indeed, towards the end of my days in Parliament, I fell ill with a virus that kept me off for months – no-one could have been more understanding or supportive than Tommy McAvoy, who has a hard-nosed reputation, and whom I had annoyed exceedingly from time to time. And no, it wasn't because he was happier if I was away. I did vote the party line most of the time.

I enjoyed the largely unsung hard slog of the standing committees on Bills. On one of the local government bills, we put down over 800 amendments, not one of which was accepted by the Government. But it slowed down their progress through their agenda for legislation. The Tory backbenchers were even more right wing than the Government, wanting to extend the privatisation of council facilities. Not surprising, as many of them had contacts with companies involved in cleaning services that were trying to pick up contracts. One of our fiercest rows took place when Labour MPs called for more information to be made available about the business interests of MPs. If MPs were covered by the kind of rules that applied to local councillors, they would be forced to declare an interest and abstain from voting. The Tories fought tooth and nail against having to make such financial disclosures, insisting on the right to privacy. Besides, were we not all honourable members? Little did I imagine that the day would come when antique furniture and mortgages for houses not actually lived in were considered suitable expenses claims by some Hon. Members, thereby blackening the characters of all the Members who never claimed an inappropriate penny, and creating an unbelievable shambles in the effort to clean up the system. When fraudulent claims were in the news for months on end, I was forcibly struck by the contrast this made with what I knew of other members, whose flats remained meagrely furnished for years because they would not take the time to shop when there was work to do, or stay in their flat all day waiting in for a delivery. One extreme example of this I heard from a colleague – a party worker who wanted to borrow my London flat during the following general election, when I was away in Scotland for the duration. The flat she had been housed in during the previous election belonged to a MP who just had a mattress on the floor – no bedstead.

Noising up Tory ministers on committees was something to be enjoyed. The Scottish Office ministers came in for a lot of stick. Michael Forsyth, combative, intelligent and ideological, was so Thatcherite he was a constant source of quotes we would gleefully seize upon for the benefit of the *Daily Record*. Ian Lang, who looked such a smoothie, had a habit of addressing a committee with one foot placed on a wooden bench seat while he held forth, for all the world like an illustration for a gent's pullover knitting pattern in the 1950s. I couldn't resist taking the mickey. 'Isn't he masterful?' I cooed. My fellow committee member Adam Ingram said, 'You could say that. I couldn't.' James Douglas Hamilton was genuinely nice and, to the annoyance of his colleagues, now and again actually took on board suggestions that we made for amendments to clauses. On my first standing committee I discovered that Ministers seldom (if ever) admitted that a New Clause or amendment submitted by the Opposition could conceivably be an idea worth exploring. It would be rejected out of hand. Later, if they thought there really was something worthwhile in it, they would introduce it in their own words.

You couldn't really lose putting down amendments and new clauses. If, as rarely happened, the Government accepted it, you could claim a victory. If they rejected it, you could go to the media and reveal how the Government had turned down something which deserved support. Backbench speeches by Tory MPs could be a great source of mischief for us. No wonder they are told to sit there, keep quiet, and not leave the room in case someone calls for a vote. We would do our level best to provoke them into saying something better left unsaid, and then send it to their local media. We fired questions we had spent ages dreaming up to every Minister, and relished it when he had to reply from handwritten notes hurriedly passed to him by the civil servants. It is an unusually well briefed minister who can give confident, well informed answers on every possible implication of each and every clause of his Bill.

My first Standing Committee, on the Local Government Finance Bill, was the one that brought in the Poll Tax for England and Wales. That particular fiasco is covered in Chapter Three.

I spent a lot of time on Standing Committees. They seldom hit the headlines, but another one on Local Government did, because of the Tories adding on the notorious Section 28. This clause, since repealed by Labour at both Westminster and Holyrood, was simply a ruse to embarrass us about our councillors in London boroughs in particular who were – shock, horror – giving equal rights to gays. Michael Howard thought he was on a winner when he tabled a clause forbidding teachers from disseminating gay pornography in schools. At one meeting of the committee, he threw down a copy of one such magazine allegedly circulated by a teacher in a London school. Jack Straw, our lead shadow minister, seemed at a loss as to how to handle this. Of course we were against any adult *in loco parentis* giving children pornographic books or magazines – gay or otherwise. But to agree to the clause implied we accepted any such thing was happening on any scale, permitted – nay, encouraged – by loony left Labour members of the education authorities. But hang on, I thought. There is no need for fresh law. Normal disciplinary procedures were quite sufficient to deal with any teacher who handed out any sort of pornographic material to pupils, and while it is rare to sack teachers, such behaviour would most certainly constitute a sackable offence. I pointed out that I would also object to 'straight' pornography being given out, but in my experience as a longstanding member of the Educational Institute of Scotland, it had never happened. So we asked Howard why he had not seen fit to make his clause cover pornography as such, whether gay or straight. To which he had no answer. This nasty piece of legislation was passed, though, simply because of the huge Tory majority.

It was not all hard work and no play on these committees. We had chats over the coffee cups when we took brief rests before plodding on. One night, still hard at work at 2am, one of our number paid a visit to the Commons post office, which always remained open when the House was at work, no matter how ungodly the hour. He took a pile of letters back to the committee room and opened one which demanded that he phone the writer immediately upon receiving it. So he did. 'You know,' he said, 'this would be a great job if it wasn't for the constituents.' I assumed he had a very large majority.

It was on one of my earliest committees that I met Nicholas Soames, who was interested to meet the new girl from Glasgow, as he had many years ago been the Tory candidate in Clydebank, just a few miles down the Clyde from Maryhill. He had never been anywhere like that before.

The Council had a Labour majority, as was to be expected, but to his astonishment the official Opposition were the Communists. He spent weeks knocking on doors in streets named after Clement Attlee and other Labour luminaries without finding a single Tory voter. Then – disaster. The SNP had discovered a photograph of him in *The Tatler*, the victor of a polo competition, holding aloft a silver cup overflowing with champagne, horse at one side, a blonde beauty at the other. They distributed a leaflet with the caption, 'Do You Want This for Your MP in Clydebank?' The next day, out once more in gloomy spirits as he tried to garner votes, a man in a multi-storey flat answered his knock and confirmed he would indeed be voting Conservative. Soames was astonished, and asked him why. It had occurred to him that whatever had appealed to this voter, he ought to know, in the hope of encouraging others. 'Well,' said the guy, 'Any man who likes horses, booze and women can't be all bad.'

When driving along one day in his campaign car – covered in blue Conservative posters – he saw to his horror a wee boy of around three years old, riding a tricycle and heading straight out into the road in front of him. Soames knew with total certainty he had stopped the car in time and the lad had not been injured, but he thought it would be a good idea to get out and show some concern, especially for the benefit of anyone looking out from behind their lace curtains. So he bent over the little fellow, and asked him if he was all right. The tot looked up, noted the Tory posters on the car and Soames's blue rosette, and scowling as he pushed his trike back onto the pavement he shot back, 'Fuck off!' As Nicholas said, 'They're fighting the class war before they're at school in that place.' He also told me that, if he had been born in a place like that, he would have been a socialist too.

CHAPTER THREE

The Poll Tax

THERE IS NOTHING to be said in favour of the Poll Tax. It was one of the worst pieces of legislation this country has ever endured. It cost us millions that could have been much better spent elsewhere.

The Bill introducing the Poll Tax for England and Wales was my first introduction to the work of a standing committee. This is a committee that sits in an upstairs room, debates and votes on each clause of a Bill, then sends the Bill back to the Chamber for debate open to all the Members, not just those who served on the committee. A similar Act had already been passed in separate legislation for Scotland before I had entered the House of Commons, so I at least had some foreknowledge of what it was all about.

Nicholas Ridley, the Environment Secretary, or 'Old Fag Ash', as Tony Banks dubbed him (because his suits were always covered in a fine dust from his incessant smoking), assured us that the tax was perfectly fair. If you buy a bottle of whisky, he reasoned, you pay the same price for it as any other customer, regardless of your income. Therefore people should pay the same amount for their local services. Wow, what a quote that was for campaigning!

So one day when I was called to speak, I invited Ridley to visit Maryhill and discuss his policy with people there. He countered I should go to Cirencester, in his constituency, and explain why I was opposed to letting people have the benefit of this change. I took him up at once, but he never made any visit to Maryhill. In a letter to me he wrote

> I doubt if you would be very welcome in The Cotswolds if you were to speak against my constituents getting relief from their excessive rate burdens. I would not impose such an unpleasant experience on you. I am far too fond of you! On the other hand, it would be unfair if I went to Maryhill and persuaded your constituents that they were not being well served by their MP. It would be very unkind of me to do that. So shall we call it all off?

I thought, what an extraordinary letter. He not only writes to me in patronising tones – fond of me, indeed! Does he take me for an idiot? – but he clearly has no understanding of a part of the United Kingdom that he takes part in governing.

Indeed, at one stage it was pointed out to him that, as the son of a viscount, he may not understand that a lot of people simply could not pay such financial rates. To which he replied, 'Well, they could always sell a picture.'

I took the bus to Cirencester, where the local Labour Party held a meeting in the Corn Exchange, with hundreds in attendance and every seat filled. They were not used to political meetings in Cirencester, and that was why the hall was full. I told them that, under this proposed legislation, already an Act in Scotland, Mr Vestey the butcher shop chain multi-millionaire – who owned a large house up a hill nearby – would pay the same Poll Tax as his cleaner and the postman. He had been in the papers on account of his ability to get away with paying a remarkably low amount of national taxes. Not only that, a millionaire living alone in a mansion would pay half the sum taken from an ordinary, wage-earning couple who lived in a cottage.

How could this new Poll Tax be? Why would anyone think that was fair? I told them Ridley's argument was that we all benefited from local government services. The street lights were equally helpful to one and all. We all got our bins emptied. Road repairs were equally necessary to the bus passenger and the Rolls Royce owner. And everyone paid the same amount when they bought a bottle of whisky.

They were so enraged by this, I could see them marching on the Big House with pitchforks at the ready. I knew that night the Poll Tax would not last, if people in the heart of The Cotswolds were up in arms.

As its proceedings are not often in the sight of the general public, anyone could be forgiven for assuming a standing committee was a body that met now and again for a few hours, like most committees. Not so. This particular committee's sessions went on for most of the day, into the evening and late night, sometimes the small hours, twice a week, for months, to get through the work on umpteen clauses. So Labour Members had ample opportunity, while Ministers spoke at length, to dream up awkward questions and alert the public to the basic injustices of this tax. For example, the joint and several liability rule. This meant that if the spouse of a person suffering any kind of severe mental impairment who was personally exempt dodged paying his or her tax, the responsibility to pay it would then fall on someone who would not have had to pay it in their own right. Couples whose marriage had broken up would be responsible for paying their spouse's Poll Tax as well as their own, even if their spouse had moved away from the marital home. As Jo Richardson (shadow Minister for Women) pointed out, this completely undermined the principle of individual financial responsibility on which the Poll Tax was supposedly based. The Tory backbenchers supported to the hilt Nicholas Ridley's argument that a bottle of whisky cost the same whoever bought it, so why shouldn't the duke pay the same as the dustman? One Tory argued with me on television that we could keep the community charge bill down for everyone by charging for services that were currently free. Like what? Entry to public parks could be one, he replied. Not everyone used them, and some did more frequently than others. The media loved that one.

'Hey Mum,' I envisaged children saying, 'Can we have money to go to the swings?'

'No. You've been twice already this week, and I need the money to buy your dinner.'

However, one night I tackled them on a point that had been raised by the British Council of Churches, but so far had gone unheeded. What about the case of convents and monasteries? These people took vows of poverty, and yet each would be expected to pay the Poll Tax. Moreover, some people in religious orders were elderly and no longer working, so their brothers or sisters, with joint and several liability imposed upon them, would have to pay their Poll Tax for them. Their Orders frequently worked in health, education and social work in areas where poverty was greatest, and that usually meant the local authority set higher rates than they would like, to make up for Tory Government underfunding. Needless to say, I sent a copy of the relevant pages of Hansard to Archbishop Thomas Winning and to the two convents in my constituency. One Sister wrote back to say that in many cases they would require to discontinue their charitable works due to lack of finance, as the money presently used to help those in need would be directed to payment of the Poll Tax. They would pray for my success. This was one amendment I achieved.

I spent many a night setting off by train or bus to campaign and address meetings all over the south of England. Then home at the weekends to Scotland, where the Labour Party, following its special conference on the Poll Tax in Govan Town Hall, launched its Stop It campaign, chaired by Brian Wilson. My own constituency party took part by holding a meeting in our local burgh hall. Queues of people formed to sign up, and the audience was over a hundred at a time when local political meetings were usually lucky to have more in the audience than on the platform. Our local party newsletter highlighted how we were considering going a bit further, however. Our front page noted that many people had already declared they would not pay it, and many others would not pay simply because they could not afford to. Our newsletter went on to highlight the huge extra cost for typical families in our area. We had managed to source the figures for what Malcolm Rifkind, the Secretary of State for Scotland, would personally save – £522 a year – and Michael Forsyth, Minister for Housing, Education and Health, a whopping £1,229. We concluded:

> In the end it is the power of the people which will stop this unjust tax. Labour wants YOU to fight the Poll Tax with us. Write to Rifkind. Sign the petition. Organise, demonstrate and vote against it. Help us resist the Poll Tax in every way you can. Let's dump the Poll Tax back in the 14th century where the Tories dredged it up from!

Poll Tax, of course, was not its official name. It had been designated the title 'community charge'. I believe Glasgow District Council's Finance Director, Bill English, may have been the first to dub it 'the Poll Tax'. Early on, when the new tax proposed by Scottish Tory MPs had gained Margaret Thatcher's support, he commented, 'This is the kind of tax they had in the Middle Ages. It's a revival of the Poll Tax!'

Labour's official party line was articulated by Donald Dewar: law makers should never be law breakers. I couldn't resist teasing him about his fine for speeding, albeit only a few miles over the limit, as he hurried one night from one meeting to another along Great Western Road. The party would campaign against the Poll Tax, but rejected non-payment by a large majority. It did, however, agree that individuals could take that step on grounds of conscience. There was entirely justifiable worry that people would get into massive debt, and the councils would run out of money. So the official line was to encourage people to send back blank Poll Tax registration forms, and enclose letters asking, for instance, why has the householder been appointed to gather in these taxes, and why must they supply their date of birth when the people in England and Wales do not have to? Such action would be disruptive, but perfectly legal. I took part in that, but felt further action was needed. I argued that if government does not reflect the will of the people, then you have a right to resist by any reasonable means open to you, including civil disobedience. Many of us felt we could sustain a non-payment campaign at least for a while, as well as all the other campaigning ideas.

Despite the comradely decision made at Govan, those of us who signed up for non-payment found ourselves under attack by people in our own party. Not willing to put up with this, I commented at a fringe meeting at our annual conference in Blackpool that I was fed up with people who praised the breaking of unjust laws in other countries, or in past times, but never here and never now. George Galloway, who was on the platform with me, said he wished he had said that. 'Never mind, George, you will,' came an amused voice from the audience. But George pointed out we were not asking people to stand in front of tanks, or throw stones at soldiers firing bullets. Non-payment was hardly revolutionary. That was one of the few times I ever agreed with George Galloway.

There is a myth that the Poll Tax was imposed by Margaret Thatcher as an experiment on Scotland to see how it panned out before implementing it in England. Many believe that to this day. But the truth of the matter is, the Scottish Tories wanted the Poll Tax in Scotland ahead of England and Wales, and they persuaded Mrs Thatcher to implement it. They believed it would win votes in the leafy suburbs, whose residents had been fearing the impending rating revaluation would vastly increase their rates bill. They calculated richer households with high rateable values for their properties would be grateful to have their share of paying for local services reduced. Thatcher was dubious at first, but gave them the go-ahead with this chance to increase the Tory vote. In the end it became clear that voters in our more affluent areas were not that selfish. They, too, opposed this legislation and the Tories suffered even greater losses at subsequent elections.

We campaigned against the tax in all kinds of ways. Maryhill Labour people sat down in the middle of Maryhill Road – the main thoroughfare through my constituency – and invited motorists to blow their horns if they agreed. Naturally, some blew their horns to indicate annoyance at our being in the road. A local policeman came plodding along towards us, very slowly and deliberately, then with great politeness told me that he would have to arrest us if we kept this up much longer, but as the press had their photos, would that do us for now?

Tommy Sheridan was, of course, the most famous of anti-Poll Tax protestors, but we disagreed with his line. At an open meeting in Glasgow to consider how to fight against it, when a majority supported non-payment, he wanted everyone present to hold themselves committed to non-payment. Well, of course, he was not speaking at a meeting of an organisation making a decision for the organisation. I argued you could not impose that decision on any individual. People should be encouraged to refuse to pay, as an act of solidarity, but we had to recognise some people, for perfectly good reasons, just could not commit themselves in that way. For one thing, not everyone could be certain to put the money away and leave it untouched until the day when you had to pay up. Many could not do that. There was always the pressure of other bills to pay. Many people would end up getting their benefits deducted at source. Others were on a very low income indeed (there was no national minimum wage then) and could not face even a small amount of penalty. Some thought that they would get away with never paying anything, not even the amount they had previously paid in rates – a fine principle, indeed. Weren't we supposed to be defenders of local government services?

The legislation at the time in Scotland permitted bailiffs to enter a debtor's house and take away non-essentials in lieu of payment of the money. 'Essentials' were defined rigorously, so they would leave behind a very barely furnished house indeed.

I had an elderly couple in great distress at my surgery, and the old lady was in tears. They had a piano that was a family heirloom, and although it was not particularly valuable, they knew they would lose it if the bailiffs came to call. They were not refuseniks. The Poll Tax was a huge increase on their former rates bill, and they simply didn't have the money to pay. And now they had a warning letter from the Sheriff. So I advised them to put any jewellery such as her mother's rings, ornaments, or anything else precious to them into someone's safekeeping. Meanwhile I would get the Sheriff off their backs for a short time, while they found someone to look after the piano. If need be, I would put it in storage.

'But keep it under your hat,' I said. Talk about laughter through tears. The husband said, 'I don't think it will fit under that!'

Tommy was keen on demos outside debtors' doors, trying to keep the bailiffs out, and that is fine for those who can tackle that sort of thing, but this was a quiet, elderly couple, not in great health, who would have been embarrassed and upset at such a kerfuffle.

But that was not the only point of disagreement with the Militant Tendency, led by Tommy. He also led a federation of non-payers, including Communists, Anarchists and the Socialist Workers' Party, but Militant excluded all of these others from committee positions. Why they put up with this I never discovered. The federation lobbied regional councils to ask them not to collect the Poll Tax, and Campbell Christie, then General Secretary of the Scottish TUC, had to point out this would lead to surcharge and disqualification of the people needed to help those in hardship.

I took advice from Bill English on the impact of non-payment on council services and jobs. It was his view that a non-payment campaign would take quite a while to create loss of service or force redundancies, but eventually, of course, it would. Meantime, the very fact that central government provided around 80 per cent of the cost of running council services meant crunch time would be some distance off. So some of us were always committed to non-payment, up until we were close to that point. We did not have a right, in my view, to throw low paid council workers out of work in pursuit of our aims. People could choose, if they wished, to be casualties. They could not reasonably decide to make other people casualties as if they were generals calculating how many lives were worth losing in a battle. People like Tommy think they are this genera-tion's John McLean because they went to jail over the Poll Tax. But John McLean spoke truth to power. Tommy ended up committing perjury.

In September 1988 a steering committee instigated by John McAllion, MP for Dundee East, Dick Douglas, MP for Dunfermline West, and myself as secretary/treasurer, was formed to seek out names of people in every sector of public life – arts, entertainment, sport, churches, universities, trade unions – who would join us in launching the first Committee of 100 against the Poll Tax. There is many a name on that original list that has since become prominent in our political life. We wanted to encourage 'hundreds' in communities all around Scotland, and we were successful in that aim.

The Govan by-election had delayed our launch. As Labour MPs, our first task was to hold on to that seat, and we knew from people's reactions on the doorsteps that the Nationalists were ahead. The SNP won, with Jim Sillars overturning a Labour majority of 19,500. The Nationalists were campaigning to recruit 100,000 people willing to declare they would not pay. They were coming across as active, and the Labour Party as too cautious. This only served to convince some of us that tougher action needed to be taken, by those willing and able to do so.

The launch on 21 November got plenty of media coverage, but not as we had hoped. We had chosen to have it in Glasgow's Winter Palace, on

Glasgow Green, site of many a historic event in the creation of our democracy. We knew the building was being refurbished, but had been assured work would stop for the duration of our press conference, for which we were paying a good fee to the Council. But the hammering and drilling went on and on, and no-one could hear any of our speakers for the din. Media people had come all the way from London, so it was particularly frustrating. I tried phoning various officials to sort things out, but no-one would take responsibility, and the clock was ticking on. In the end I had to suggest that the media people do one-on-one interviews in another, quieter, part of the building. Later I was told by a person working in the bookings office that Pat Lally, the council leader, had instructed that nothing was to be allowed to disrupt the works being carried out. If that was so, then they should not have accepted a booking for that place at that time. I demanded our money back, and got it. Small consolation. Was this a mistake, contrived by a person or persons unknown? I never found out.

By September 1989, local authorities reported that around 15 per cent of those liable had paid precisely nothing. That was nearly 600,000 people. As a *Scotsman* editorial pointed out, the real test would come when debt collection enforcement was put into action. In the same month, I was appointed by Neil Kinnock, Labour Party leader, as front bench Spokesperson on Women's Rights, working with Jo Richardson, the shadow Secretary of State for Women. Not that the Tories had any such Minister in their team until David Cameron became their leader, all those years later. It says something about the difference between Neil Kinnock and Tony Blair. Neil did not suggest in any way that I give up my anti-Poll Tax activity. Tony would not have tolerated it for a moment.

Nevertheless, by July 1990 I was arguing it was time for our Committees of 100 to be wound up. Strathclyde Regional Council had just announced, on legal advice, that they would have to enforce warrant sales even in cases of hardship, something they had always hoped to avoid. Other regional councils were announcing they would have to put up the Poll Tax the following year to cover for unpaid Poll Tax, or alternatively cut services and jobs. We needed to discuss our response to this news. When we had launched, everyone thought non-payers would be caught up with long before now, and here we were, in July 1990, and I for one still had not paid a penny. But we had made it clear from the start that our campaign was always going to stop if jobs and services were at risk.

By late 1991 the anti Poll Tax campaigning had succeeded. There had been a riot in London in March 1990, and demonstrations everywhere. Tory MPs had begun to realise how deeply unpopular it was. Their jobs were at risk. Margaret Thatcher would go before they did. By the 1992 General Election, an estimated 700,000 people had not put themselves on the electoral register. In April 1993, the Poll Tax was abolished.

Then John Major introduced the Council Tax, which at least was an improvement, but still needs reform. Late one night on the standing committee to consider this change in the law, I innocently asked how houses could be assessed for banding when they were not being inspected individually. Similar frontages might have quite different sizes of flats inside, as for example when a Victorian terrace is divided up. There could, indeed, still be a single household taking up every floor. The minister, Christopher Chope, replied that aerial photography would overcome this problem. Eh? Another one to feed to the media.

And now here we are in 2014, and we still have not solved the problem of how to pay for local government. The SNP spent years trying to persuade us that a local income tax was the best way. But there were two key questions they could not answer. If it was genuinely local, then large employers would have to deduct different amounts from all of their staff according to which local authority each one lived in. Did anyone believe they would bother to get it right, year after year, when it added nothing to their benefit and only added costs? And there was a killer objection: why should rich people, who did not have tax deducted by PAYE, get away with paying nothing at all to their local council? Many were already adept at avoiding or evading their national taxes. The Tories were rightly never forgiven for creating a system where the rich paid a lot less than their fair share. Here were the Nats proposing they should pay nothing at all!

My own preference is keeping a property-based tax, but with a larger number of bands so that more is paid for the more expensive properties than has been the case all these years. Those on very low incomes could pay little, or nothing at all. Any such system can have discounts for as many reasons as are thought relevant.

People talk about the high cost of local services, but two aspects are frequently ignored. One is that if we all paid for them as individuals, the cost would be astronomical compared to what we pay our council. The second aspect is that if everyone paid their share of national taxes, and tax dodgers didn't get away with it, central government could afford to spend a great deal more on people's welfare.

In April 1995, Ian Hernon reported in Glasgow's *Evening Times* a ministerial written reply to a question I had tabled, that the real cost of the Poll Tax fiasco to Scotland amounted to a staggering £1.5 billion. That wasted money could have been far better spent on schools, or housing, or the NHS. At that time, long waiting lists for hospital treatment were the norm, schools were in a bad state of disrepair and thousands of people lived in houses with damp running down the walls. That sum could have doubled the education budget, wiped out hospital waiting lists dozens of times over, or tackled all the work necessary to bring Glasgow housing up to an acceptable standard, and have some left over. We were not to see these issues addressed until Labour came to power in 1997.

CHAPTER FOUR

Changing the Recipe

1988

NEW YEAR 1988, and I must have been settling in quite well. I had been elected chair of the Glasgow Group of Labour MPs, and had helped to set up the newly formed Labour women's caucus for both the Commons and the Lords. I began campaigning against the Economic League's blacklisting when I discovered that one of my constituents, Carol Meikle, had been branded by them as 'a subversive trouble-maker' on account of her membership of the Anti-Apartheid Movement. It was great to realise that, just because I had 'MP' after my name, I had much more opportunity to draw public attention to the activities of the Economic League. A lot of people, famous and not at all famous, were involved in that campaign, described in Chapter Five.

Nevertheless, there were occasions in the House when I thought, 'What am I doing here?' Like the time when Ron Brown, MP for Leith, thought the best way to oppose the Poll Tax was to pick up the Mace and throw it to the floor of the Chamber. He then had to pay an estimated bill of £1,500 for its repair. His speech of apology was generally regarded as insincere, and all this led to a motion to suspend him. The Chamber was full to bursting. You didn't see that kind of attendance for boring issues like injustices in the benefits system. Tory MPs were baying for his blood. I personally thought of course he should pay for the damage, but this was way over the top. Nobody had died. Eric Heffer, one of the Liverpool MPs, tried to ameliorate things by saying the motion was taking a hammer to crack a nut. A nut was precisely what many of those present thought Ron was, so this provoked some hilarity. I looked around in distaste and caught the eye of my old friend, Norman Buchan. He jerked his head towards the nearest door, and I joined him outside. We headed for the smoking room, which was for once empty, and had a glass or two while we took some comfort in shared attitudes. Norman was a real comrade and friend.

In March the Government brought in a parsimonious training scheme for the unemployed. It had allocated no extra funds, yet the number attending were planned to increase by a third. The whole idea was just a way of fiddling the dole figures. Benefit would be withdrawn from those who did not participate in the scheme, but if they did they would be working for only £5 a week more than their benefit level. Considering travel costs added on, this was hardly the great incentive it was cracked up to be. What we needed was real job opportunities, and they were nowhere in sight.

The same month was notable for other reasons. Nigel Lawson began his budget speech by commenting that it would be the last time this event was 'untelevised'. Going through a list of Tory measures, he got to the point when he announced the rate of corporation tax for small companies would be reduced to 25 per cent. Alex Salmond jumped to his feet to protest against the entire budget and was then suspended for a week. Interesting, because in 2011, re-elected as First Minister in the Scottish Parliament, he was now demanding that Westminster allow him to reduce the corporation tax in Scotland to 10 per cent. Why a reduction to 10 per cent was desirable, even necessary, for Scotland, but 25 per cent was so outrageous for the UK that he got himself thrown out on account of it has never been explained. Never mind, it got his name in the papers. He has even claimed that, as he remembers it, his action was against the Poll Tax. There are three small objections to this version of events. First, neither in Lawson's speech nor Alex's interventions was it even mentioned. Second, the Poll Tax legislation affecting Scotland had already been passed before Alex even entered Parliament, and the SNP makes a virtue of staying out of English business. Third, Nigel Lawson was strongly opposed to the Poll Tax, and expressed his views frequently at cabinet meetings, to no avail.

In June that year, Ian Lang, Minister of State at the Scottish Office, was claiming that there were signs of improvement, and that unemployment in Maryhill had fallen by 848 during the past year. I asked where people had found these jobs, but no answer was forthcoming. It certainly was not industry in Maryhill – there was very little left. He went on to outline the urban programmes for Glasgow, 11 of which would be based in Maryhill. Sounds good? Not in reality. The only definite, guaranteed new jobs were 41 full-time and 11 part-time. It was true that the West of Scotland Science Park's funding would create high-skilled and professional jobs, but nearly all of them would be filled from outside my constituency. Meanwhile, 47 jobs would be lost when the community programme closed.

* * *

In April 1988, four months after the Intifada had begun, I was part of a delegation along with Clare Short and Mo Mowlam, to the West Bank and Gaza, as members of the Labour Middle East Council. We flew to Amman in Jordan, and crossed the Allenby Bridge into the Occupied Territories. The following day we were unable to meet our host, the General Secretary of the Federation of Trade Unions in the West Bank, because of a blanket curfew inhibiting any movement between towns and villages in the West Bank and Gaza. I was more than ordinarily anxious to meet someone at a senior level in the trade union federation: when our delegation was seen off at Heathrow, we were asked if we would take a large sum of money to hand over to them. Obviously we did not want to declare it when entering Israel, as it would probably be confiscated. I went over to the Boots branch a few yards away from where we stood and bought a box of sanitary towels, and then stuffed the notes well down inside. When my luggage was checked on arrival in Israel the male security officer recoiled a little, an expression of distaste on his face, and gingerly pushed the box aside when he recognised what it was. I stood at the table trying to look casual.

So, on to Jerusalem, the box never out of my sight, wherever I went. We stayed in a hotel in the east of the city well known to Scottish trade union delegations, and at last I was able to hand over the money to someone in authority, who laughed incredulously when he heard how I had got it through. We sat around a table in the hotel, discussing the difficulties under which their trade union officials were operating. Mo, I noticed, was behaving a bit oddly, putting her feet up on the table, crossing and uncrossing her legs, and showing a great deal of leg in the process. Yet not in a seductive way. It was more reminiscent of a little girl unselfconsciously throwing her limbs about. It was obviously disconcerting our hosts, so when I had the chance I said to Mo, 'Didn't your Mum ever tell you not to let the boys see your knickers?' To which she replied, 'My Mum gave up trying to make me act like a lady a long time ago.' It obviously hadn't occurred to Mo that she was embarrassing our hosts. It is only recently that I learned showing the soles of one's shoes is considered deeply insulting in the Middle East, but I am certain they would have realised she wasn't intending anything of the kind.

We visited Arab cultural and youth organisations, met representatives of the General Union of Palestinian Women, the deputy editor of the Palestinian Press Service, whose office had been closed by the Israeli authorities the day before, and finally visited the Makassed Hospital. We heard numerous accounts, by people in positions of responsibility, of dreadful deeds carried out by Israeli soldiers, well documented elsewhere. I have no reason to disbelieve them, especially since it corresponded with what we saw ourselves, and what follows is precisely what we witnessed.

What we found in that first hospital we visited shocked us, and the report we drew up contained the evidence of all three of us. We saw bed after bed after bed occupied by boys between ten and fourteen years old with severe bullet wounds, chiefly to their legs. They would be crippled for life and therefore find it hard to get work. Yet, lying there in their beds, they would smile at us and lift their hands to make the Victory 'V' sign. Another youth had such dreadful injuries to his stomach and bowels from high velocity bullets that the doctor said he would not live. Bernard Mills, the Director of the United Nations Relief and Works Agency for Palestine Refugees, told us he had repeatedly complained to the civil and military authorities about the beating of children under ten years old, but to no avail. In Hebron Hospital the following day, after our meeting with the mayor, we talked with a youth who had been shot in the leg while praying in the mosque. A woman of 50 had injuries to her arms and legs from rubber bullets, sustained while trying to protect children from being beaten. She was also suffering the effects of toxic gas. Out in the street we could see several soldiers, all of them armed, standing on rooftops overlooking the mosque as a helicopter flew overhead. Then, as we were leaving Hebron, we saw several injured people being taken to the hospital. There were three being carried on rough and ready stretchers, clearly dead as they were covered from head to toe. The military would not allow us to return to the hospital, where we had hoped to lend a hand in any way we could. Later we went to Nablus and met trade unionists, doctors, lawyers and professors. We visited Litihad Hospital and again saw rows and rows of youngsters in beds, suffering from terrible wounds. One woman had been thrown off the roof of her house when she was hanging out washing. At one hospital we were told by senior administrators that soldiers had raided the hospital only recently. They had even broken into the theatre while an operation was going on and forced the surgeon out. The patient died.

The day after the 40-day siege ended we visited a village, which I will not name. As we travelled around in the dark at night, with no other cars to be seen on the road, I was feeling a bit concerned about our safety, which one of our hosts noticed. Maybe it was the way I kept biting my lip and chewing my nails. Sitting beside me as we bumped along a country road with hundreds of olive trees on either side, he said in a gravelly voice that I can hear in my mind's ear to this day, 'Do not worry, Maria. We will protect you.' Considering what we had witnessed in the hospitals, this reassurance seemed a bit optimistic. But, I thought, this is what they live with all the time. Then he joked, 'If the soldiers spot you three, they'll run away!'

We sat talking around an outdoor fire, the stars shining above us in a clear sky. We met bereaved parents, families and friends. Their words had to be translated for us, but anyone could read the pride and determination in their eyes. Our hosts told us of the economic and trade union repression. They had served long and repeated jail sentences, frequently without trial, for defending rights we take for granted. A traitor had been executed in this village. We told them frankly we disagreed with capital punishment, and they answered they had no jail to put him in, so what else could they do? We timorous souls were, as promised, eventually delivered back to our hotel unscathed.

Finally we visited Gaza City and the refugee camps of Beach and Jabalia with the assistance of the relief agencies, including UNWRA. In Gaza we met an elderly woman who had fallen foul of the Israeli authorities for running a sewing class and possession of suspicious sewing materials. To wit, her box of remnants contained some that were black, white, green and red, the colours of the Palestinian flag. No doubt she had been making Palestinian flags. So what? Is that anything to hassle an old woman about? We met yet more patients who were blind, paraplegic, quadriplegic, and lame for life.

Our last meeting was in Amman, where we discussed with a number of members of the Palestinian National Council what needed to be done to achieve a lasting solution, and afterwards had an interview with Reuters. I was surprised when the PNC asked us if we had any advice. What did I know that could be of any use to them? Clare offered one small thing: 'Could they ask Yasser Arafat to shave every day? That unshaven look he had did nothing for his presentation.' Either the message was not passed on, I hope, or it was and he ignored it. I then travelled back to London a day ahead of the others, because I had a meeting I could not miss. I had a hairy time at Tel Aviv airport security, when I told the man I had been on a holiday. He commented it was a very short holiday, wasn't it? I just nodded and said yes, so it was. Pressed further, I told him and one of his colleagues I had visited the Dead Sea, Nazareth and Bethlehem, which was true. We had made short visits to these historic places. They delayed and delayed, and searched my case over again, while they continued to question me and I provided vague answers. Oddly enough, they paid no heed to my notebook, where (if they had someone who could read Pitman's shorthand) they would have found plenty of evidence of where I had been and whom I had met. The comical thing was, even if I had been prevailed upon to tell them, I couldn't have told them much. My memory for names of people I have met only once is shocking. I finally had to say to them that if I missed that flight and returned to London too late for my meeting, there would be repercussions from Her Majesty's Government. I had no idea whether that was true or not, never having been abroad before as an MP. Anyway, it worked. I got on board in the nick of time. When Clare returned she showed me a dum-dum bullet she had picked up in the road. When questioned at the airport why she had this on her, she said it was a souvenir. Again, she was questioned at great length.

* * *

That May, during the Whitsun recess, I visited Nicaragua along with Audrey Wise, Alice Mahon and Dawn Primarolo as guests of the Sandinista women members of the National Assembly who wanted to have discussions with Labour women MPs. No, not a junket. We paid our air fares out of our own pockets, and lived modestly throughout. They told us that current issues they were working on included rights of mothers as workers, reducing health risks in maternity, and family planning. There were a lot of illegal abortions and the hospitals regularly treated women who were almost dying. Abortion was only legal if the mother's life was in danger. Nowadays, sadly, even that right has been repealed. A woman will now be allowed to die, even in the case of an ectopic pregnancy when the foetus cannot survive anyway, and even if already existing children are left motherless. The penalties are so severe that only a tiny few doctors dare break the law to save her. I wonder if Daniel Ortega, who raised such high hopes around the world, realises how badly let down many women feel about such a backward step. At that time, however, progress seemed to be taking place. Wives had the same rights as their husbands. Sexist language was forbidden, and the laws written accordingly. This reminded me of a spat I had once with an official back in the UK, who assured me that 'he' was always to be understood as including 'she' in Acts of Parliament. So I looked forward to one day tabling a clause in a Bill to enforce 'his' right to breastfeed in restaurants and public places. The Nicaraguan women's battle on media images of women seemed to have been won. Neither newspapers nor posters featured women's bodies being used to sell products, nor were there any 'page three' pictures of women in popular newspapers.

We learned from them, too, about their organisation of parliamentary democracy. Each National Assembly Member had a twin member, who could vote when the other had to be away. If a Member failed to turn up over a period of some length without reasonable cause, he would be deemed no longer in office and a by-election would be held.

On our way to Nicaragua, we had to transfer flights in Costa Rica, where the British ambassador was to greet us and look after us until it was time for our plane to Managua, the capital of Nicaragua. So we were taken in a limousine to the Embassy, where, you might think, we could expect a little food so many hours after we had last eaten. No chance. We were offered tea, coffee and a small plate of biscuits by the wife of the ambassador, whose sole topic of conversation was the impossibility of getting decent staff. I nearly choked on my biscuit when Alice, with an air of innocence, asked if she had made the biscuits herself. The ambassador did not impress us. He took it as his duty to warn us that the Sandinistas could be very charming and persuasive. Who did he think he was talking to? Daft wee lassies going out to our first disco?

Audrey had brought two large suitcases full of pins, needles, buttons and zips, which were fallen upon with great delight when we finally got to Nicaragua. Such items were subject to the embargo imposed by the United States, and they were needed for their clothes-making co-ops. We visited a wheelchair repair workshop, where they were desperate for parts – again, barred by the USA. People told us that they had lived in poverty and fear under the Somoza regime. They were still in poverty, largely due to the embargo, but now they lived in hope. We attended a public meeting in the open air, convened by Sandinista women, where one peasant woman conveyed her delight at acquiring literacy, having been taught by her primary school aged children. She had never dared before to approach the archbishop over something that was bothering her, but now she could write. And she wrote again when she did not get an answer. Then she sat in his waiting room and refused to go away until he saw her. The fight against 'machismo' had made Nicaraguan women more independent and confident.

As we walked around we saw the best graffito that I have ever seen. It has become quite famous since. On a poster reading 'The Man from Del Monte Says Yes', someone had written, 'But the People Say No!'

We were told that European politicians usually stayed in the best hotel in Managua, and did not travel elsewhere. We did not want to go all the way across the Atlantic just for talks, seeing practically nothing of the Sandinistas' achievements, so we had a number of visits lined up. We went to what in Britain we would call a cottage hospital where it was two to a bed, in turns. Contra forces had bombed so many hospitals that the medical authorities were forced into having beds that had to be shared in those that remained. In spite of this, the World Health Organisation, a few years before, had awarded Nicaragua its prize for the greatest achievement in healthcare by a third world nation. I was proud and pleased to see Scottish Medical Aid running a health centre. We visited a school with no roof, but there had been no school at all before. We even dropped in on an open prison where the inmates did hard but necessary work in the sugar cane fields.

Then it was time to visit a town called Bluefields on the Atlantic coast. So off we set to a small airport, where we stared in disbelief at the plane we were to travel on. I had never seen anything like it except in films about the Second World War. It was indeed a Douglas DC3 that, sure enough, had seen service against the Nazis. We watched in fascination as its propellers were started up by hand. Gulp. But later on my brother Jim, who spent most of his working life in the aircraft industry, told me they were reliable workhorses and had a great reputation for safety.

When we arrived we were met by our host, Ray Hooker, a Sandinista member of the National Assembly. He had become famous for his experience as a prisoner of the Contra. He had been allowed to live, when they might otherwise have killed him, because he told them stories or set them riddles night after night. He had got the idea from the Arabian Nights tales.

The next day the rain – a deluge such as I had never seen even in the West of Scotland – had us wet through before we even left the steps of our hotel. No raincoat was capable of resisting such a downpour. Nevertheless, we set off down the river to visit a village that had historic connections with Scottish settlers, where Ray showed me, with much amusement, a gravestone dated over 200 years before with the name 'Maria Fyfe' on it. On the way there we noticed that the Sandinista soldier, rifle in hand at the back of our speedboat, kept looking from left to right. 'Was he looking out for logs in the water?' Alice asked. We had been told that if we hit a log we would capsize, so we were provided with life jackets. 'Not logs,' came the answer. 'He's looking for Contra in the bushes.' We were urged to speak loudly, because if there were any Contra they would assume we were American when they heard English being spoken. Also, it would be a good idea if we sang. So we belted out 'My Old Man's a Dustman', 'On Ilkley Moor Baht 'at' and 'I Belong to Glasgow'.

We had a party that night at Ray Hooker's home. Among the fruits plucked from the trees and the fish freshly caught, we were told laughingly there was a particular item that had a reputation as an aphrodisiac. At that moment I was up dancing with some local man. 'Pity it's going to waste, then,' I remarked. 'Maria!' Audrey cried. 'Behave yourself!' Only joking.

Dark falls early in the Tropics. And if you have never experienced it before, it is unbelievably dark. We had already been appalled by the sight of cockroaches scuttling around the lobby of our hotel, so when the lights suddenly went out and we knew that power would probably not be restored for hours, we felt nervous. Alice, in the bed next to mine, thought that a cockroach was walking over her legs. Or maybe it was only sweat dripping in the intense heat. But she couldn't even see her hand before her face, and was extremely reluctant to put her hand down under the sheet to settle the matter one way or the other. We both passed a sleepless night. The local paper, on hearing of this, ran a front page headline: 'British women MPs more afraid of cockroaches than the Contra.' Bluefields has been torn apart again and again by successive hurricanes, but it still struggles on.

On the day of our return home I fell foul of some bug or other. Between diarrhoea and vomiting endlessly, I was monopolising one of the toilets at the back of the plane. I had been offered a bed in one of the hospitals in Nicaragua, but aware of their limited supplies and having seeing the conditions there, I thought, no fear. I would get back home by hook or by crook. Alice nursed me all the way across the Atlantic, and told me later she actually thought I might die as she watched over me on the flight, but wisely kept her thoughts to herself. She continually gave me Immodium and forced me to drink water, which I found hard to do.

I don't remember anything that happened at Amsterdam airport, or how long we waited for the flight to London. Possibly I fell asleep. An ambulance drove up to take me off the plane when we arrived at Heathrow, and they put me on a drip immediately in a small medical room in the airport grounds before setting off for St Thomas's. At the hospital they were unable to identify what bug had assailed me, as, thanks to Alice's insistence, it had been washed out of my system by the time they took my samples. But I was so shattered they told me to spend a week in bed in my London flat before attempting the journey back home to Glasgow. On about the third or fourth day I thought, how hard can it be to take a taxi to Heathrow? It would be so much better getting back to my real home. It was the Whitsun recess and nobody was about in my block of flats. So I disobeyed doctors' orders and by the time I got home I was so weak I could hardly stand. But it was so good to be home. Then the phone rang: it was my friend, Ali Syed, who worked at the Western Infirmary, asking me to go to a meeting. I told him I felt too ill, and he asked me what was wrong. He left work that instant and brought me packets of rehydration powders, which began to take immediate effect. When I felt up to getting dressed I discovered I had dropped two dress sizes. There are better ways to lose weight. But not even that experience could ever make me regret going to Nicaragua. Who could forget hearing a villager say, 'When you have danced, no-one can make you forget you have danced.'

* * *

Earlier that month something I will never forget happened. Jo Richardson was the main speaker at Glasgow's May Day rally, and she told the crowd that Scotland's rejection of the Tories was an inspiration to England and Wales. I was a speaker on the platform for the first time, having faithfully been in the audience for too many years to remember, and my general theme was how, around the world and in our past history, people had fought repression and injustice and we honoured them that day and took courage from them.

Later the same month a Tory MP, John Stokes, tabled an Early Day Motion criticising the way the French had celebrated the election of President Mitterand, with blaring of motor horns and waving of tricolours, opining that 'this House is glad not to be composed of Frenchmen, but of Englishmen who conduct themselves differently after general elections'. I put down an amendment to congratulate Mitterand, and to remind Stokes that 'this House includes Members who are neither English nor men'.

As Labour's sole woman MP in Scotland, I began to find I was constantly asked by reporters for quotes on issues they thought particularly suitable to ask a woman about. I thought, fine, but wouldn't it be a good idea to ask some of my male colleagues what they thought of cases like the one that arose in February 1989? That month, some of us women MPs had a talk with Lord Mackay of Clashfern, the Lord Chancellor, concerning the sentencing of child killers and abusers. I also took the argument to Lord Advocate Lord Fraser, who had oversight of the Scottish judges. There had been many a light sentence before, but this was the last straw. A judge had given two years probation to a man who had sexually abused his 12 year old daughter, who was epileptic and had a mental age of seven. In passing sentence, he told the accused that the fact his wife was pregnant and off sex was a mitigating factor. Those were days when it was common to hear of judges opining that women who went out without a bra on, or wore short skirts or low necklines, were inviting rape. Two safe deposit robbers had only recently been sentenced to 18 and 22 years respectively, when no-one had been hurt. Why was justice in our courts so skewed? Obviously because the judges value property more than people. Lord Mackay was very sympathetic to our concerns. We knew he meant it when he sacked the judge in the 12 year old girl's case within a couple of days. He also agreed to give our message to the Judicial Studies Board, who train English judges, and urge them to require their students to meet women's groups during their training. All in all, a very satisfactory meeting. A few hours afterwards I was phoned by a reporter who asked me if it was not a bit intimidating meeting such an eminent man as Lord Mackay in his very grand suite of offices. Never thinking for a moment that I would be quoted word for word, I replied, 'Och, no. He was great. He's a lovely teddy bear of a man.' I don't know what His Lordship thought of it, but I was forever afterwards much more careful of what I said to the media.

I still seemed to shock some people when it came to defending abortion rights against David Alton's Bill. In January 1988, Jo Richardson came up to Glasgow to speak at a Fight Alton's Bill rally in the City Halls, which I chaired, following a march through the city. The hall was packed. Alton's intention was to ban all abortions after 18 weeks of pregnancy, cutting the limit from the current 28 weeks, but in effect really reducing to 16 weeks to ensure erring on the safe side. I pointed out that many tests to determine abnormality were not carried out until 20 weeks of pregnancy.

Of more than 10,000 abortions carried out in Scotland during 1986, only one per cent were carried out after 20 weeks. The largest group of women requiring late abortions were those with a severely deformed foetus.

While I received numerous letters in support, there were a few that were very hostile. Archbishop Thomas Winning sent me a friendly little note, simply asking me to explain my stance, but two of the parish priests in Maryhill accused me of 'liking' abortion. I wrote back to them to say that in all kinds of civilisations, at all times in history, desperate women had done dreadful things to themselves when abortion was not permitted. Bills like Alton's did not stop abortion: they were more likely to send women to back street abortionists, or attempt to do it themselves. If it was going to happen, I preferred it be carried out in sterile conditions by people who knew what they were doing.

I had a little personal experience in my '20s, before David Steel's 1967 Act came into force, which brought this home to me. One day I heard an urgent knocking on my door, and standing there was a distraught friend. She had been to a back street abortionist earlier that day, who had then told her to go home. But on the way she began to bleed badly, so she headed to my door, simply hoping I would be at home with my young sons. I was really worried for her, and said she couldn't take such a risk with her life. If the bleeding didn't stop soon I was going to get her an ambulance. Fortunately it did stop, and I took her to see my GP, who confirmed she would be safe to go home.

Recalling her nursing experience in a gynaecological ward, my friend Alice Mahon revealed the dreadful things she had seen all too often before David Steel's Act made legal abortion possible. Women did die, or were left unable to have a child, as a result of methods so grim and dangerous we can only speculate what state they must have been in.

There was another thing that irked me about some of the 'pro life' MPs and others. Why did they care so little about those children already born? Why should families in my constituency have to live several floors up in multi-storey blocks, in flats ridden with damp, without a safe place to play, when some had so much money they could never live to spend it?

Jo and I benefited hugely from the experience of Ian Mikardo, a former MP and good friend of Jo's, who taught us how to organise whipping. We had to draw up short briefings on each clause of the Bill and on any amendments that had been tabled, circulate them, and phone round to gather support. There would be many members on our side of the argument, or minded to compromise at some point, who would not be in the Chamber hearing the debate. When the division bell rang they wanted to be clear on which lobby to enter, especially if the doors were just about to be closed. The party whips were standing aside from the whole thing, as 'conscience' issues are given a free vote by all of the parties. Neither Jo nor I had any experience of whipping, so we really needed this kind of help. Tony Banks warmed to the task we gave him. He stood outside one of the doors to the voting lobbies, declaiming: 'Pope and Paisley that side, women and choice this side!' But the contribution to the debate that I will always remember was Teresa Gorman, someone with whom I was normally in disagreement about everything under the sun. But on this occasion she put the case for a woman's right to choose: 'How dare you treat me, and every other woman in this country, as if we should have no more say than a plant pot?'

The Bill worked its way through the system until May, when on the day of the final debate Alton's opponents scuppered it by parliamentary tactics. We presented no less than 11 petitions on constituency matters and 13 points of order, taking up 40 minutes before he could even begin his speech, and so making the Bill run out of time and unable to complete its report stage. This was attacked as 'dirty tricks'. But coming from people who were hiding the fact that they were really opposed to abortion full stop, no matter how grave the situation, this cut no ice with us. Anyone who could even think of forbidding abortion to a girl barely old enough to conceive, but who was pregnant as a result of her father committing incest, was not someone I felt inclined to listen to. The Fight the Alton Bill (FAB) campaign office was deluged with telephone calls from women who wanted to express their relief and thanks.

With all this going on, perhaps I shouldn't have been surprised to be invited to speak at the Tribune Rally at the Labour Conference in Blackpool that September, but there I was, on the platform with the likes of Michael Foot and Ron Todd, telling the audience how we had been fighting the Poll Tax in Scotland.

That November, the new joblessness figures were published. In Maryhill alone 7,861 were out of work, no less than 24 per cent of the local workforce. Maryhill had the fifth highest numbers of unemployed in the country, and between the general elections of 1983 and 1987, the jobless total had increased by nine per cent. I had calculations done for me, which revealed that the cost in foregone taxes and national insurance contributions took out £52 million from Maryhill alone.

When Neil Kinnock appointed me to the front bench as deputy to Jo Richardson, his words were, 'I want you to rattle their cages'. I needed no further encouragement. Jo had been doing far too much for one person, taking on campaigning around the country with women's groups of all kinds, at which she was brilliant, as well as keeping tabs on what was going on in Parliament. She had a favourite way of making the point that it was not only a matter of getting more women into elected bodies. What she would urge those women who succeeded was to work to change the laws and bring in new laws to the benefit of women, because a male-dominated Parliament simply did not think about some of the issues that mattered to women. 'It's not just about a fairer share of the cake. It's about changing the recipe!'

She had asked Neil to appoint me and I was delighted to be such a square peg in a square hole. There was no other job in Parliament I would rather have done. Jo's office was typical of such an unassuming woman: it had desks for her and her two assistants, with another one squashed in for me, and there was nowhere to sit visitors down. Other leading front benchers had far grander accommodation. On 27 May 1989, Jo and I launched a new policy programme to give a better deal to women. Called 'A New Future for Women', it sought to end taxation on workplace nurseries, and create high quality crèche provision for the under fives. Fathers would, under a Labour government, be entitled to ten days paternity leave when the child was born, and parents of young children would be given up to five family days off every year. We reminded people of our commitment to the national minimum wage. A new carer's benefit was proposed, to help people (usually women) who gave up their job to look after an elderly relative. There was more: better street lighting, more police on the beat, and more regular health screenings and check-ups. It is interesting to note how much of that agenda was achieved and is now taken for granted. We will see how much of it survives the Con-Dem cuts.

Jo and I went around the country, together or separately, speaking to women's groups of all kinds. On the way to a meeting somewhere in the region of the River Severn, she told me what had happened there many years before, when she had been a parliamentary candidate for the first time. She was speaking on a platform in the local hall to a large audience, when suddenly she felt her knicker elastic snap. So she tried to continue speaking, the forefinger of one hand jabbing the air as she made her points, the other hand pressed hard against her hip. Then she began to think this must look odd. But there was a solution. Along the front of the stage there was a bushy row of plants, and she thought, my French knickers would slip off quite easily if I let go, and when they drop to the floor I can step out of them and no-one, at least in the audience, will notice. So she let go, and managed to extract one foot when they landed on the floor. Now for the other foot. She kicked – and a small heap of peach satin and lace landed in the face of the local reporter. She would tell this story to new women candidates, saying don't worry – whatever you do, it won't be worse than that.

CHAPTER FIVE

Blacklists: A Blot on British Democracy

YOU MAY NEVER have heard of the Economic League. It was not an organisation that sought publicity. But for most of last century it secretly gave hundreds of major British companies information about prospective employees, and equally secretly, these companies funded them handsomely. It was responsible for keeping untold numbers of people out of work, not even aware they had been judged and sentence passed.

My own involvement in raising this matter in Parliament began in 1981, long before I entered the House of Commons. The magazine *Labour Research* revealed information sent to them by a mole, alleging that the Economic League was receiving substantial payments from a body called British United Industrialists. He listed a number of highly-placed donors in the world of industry. Yet nothing much happened in the immediate aftermath. I was working during the '80s at Central College of Commerce in Glasgow, where a trade union studies unit had been set up, teaching TUC courses to union reps. There was some awareness amongst our students of what the Economic League was up to, but there was no concerted action to deal with it by the trade union movement or at a political level. My colleagues and I at least made sure our students were forewarned.

It wasn't until 1987, when *World in Action* (the must-see current affairs TV programme), ran a series of three sensational programmes exposing what the League was up to, that all over Britain thousands sat up and took notice. Some decided action had to be taken.

The first programme to be scheduled in February that year was about the blacklists operated by the League. Entitled 'The Boys on the Blacklist', it uncovered cases where the Economic League had listed individuals on the basis of incorrect information. In one example, a member of the Conservative Party was listed as supporting the far-left Militant Tendency. In another, a labourer was listed as a member of the Communist Party – shock, horror – when he wasn't a member of any political party and had never even voted. There was a pensioner in Dundee who had lost a foot and was blinded whilst serving with a Highland regiment in the Second

World War. He came to be listed by the League because he wrote a letter to a newspaper praising Edinburgh council's decision to buy a picture of Nelson Mandela. A former printer in Glasgow applied for an industrial relations job that turned out to involve spying for the League. When he said he wasn't interested in the job, he too was blacklisted. *World in Action* went on to scroll down a long list of companies subscribing to the Economic League. Beecham, Brook Bond, Barclays Bank, Dunlop, Glaxo, GEC, Hotpoint, Pilkingtons, Plessey, Royal Bank of Scotland, Reckitt and Coleman, Shell, Taylor Woodrow, Tate and Lyle, Wimpey, Whitbread – these are just a brief selection of the names revealed to their startled viewers. We learned that the Economic League had 60 full-time employees, busily concocting this kind of rubbish from eight offices throughout the country and providing this 'service' to an incredible number of famous companies. These companies were generous donors to the League. In 1986 alone, they netted £1 million.

The second programme, 'The Secret Life of Mr Walsh', revealed how a man named Ned Walsh, who had been taken on trust as an active member of ASTMS, was in reality a spy for the League for the past 27 years. Yet more instances were revealed of people who had been blacklisted on the flimsiest of grounds. Again the programme questioned the moral right to act as the League was doing.

The third programme, entitled 'Secrets of Wine Office Court', gave us more hilarious examples of alleged dangers to society. Hamish Imlach, the Scottish folksinger, agreed it was true: he *did* have a go at Margaret Thatcher in his performances. Learning he was listed as a Communist Party member, Hamish said, 'People I know in the CP think of me as a wishy-washy liberal.' He had been in the first concert party flown out to the Falklands to entertain the troops. When the League spotted candidates they saw as subversive standing at elections, they added the names and addresses of all the people who nominated them. Solicitor Derek Ogg, a Conservative candidate at both regional and district levels and chairman of the Young Conservatives, was listed as an anarchist. He surmised this must have come about because he was the editor of a magazine that was sold in an anarchist bookshop. And so it went on and on. But the really disturbing thing was that in 1986 alone, over 200,000 people were checked through the League's records by member companies, each one totally unaware that allegations, true or false, were being made against them.

In October 1987, *Labour Research* returned to the fray, this time in an article entitled 'Around the Right'. It showed that the League had helped recruit 'politically reliable people' for Rupert Murdoch's Wapping plant.

But now, as a MP, I could do something that had not been open to me before. In February 1988 I tabled Early Day Motion No. 614 congratulating the *World in Action* team on their recent programme, and it was signed by 76 Members. Then in April I had an unexpected opportunity to raise the issue of blacklisting in a Ten Minute Rule Bill. This kind of Bill is a way of allowing backbenchers to raise issues in a brief debate, which in theory can win through to legislation being passed, but in reality is unlikely to succeed if the government of the day is opposed to its contents. Clare Short had asked me if I would queue for her to ensure she did not lose her chance of bringing forward a Bill of her own. She was detained elsewhere, and needed someone to take her place in the queue outside an upstairs office in the House of Commons at the ungodly hour of 6am, so as to prevent any Tory MP, some of whom had offices nearby, from sneaking into the queue ahead of her. Such were the childish tricks of some members. They didn't necessarily have any serious intention of pursuing a Bill of their own, but might just want to prevent a Labour member from getting a Bill on its way to being debated. But while I patiently waited, longing for my breakfast, a Labour whip hurried up the stairs to tell me that Clare could not get away in time to present her Bill to the clerk after all. I could use this opportunity to present a Bill of my own. I knew at once what I would do. I would seek an amendment to the Data Protection Act to give anyone a right of access to information held by any organisation for the purposes of blacklisting. Before any employer could seek information on a prospective employee, he would have to obtain the permission of the applicant before doing so. Applicants would be given a copy of all information held about them.

Two points were at stake here. The Data Protection Act only gave people the right to see computerised data held on them, not files, manually constructed lists or index cards. So blacklisting organisations could easily get around the provisions of the Act. The second point, I surmised, was that if such organisations had to fulfil the requirements of my amendment it would destroy them. Big firms would be embarrassed at having their connection with the Economic League exposed.

My big day arrived on 12 April 1988, when I introduced my Blacklists (Access to Information) Bill for its First Reading, the first ever Bill I had brought forward. I drew attention to the case of one of my own constituents, who had been blacklisted on account of her voluntary work for Anti-Apartheid. Until a TV producer showed her the Economic League's blacklist, she had no idea she had come to the League's attention. I went on to point out that she had received neither apology nor explanation from that body. Nor was this an isolated case. The League's own publication, *Companies Under Attack*, listed organisations such as Oxfam, Christian Aid, CND, the Child Poverty Action Group, the Low Pay Unit and many more as suspect. I would imagine many employers would see an interest in at least some of these matters as praiseworthy, if anything, but I suppose the League would know its own paymasters' attitudes. I had not expected the drama that was to follow. As the *Financial Times*, *Guardian*, *The Herald* and *The Scotsman* all reported (to my glee), the Conservative Member for Colne Valley Graham Riddick stood up to speak against my Bill and implied that Labour Members were against the Economic League because we had something to hide. At once Willie McKelvey and Max Madden raised points of order. The Speaker (although a Tory himself) agreed with them, and rebuked Riddick for his 'veiled allegation' that the Economic League might have anything 'on' anyone in the House. Riddick nevertheless called for a vote, which was silly of him, because not enough like-minded MPs were around to troop in and vote to support him, and we won by 138 to 49. Some of the 'extremists' who voted for my Bill that day included John Smith, Donald Dewar, Alastair Darling, Michael Foot, Neil Kinnock, John Prescott, George Robertson, Alex Salmond, John Reid, David Steel, and even, to my surprise, the Rev. Ian Paisley.

On 12 July I called a meeting in support of my Bill's Second Reading, which was to take place on 15 July. The platform included Michael Meacher, at that time Shadow Secretary of State for Employment, Madeleine Colvin, the legal officer of the National Council for Civil Liberties, and Richard Norton-Taylor of the *Guardian*. The room was filled with supporters of the campaign from far and wide, including members of the public. But on that day the Tory majority was organised and, of course, my Bill failed. But a large turnout of Labour Members, with support from some Plaid Cymru, Scottish Nationalists, Liberals, SDLP and others gave me great encouragement. Neither that day, nor any other, did even one Conservative Member support our counter-attack on McCarthyism in Britain.

Other developments were on the go. In September that year, Ron Todd wrote an article in the Transport and General Workers' Union magazine praising the initiative of one of its sponsored members, and called on those involved in collective bargaining to put an end to the use of Economic League information by their employer on their agenda for negotiations. Several companies announced they had already ended their subscriptions.

In the same month, the *Observer* pointed out that the Economic League's blacklist included one Wendy Henry, editor of *News of the World*, presumably because in her youth she had been a member of a Trotskyist sect, the International Socialists. Also listed was Roger Rosewell, lead writer for the *Daily Mail*, who had been a full-time official of the International Socialists and was the author of a pamphlet entitled *The Struggle for Workers' Power*. For an organisation that purported to provide sophisticated knowledge of all that goes on in the Left, it seemed strange that it should be unaware of the well known phenomenon of people being ultra-left in their youth, condemning any and all Labour people as sell-out merchants, only to fly – as their careers developed – straight over into the ranks of the Tory Right.

Richard Norton Taylor of the *Guardian* and Mark Hollingsworth of Granada TV were joint authors of a newly published book, entitled *Blacklist*. They pointed out that the conventional wisdom had always been that Britain escaped 'relatively unscathed from the political witch hunt'. Not so. It was hidden. The authors detailed collaboration between MI5, local police forces and private detectives working for the Economic League.

The *Observer* also reported that the Economic League was to hold a crisis meeting. It was finding itself hard pressed after withdrawal by many companies following media disclosures of their donations and the recent publication by the *Observer* of the contents of the organisation's list of alleged subversives.

Leeds Trades Council stepped forward with a great initiative of their own. They hosted a national conference in November 1988 on the Economic League, sponsored by MSF, ISTC and NACODS. There it was revealed that the League, founded in 1919 when some right wing alarmists got together to prevent revolution from breaking out in Britain, had some 2,000 British companies, employing between two and five million people, subscribing to it. The League was the oldest member of the Radical Right network of fundamentalist pro-Conservative organisations. In its own account of its history, it records an initial meeting called by an admiral who had recently been head of naval intelligence. Others in attendance that day were top industrialists in mining, shipping, engineering and brewing. One can't help wondering if they had been imbibing a little too much of the latter's products.

And here it was, still fantasising, in 1988. In offices in London and seven other areas in mainland Britain, including my own city of Glasgow, it held files with details on a quarter of a million people. On at least 40,000 occasions since 1979, the League had discouraged companies from employing people on the basis of their secretly held information. The whole set-up was described as 'McCarthyism in Britain'. In reality, it was worse. These British McCarthyites' victims had never been notified of any judgement on them. No opportunity to defend themselves. No appeal.

On 24 November 1988 I convened the first meeting of the Anti-Black-listing Campaign. I was surprised and delighted that so many fellow MPs joined in, while I wondered why a campaign of this kind had never surfaced before. But then, some of us new members had entered Parliament from a campaigning background, respecting what the good MPs did, but realising the fight against the Tories had to be on a much broader front than Parliament alone. Over 130 Labour MPs joined, including Alastair Darling, Donald Dewar, Robin Cook, Derek Foster (the Labour chief whip), Michael Foot, Dennis Skinner and John Smith. Liberals, Welsh and Scottish Nationalists including Alex Salmond signed up. Quite a large number of the wider public joined too. They came from universities and colleges, trade union branches and trade clubs. Trade union movement big names like Ron Todd and John Monks, journalists including the producer of *World in Action*, and several individuals who were simply outraged at this sort of thing being legal in modern Britain all flocked to join.

I challenged the Economic League to a debate any time, anywhere, where they could justify their spying on British citizens. I was able to include a great quote from John Alderson, former Chief Constable of Devon and Cornwall on our leaflet:

> I would regard the Economic League – which is an organisation unaccountable, unofficial, funded by business management – prying into legitimate political activity as absolutely outrageous... I think the whole business of unofficial organisations taking this on themselves is highly dangerous. We've seen this in Europe before – unofficial organisations

becoming a police force which is unaccountable. It's highly dangerous and quite improper.

Even the *Press and Journal* covered our meeting, delighted to announce that an Easter Ross man, Paul Mack, who was president of his Boilermakers' Union branch, had been elected as one of its office bearers. He had been drawn to participating in this new campaign because it was particularly relevant to the oil and construction industries. Our meeting drew attention to my second effort at a Ten Minute Rule Bill, due to have its first reading on the 28 of the month. That failed too, a large Tory majority having turned out against it. Still, I was determined to keep at it until success was achieved, even if that meant waiting for the election of a Labour government.

The Tories seemed to feel no embarrassment over the further idiocies of the Economic League that continued to be revealed. In 1989, *Scotland on Sunday* ran a story that the League was now targeting Greens, on the grounds that the class war was no longer where the most active subversives were at work, and Britain's interests were being undermined by clever people working on environmental issues.

As *Scotland on Sunday* reported, that April the League had decided on a change in strategy, and now focussed its attention on the environmental lobby. It announced it would prepare dossiers on Green activists and provide companies with intelligence about campaigns aimed at them or their products. Mr Michael Noar, their director-general, said in a rare interview with the paper:

> It's environmental issues that are attracting the sophisticated left. It is realising the old class battle on the shop floor isn't worth fighting any more... One of the features of extremist politics is that the members are becoming increasingly middle class. These firms are natural targets for this much more highly educated and articulate revolutionary.

Then the League offered a new service: to spy on gays, to discover for the benefit of insurance companies whether or not they were health risks.

We had another meeting on 12 May 1989 at which Richard Brett, a former military intelligence officer who had been the League director in the North West of England until he left them over disagreements spoke to our gathering. He commented:

> I cannot recall a similar power being held by any single non-Government official in this country even in wartime, let alone peacetime... I consider

it presents a most serious threat to our way of life and our democratic traditions.

Then came another startling development. On 4 October 1989 the Glasgow *Herald* exposed the fact that Michael Forsyth, the Scottish Secretary, had appointed a Mr Russell Walters as his new Chief of Staff, whose previous employment had been as a research/intelligence officer with the Economic League. Mr Forsyth asserted that Walters was a mainstream Conservative and that the League 'does some very excellent work'.

As 1989 came and went I had another go with a new clause in the Employment Bill. In that debate great contributions were made by Chris Mullin, Bob Hughes, David Clelland, Jim Wallace and Audrey Wise. For my own part, I pointed out that leaders of the Economic League had been secretly advising the Prime Minister on anti-union laws. Its Director-General was secretary of a small group of industrial representatives who told the Prime Minister what they wanted. Yet again, we were defeated by a large Tory majority.

January 1990 saw Tony Blair leading for Labour in debate, on yet another Tory Employment Bill. He was sparring with Michael Howard, then Secretary of State for Employment, on a wide range of issues, including blacklisting for union activities. He exposed the weakness in the Government's case, which amounted to saying the activities of the Economic League were legal. So they were. But that was the whole point. They were legal because the Tories had set their faces against changing the law and making this McCarthyism unlawful.

Yet more efforts against the huge Tory majority were mounted throughout that year and the next, all to no avail. However, now I had an important promise: Labour would legislate when it came to power to tackle this gross injustice once and for all.

In the early months of 1990 our campaign took a new tack. I wrote polite little letters to the chairmen of leading companies, asking them if they still used the League's screening service. I mentioned that the League's information had been shown to be extremely unreliable, and individuals had been listed for the flimsiest of reasons. I went on to say I was sure that their own experience had taught them that, generally speaking, trade unionists are reliable and competent workers. Replies poured in, confirming that their company had ceased subscribing, in some cases two or three years before, or even as long ago as the '70s. Only one reply was unfriendly. Lord Weir, on behalf of the Weir Group, wrote:

I am afraid that we view our hiring practices as being our own affair, and a matter between ourselves and those we employ or seek to employ. Certainly, we do not see them as having anything to do with individual members of Parliament.

I happily sent that off to the media.

25 September 1991 saw fantastic coverage for our Anti-Blacklisting Campaign: Paul Foot, whom I had known since his days as a young reporter on the *Daily Record* in Glasgow and as a fellow member of the Young Socialists, took up the entire front page of *The Mirror* with a headline in gigantic capitals – 'Big Brother's Blacklist'. It ran for five consecutive days. He and his colleague Bryan Rostron catalogued their efforts to get answers from the Economic League, and exposed their lies. With four other reporters, they got in touch with all sorts of people on the League's list. They listed several MPs and others in public life, but also a number of people whose lives had been wrecked by the League. Their article began: 'The "subversives" on the Economic League's Big Brother blacklist range from top politicians to troubled teenagers and pensioners who want to save the whale.' They included a 15 year old lad who played truant from school, an Oxford University professor, Labour MPs such as Robin Cook, Peter Hain, Tony Benn and Ken Livingstone, trade union leaders, liberal journalists and campaigners for civil liberties.

Among the unknown were countless building workers, a blind war hero, an 82 year old animal lover and a retired missionary.

Paul reported on 26 September that in 12 years of writing his page, he had never known so many people respond so angrily. Neil Kinnock challenged John Major to take action, but of course he did nothing. On 27 September the *Mirror* Comment went for John Major. It pointed out, 'If John Major really wants, as he says, an open society he can start by condemning the Economic League and its secret blacklist'. It went on to say two days had gone by since the story had been revealed, and Neil Kinnock had demanded action the day before. The *Mirror* editorial also put this point:

The Tories are quick to condemn trade unions for being the so-called paymasters of the Labour Party but they won't condemn the League because the people who have financed it are among their paymasters. Over the years, the Tories won votes by denouncing trade union 'kangaroo courts' but the League's blacklist is the worst of all secret courts. No charge, no trial, no defence. Only a verdict of guilty and a life-long sentence on people unaware they had even been accused.

The *Daily Record* ran a front page headline, 'Scots Smeared by the Black-list', and its editorial got torn in. Headed 'Evil List Must Go', it declared the Economic League should be shut down *now* and its evil list torn up. Across a double page spread it set out a number of brief biographies with photographs of people in public life in Scotland who had been blacklisted by the Economic League. Examples included Adam Ingram, MP for East Kilbride, PPS to Neil Kinnock, listed as 'Militant'. This is a man who was widely known as 'Hammer of the Trots'. Margo MacDonald, but oddly not her husband Jim Sillars. Myself, not surprisingly, considering my long-standing campaign against them. But, incredibly, my elder son Stephen was also described as 'Militant'. He commented, 'They couldn't be more wrong! I am against Militant and have often spoken against it publicly.' Pat Lally, then leader of the Labour Group on Glasgow's council, was similarly defamed. He had helped expel several Militant supporters from his local party. Kenneth McLellan, ex-president of the Educational Institute of Scotland. Tom Clarke, MP for West Monklands, who was outraged:

> Communist Party supporter? What, me? And me a former altar boy. I thought I was known as a moderate. If people like me, with my views, are on that list it's an absolute disgrace, and there should be legislation forcing all such organisations to make their information public.

For variety, I suppose, Professor Sir Kenneth Alexander was listed as something different: in his case allegedly a member of the Socialist Workers' Party, with which he had never had any connection whatsoever. Author William McIlvanney, described as 'Marxist', had never been in any political party. He commented: 'I am a socialist and not a Marxist. But they probably don't know the difference. What I find pernicious is that it's obviously not acceptable to even have opinions.'

Jimmy Hood MP, a former miner who had been one of the principal leaders of the striking Nottinghamshire miners in 1984, spoke for all his parliamentary colleagues who had come to the attention of the League when he said, 'I suppose in a way I would be disappointed if I was not listed. But really this type of thing is absolutely despicable.' There were more and more names of fellow MPs, two of whom, Allen Adams and Norman Buchan, had died. Colleagues who were not listed said they were jealous, and wanted to enhance their street cred by getting themselves blacklisted. Why, they demanded, had they been left out? Finally – you couldn't make it up – the *Record* discovered that its own chief reporter, Gordon Airs, was blacklisted! The only reason he could think of was that he had once spent a night in jail and fined for contempt of court for adhering to the journalist's principle of not revealing a source, although top judges later on accepted he had honourable, principled reasons.

At the end of all this, in 1994 *Tribune* joyfully proclaimed the demise of the Economic League in its editorial. Under the weight of all the superb work done by sectors of the media, the placing of the issue on the bargaining agenda by the unions, and our campaign's exposure, financial support for the League had collapsed. This campaign showed investigative journalism at its best: hard hitting, putting substantial resources into investigating the details, demanding action.

Meanwhile, I had been successful in persuading the Select Committee on Employment to enquire into recruitment practices. It called in League representatives to meet them, who were not impressed. On behalf of the TUC, John Monks put a clear and convincing case. HR experts told the committee they strongly disapproved of secret lists. Employers had no legitimate need for such methods.

The committee, not surprisingly, recognised that the activities of the Economic League posed serious civil rights and professional personnel problems. It recommended that the Government make such agencies subject to legislation similar to the Consumer Credit Act. It did not set out safeguards such as I had proposed in my Bills, which would have fatally weakened secretive vetting organisations, but even this relatively weak recommendation was not acted on anyway, despite Dundee MP Ernie Ross's vigorous demolition of the League in committee.

On 30 March 1999, we thought all our efforts had come to fruition. The Labour Government's Employment Relations Bill changed the law. Speaking in the debate, Stephen Byers, the new Secretary of State for Employment, declared:

> To be blacklisted from employment – to be unable to work in one's profession or trade – simply because of trade union membership or activity is entirely unacceptable, and many of my Honourable Friends have fought and campaigned for years for the day when, through legislation, we can ensure that such blacklisting is no more.

Clause Three, 'Blacklists', was passed without a vote.

But that is not the end of the story. A few years ago I began to read about blacklisting rearing its ugly head again, particularly in the construction industry, and trade unionists saying there ought to be a law. 'What are they talking about?' I exclaimed in irritation. 'There is a law.' But apparently, so convinced New Labour ministers were that the Economic League and its minor imitators had been destroyed, they thought there was no point in bothering to complete the legislative process by seeking the Queen's consent to ban something that no longer existed. I have been told that they thought, why take action to kill something that has already died?

However, realising that it had not died, Gordon Brown's Government made blacklisting illegal by Regulations created in 2010. The Information commissioners had raided the Consulting Association's office in 2009 and discovered that 40 of Britain's biggest construction companies kept blacklists. Eight of them have now agreed to pay compensation to the fraction of the number of people affected for whom they have contact details. The Consulting Association was itself formed by a former employee of the Economic League, soon after that body disbanded, funded by £10,000 from a major construction firm.

As I write, construction workers have been bringing evidence to Ian Davidson MP, chair of the Scottish select committee, on blacklisting in their industry and the committee is pursuing the issue with vigour. The Scottish Parliament is bringing forward a Bill to prevent blacklisting where public contracts are concerned. Good, but we need to go further. There ought to be severe penalties against this evil practice, no matter what sector it is engaged in. People go to jail for less.

CHAPTER SIX

Babies and Bars

1989–1991

A NEW YEAR, and another Tory wheeze to reduce the unemployment statistics. They withdrew entitlement to income support from unemployed 16 and 17 year olds, thus wiping off thousands of young people from the records. Along with other Labour MPs, I provided those affected in my own constituency with a pack on how to go about appealing on the grounds of severe hardship. Of 254 appeals that went through one of the three Maryhill social security offices, 172 were successful.

Government-funded training schemes continued to be farcical. In the whole of 1989, £100 million had been spent on employment training in Scotland alone, but no-one knew how many trainees succeeded in finding full-time employment. No-one knew how many went back on the dole. As for the quality of the training schemes, it was a disgrace that any government saw fit to endorse them.

A Clydebank girl, Ann-Marie Campbell, had gone on a course to learn typing. She was taught to solve a murder mystery, and she was taught how to survive on the moon. Perhaps her instructors thought she would be more likely to find work there than in the Glasgow conurbation. What she did not do was sit at a keyboard even once in eleven weeks. One of my own constituents was keen on a career in gardening. Imagine his disappointment when all he did, travelling each day from Maryhill to Airdrie, was clear rubbish from a derelict site.

Trainees could not simply walk out. If they did they would lose their money. There was nowhere to complain. All this was perfectly legal. And so it went on, year in and year out. At one time, years later when Tony Blair became leader, I was asked by party apparatchiks to get in touch with all the large businesses in my constituency and ensure that they understood Labour was open to hearing their views. I had spent a lot of time over the years trying to open up job opportunities with the help of small and medium sized enterprises. The party officials from down south were incredulous when I told them there was no such thing as a large business in Maryhill, and the largest employer was the hospital.

* * *

On 7 June 1989 we had an opposition day debate that has lasted long in all our memories. The subject was the deteriorating state of the economy – a dry subject, one might think – but John Smith (then Shadow Chancellor) soon had us all in knots as he made the most of the unhappy relations between the Chancellor and the Prime Minister. John began by talking about Nigel Lawson's 'blissful ignorance' of the true state of the British economy. 'The sort of ignorance', John went on, 'demonstrated by a man on the top of a ladder who does not know he is about to fall off.' Then, following a forensic taking apart of government policy, he went on to have some fun over Mrs Thatcher's disagreement with her Chancellor. Lawson wanted Britain to join the Exchange Rate Mechanism of the European Monetary System, and she did not. They were known to be in heated disagreement, but the Prime Minister had declared, 'Nigel is a very good neighbour of mine, and a very good Chancellor.' 'Neighbours,' John half sang, half spoke: 'Neighbours. Everybody needs good neighbours. Just a little understanding…' and so on through the words of the soap opera tune. She hadn't a clue what he was on about. Her frontbenchers sat looking grim, while the Labour benches were helpless at the sight of all the very un-amused faces opposite us.

You would surely not think it possible to confuse that John Smith with any other John Smith. But once an MP for a Welsh constituency, also named John Smith, was on holiday in Cyprus, and got a phone call from the Whips' Office telling him to return immediately for an important vote. He tried all the airlines, to no avail, and phoned them back. 'Stay where you are,' they ordered. 'We'll sort something out.' And sure enough, they did. There was a RAF plane heading from their base in Cyprus over to England soon, and they had agreed to let Mr Smith travel on it, if he was ready to leave straight away. So he hurried in a taxi to the RAF Station. As he approached he could hear a brass band playing. A red carpet had been unrolled. Who could that be for? He wondered. Himself, as it turned out.

* * *

In June 1989, the Glasgow *Evening Times* ran several pages on the issue of domestic violence, reporting on the outcome of a survey they had launched the previous January into women and violence. They mentioned that I had raised the matter with the Scottish Office, only to be told it would be too expensive to separate the statistics on domestic violence as distinct from other crimes of violence.

The same month, my old friend Janey Buchan MEP (sad to say she died in January 2012) and I urged the Chancellor to lift the tax on workplace nurseries. We had discovered that the Treasury treated such a facility in the same way as a company car and imposed VAT. In this case it amounted to £20 a head each week, a staggering sum back then. At that time in Denmark 44 per cent of children under two and 87 per cent of three to six year olds benefited from publicly funded childcare. In the UK it was two per cent of under-twos and 44 per cent of three to six year olds. At that time there were only 33,000 day nursery places in the whole of the UK for more than 3.5 million children under five, the worst figure in the entire EC. Even Portugal, with its much lower GDP than ours, was streets ahead when it came to childcare. The impact on mothers who wanted to work was obvious: in Denmark 75 per cent of women with children under five went out to work. In Britain it was 28 per cent.

In October Jo Richardson and I, along with over 100 women, lobbied MPs on issues raised by the Equal Opportunities Commission. Their figures showed that more women now worked part-time than full-time (54 per cent) and yet less than half were on equal pay with their male colleagues, and working conditions such as pension rights and sick pay were ignored by employers.

In the Commons itself we were struggling to get minor improvements. One MP with young children asked if the so-called family room, which provided nothing other than a few armchairs and sofas, could be given a budget for some toys. Eventually the committee responsible allocated £200 for books and children's chairs, but nothing for toys. That same committee funded a rifle range, but rejected a request for a crèche on grounds of cost.

With all this going on, no wonder women in the Party were demanding more women in Parliament. It had become obvious that far too many matters that affected the female half of the population won scant attention in a male-dominated Parliament. At the Labour Conference in Blackpool in 1988, I had been delighted to share a platform at the Tribune Rally with Ron Todd, who had done so much to encourage me. This was an occasion when the suits lost. Conference voted to have a woman on every parliamentary shortlist. Rosina McCrae, vice-chair of the National Labour Women's Committee, called for a quota of women MPs. 'Let's face it,' she said. 'The brothers have operated men-only lists for years.' Margaret Prosser of the Transport and General Workers' Union answered the silly argument that Margaret Thatcher should put us off having a woman Prime Minister ever again. Speaking in the debate at Conference in 1989, she commented, 'No-one ever said we couldn't have a man after Adolf Hitler.' The infighting was intense. George Galloway made persistent efforts to have Johann Lamont dumped from being Hillhead constituency party chair, and remove her from membership of the Scottish executive of the party. He thought she would challenge him for his Westminster seat when it came to reselection, even though she never made any attempt to do so. Johann was, and remains, highly regarded for good sense and political honesty, rewarded in December 2011 by being elected our first-ever Leader of the Scottish Labour Party. George ended up being expelled.

Back then he had the support of only one ward in the constituency, a loss of support he had managed to achieve in a mere three years. Learning nothing, George – boasting he would show the Scottish Parliament how to do it – failed to win a seat in Glasgow when it came to the 2011 election.

In November I had a visit from a young constituent, Caroline Munro, who had been penalised for being too clever. She had overcome deafness to gain an excellent set of Highers and had won a place on an honours science degree course. If she had entered on a building surveying diploma course, which was what she had originally applied for, Strathclyde Regional Council would have paid for it. However, college officials advised her she should go for a BSc honours, and degree level courses are funded by the Scottish Education Department. Ian Lang, the Education Minister, refused to pay for her needs. It took me until the following March to get anywhere, when changes to the way grants for disabled students were administered were announced in Parliament. A brand new allowance of up to £4,000 for non-medical personal helpers, such as interpreters for the deaf, was to be introduced, along with a grant for equipment such as Braille word processors. I wonder now if payments such as these will survive the Con-Dem cuts.

Jo and I had virtually no opportunity to speak on our brief at the Despatch Box in Parliament, simply because there was no such animal as a Conservative Minister for Women to answer questions. So we relied on our front bench colleagues to allow us in occasionally. It was the day for Welsh Questions. In his *Times* column the following day, Matthew Parris fancifully portrayed Peter Walker, the Secretary of State for Wales, as a budgie contentedly trilling away, not a care in the world, in the gilded cage they called the Welsh Department. He then went on to write:

> The terrifying Maria Fyfe stamped in... but the budgie had ceased to care. The cage may keep him in, but at least it keeps Her – Her of the sharpened claws – out.

I still feel disbelief that anyone thought of me as terrifying. Soft lot down there in London.

1990

The first meeting of Maryhill Labour Party in the new year was in January, and the large crowd present voted unanimously to reselect me as their candidate. It was wonderful to have such consistent support.

In February I joined other Labour MPs in supporting Margaret Ewing's Abolition of Warrant Sales Bill. The number of warrant sales sought by local authorities had risen sharply due to non-payment of the Poll Tax. In 1988 there had been over 6,000 warrants to sell delivered, but only 714 reports of sales taking place. That meant there must have been thousands of people who, to avoid their household goods being sold up, took out loans from loan sharks, legal and illegal, to pay their Poll Tax and put themselves into an even worse financial position.

Although some reforms had been passed, I pointed out that a sheriff officer could still take away a family's television set, which might be the only entertainment they could afford, or grandmother's wedding ring, or their teenager's second-hand guitar.

Three months later, I did something that upset and disappointed some of my friends. The *Sun* had asked the Labour Party to provide a woman MP to write a review of a new TV sitcom about a female MP, acted by Penelope Keith. Our media people asked me, as junior spokesperson for women, but I felt unhappy about doing so, and sought advice from Jo. She asked Neil Kinnock, and the consensus was that we had to find a solution to a problem: our private polling showed we did not do well with female *Sun* readers, many of whom actually thought our foremost women's policies must be Thatcher's ideas, because she was a woman Prime Minister. We had to get through to them and win such women for Labour. I spent a sleepless night worrying about it. On the one hand, I could see the force of the arguments for. Against, well, how long have you got? The *Sun* was the *Sun*. It lied. It insulted the intelligence of its readers. Owned by anti-union Rupert Murdoch. At last I decided what to do, although I have thought ever since I made the wrong decision. I would write the article, taking the opportunity to put across a few messages about what Labour women MPS were doing, but ask the *Sun* to send my fee to the striking ambulance workers' fund. That way, I thought, they will be unlikely to ask me again. Someone else could do it, someone who wouldn't lose sleep over it. The paper said they could only send payment to the writer of the piece, so I then sent off a cheque for the same amount to the strike fund, telling them the source of this largesse. Then someone in a Glasgow branch of the T&GWU complained about one of its sponsored members writing for that Tory paper, but of course he was unaware of all the facts, and would naturally presume I was taking Murdoch's shilling. So I wrote an explanation to the Branch and heard no more about it. I thought I had better put this matter into my monthly written report to Maryhill CLP, and take whatever consequences were coming. No-one there had raised it, because no-one actually read the *Sun*. When I spoke to my report, this item just received nods and shrugs – no questions. But I have reasoned since that one wee article was not going to get much across to a readership fed with Tory propaganda daily (or more recently, for their readers in Scotland, Nationalist). I know Neil Kinnock meant well, in trying to use all of the media for the sake of getting our message across to millions who might otherwise never know it. And look what they did to him when it came to the 1992 General Election, with their picture of him on the front page alongside the words, 'If Neil Kinnock wins today will the last person to leave Britain switch the lights off'. Neither of us anticipated the day when we would have a party leader who actually liked Rupert Murdoch.

That year Maryhill Labour Party leafleted local bingo halls and shopping centres on the scandal of low pay. In April we had noticed the wages offered for jobs advertised in the local job centre: dry cleaning £1.97 an hour, security guard £1.15 an hour, and £65 a week for a hotel porter. This was what was going on with a woman Prime Minister – don't try to tell me Margaret Thatcher was a good thing for women or men. A national minimum wage had to wait for a Labour Government.

Some of us 'put babies before booze', as the *Glasgow Guardian* had it, when we argued for a workplace nursery to be provided when Portcullis House, the new parliamentary building was being planned. I commented at the time, 'You can drink at a bar here all day if you are so minded, but there is nowhere to feed a baby.' Women MPS were furious when we learned that the first phase of the new building plans included yet another bar and banqueting rooms, but the crèche would have to wait five years. I had recently tabled questions to our female Prime Minister on why the shooting gallery in the basement below the House of Lords was refurbished at public expense, and a room set aside to play chess, when a request for a hairdressing salon was turned down for lack of space, although there had been a barber's shop for many years. They could find money for all that, but a few toys were too much to expect. Nor were the House authorities willing to let tights be sold in the shop, although they did sell men's socks. Their problem was, and I am not making this up, where to put the Portcullis logo on the tights? All items sold in the souvenir shop had to have the logo somewhere. On the packet might seem the obvious place, but there you go. No-one would think from all this nonsense that the majority of the 10,000 who held Commons passes were women – cleaners, secretaries, librarians and waitresses. Parliament would collapse without their services. In fact it took until November 2010 to create a crèche, in a room that had been one of the many bars around Westminster. Well, it had only taken 40 years of campaigning. We shouldn't expect to rush things.

In April 1990 we were all plunged into controversy with the Human Fertilisation and Embryology Bill, and I was leading one night on the Standing Committee that was considering it clause by clause. I was in favour of its general principles. Embryo research had increased our understanding of infertility and could help to overcome genetic defects that caused a wide range of serious illnesses. A large lobby of Parliament by people who would not have had children if they had known what their children would suffer made their points forcefully. Not all people seemed to realise that an embryo is not a human being, but a number of cells clustered together, no larger than a full stop. Some of the local church leaders were angry about it, and condemned Donald Dewar and me for supporting the Bill. George Galloway voted for an amendment calling for the research to be banned. In the debate I made the point that we were not talking about perfecting human beings. This was not about flawlessness – as if there could be consensus about what constituted flawlessness. We were talking, for one thing, about recognising the desire of someone who cares for a child with severe illness or incapacity, day after day, to be allowed the small human happiness of certainty that their next child would not suffer likewise. I can't remember who argued – it may have been Edwina Currie – that the men who were opposed to this were showing their ignorance of women's bodies. Nature itself, unassisted, got rid of embryos all the time. So why shouldn't some be saved for such a good purpose, when so many went down the toilet pan? There were yet more amendments proposing reduction of the ceiling times for abortion, and once again we benefited from Ian Mikardo's help and the goodwill of many of our male colleagues as well as those women who would stand up for women.

Life on this committee was not always deeply serious. We could rely on certain members of the Lords to create some unintentional amuse-ment, as they did when Scottish clan chiefs set about attempting to enshrine their claims to blood purity in the law. They had tabled a clause precluding the possibility of test tube babies succeeding to clan titles and coats of arms because they were not of the blood line. Brian Wilson condemned this as 'genetic fascism', and in the West Highland Free Press he quoted me at some length. I attacked the arrogance of a few highly privileged people in the House of Lords, who could impose their obses-sions on the time of Parliament. Would that my constituents, who did not have that sort of class-based advantage, could impose their needs on Parliament's attention. I went on to say the Roman emperors often adopted heirs. If that was good enough for the Roman Empire, might it not be good enough to rule the clans which matter to nobody nowadays. Peter Thurnham, though, came up with an argument that really foxed them. He said:

> From what we know from DNA these days, among the population as a whole, between one in five and one in twenty people do not have the genetic father who is shown on the birth certificate. Applying that to the House of Lords, it means a good few people should not be there.

But never mind logic and facts. Summing up for the Government, Solicitor General Sir Nicholas Lyall said that if my amendment was accepted, 'a peerage might be inherited by the non-genetic son of a peer who had resulted from the artificial insemination of the peer's wife using donated sperm'. As Brian commented, the committee did not appear to be appalled by this prospect and voted 10–6 to throw out the clan chiefs' clause.

In July 1990, Jo and I decided to have a go on an issue that would never occur to our male colleagues. We had received letters from women who were concerned about toxic shock syndrome, associated with the incorrect use of tampons, which had killed a small number of women. TSS was not mentioned on the outside of tampon packs. Users were simply instructed to read and retain the leaflet inside. While the leaflets generally gave details on the safe use of tampons, and information on TSS, the importance of changing tampons regularly and using the lowest absorbency possible was not explicitly linked with TSS. The manufacturers said that to put explicit warnings about TSS on tampon packs would scare people unnecessarily given the rarity of the disease.

It was common then for young women not to know they should not keep them in all night. The symptoms of TSS were not widely known, yet speed in getting medical treatment was essential.

Then I was lucky with my application for a Ten Minute Rule Bill. This meant I was required to stand at the right of the Speaker's chair, while the Clerk read out the name of my Bill and asked what day I wished it to be debated. As I stood there waiting while other business was being conducted, Nicholas Soames, seated on the government benches, said to me jovially, 'See you've got a Bill up today, Maria. What's it about?'

'Wait and see,' I replied.

Then the Clerk, as is customary, shouted the name of the Bill in a loud voice. 'Tampon Safety. What Day?' As I gave a date for my Bill to be debated I saw Nicholas shaking his head in disbelief. 'What is this place coming to?' he groaned. Upstairs on the committee corridor I held a press conference. Donald Dewar came walking along, and asked me why all these reporters were milling about. I told him, and he shuddered and walked on. Inside, a reporter had the cheek to ask me whether I used tampons. I told him I considered that no business of his. I had no wish to either promote or disfavour tampons, merely ensure their use was safe. My personal habits were irrelevant. But thanks for the compliment – I was now some years into the menopause. He looked bemused until the penny dropped.

The manufacturers responded. In 1992 they agreed with the Department of Health and decided to upgrade the information both on the pack and the leaflet, and from January 1993 all the major UK companies put easily noticed warnings on the outside of the packets. I had taken this issue up because somebody had to do it. But I will admit I was also enjoying noising up male colleagues who thought such things were unmentionable.

That October, Norman Buchan died after a long illness. In a brief potted history of his life, Janey recounted a story I had told her of a day in the Members' tea room some months before, where a group of Labour women MPs were sitting. Norman was just about to go to a TV studio for an interview, and a button had come off his jacket. He asked, 'Any of you lot handy with a needle and thread?' and got a roar of laughter. We would have told most of our male colleagues if they thought they could run the country they could learn to sew on a button, but we knew Norman really cared for women's rights. Someone did produce a needle and thread, seeing it was Norman and time was short.

I for one recalled the night 20 years before, when I was a speaker for the first time at an election meeting. Norman, having to cover a very large constituency with a lot of villages, needed to get round two or three meetings on the same night, so he needed speakers to keep things going in any one hall until he turned up from the previous meeting elsewhere. So he asked me to help, even though I was inexperienced. I tried to ignore the butterflies in my stomach, and made my theme the unfair division of wealth in our society, referring to the recently formed 7:84 Theatre Company, whose name illustrated the point that seven per cent of the population owned 84 per cent of the wealth. Time went on. It was now ten minutes past Norman's estimated time of arrival. What to do? I found out three things that night. I could keep talking, and not dry up. I could encourage questions and give answers. And I could improvise. I brought out a round sponge cake from my shopping bag and cut it up to illustrate the 'world's ill-divided' point. Norman came in the door, bemused to find us all munching slices of cake.

Then in November 1990 Margaret Thatcher was forced to stand down. The Poll Tax had been her undoing. I was sitting in a local hairdresser's near my flat in Kennington, getting my messy hair tidied up, and the radio was on. They interrupted a music programme to announce her defeat. At once shouts of joy arose from all the women there, staff and customers alike.

My everlasting memory of the Thatcher years was when, during a surgery in Maryhill, a local man asked me, 'By the way, do you never feel like shooting That Woman?' Everyone knew who That Woman was. I replied, 'Often, but I don't want to spend the next ten years in jail.' He looked at me as if he thought his MP was a bit dim. 'But do you no' understand? No jury in Scotland would convict you!'

Then there was the problem of a nation divided by its numerous dialects. My assistant Vicky, a southern Englishwoman, asked me one day, what is an oxter? 'An armpit,' I replied. 'What brought that up?' 'Well,' Vicky said, 'Mrs Fraser was on the phone, saying she had lost the file with all the documents she was going to bring to your constituency office, and she definitely put them under her oxter when she went out. I thought she was talking about a piece of furniture.'

At my surgery one morning I had my comeuppance. A couple had come along for the umpteenth time. They simply could not, or would not, grasp that their housing points came nowhere near the total required to get a transfer to Jordanhill. This is one of the most desirable areas in the city, where only a small number of public sector houses can be found. I had tried and tried to help them, pointing out it would be another ten years before their points total came within range. Yet they could, straight away, have a house in an area a lot better than their own, if not as desirable as Jordanhill. But no, it was Jordanhill or nothing. Concluding my remarks, I said, 'Getting you a house in Jordanhill just can't be done. There's no magic wand.'

As they left the room, I heard the man say to the assembled queue, 'No use going to her. She says she hasnae got a magic wand.'

1991

1991 was the year of the first Gulf War. The memory of that crowds out what else happened that year. I enjoyed a little amusement when in May 1991 I read a piece by Edward Pearce in the London *Evening Standard*, telling us why virtually all women MPs were not up to scratch. He was against putting any women at all in the Tory cabinet, except Gillian Shepherd. John Major was now PM, and his first cabinet, being all-male, had attracted some criticism. The sole Labour woman Pearce thought worthy of the shadow cabinet was Margaret Beckett. As for the handful of us that he deigned to even consider before rejection, he wrote about me: 'The intimidating Maria Fyfe sounds like strong Scottish domestic drama'. Here we go again, I thought. Men get praised for attacking their opponents, women are supposed to be – what? Maryhill didn't send me down there to be meek and mild. Certainly Jimmy Allison, the Labour Party's Scottish Organiser, did not think so. He retired after 14 years' service that September. He was the best party official in Scotland that we had ever had, down to earth, forthright, realistic and committed to Labour values.

CHAPTER SEVEN

The First Gulf War

BY MID-1990 we were on a countdown to the First Gulf War.

August: Saddam Hussein invaded Kuwait, and sanctions were imposed. One of my constituents wrote to ask if I would oppose sanctions, as they were brutal and affected ordinary Iraqis who did not have any say in the dictator's policies. I had to tell him that with some reluctance I supported sanctions, because some kind of pressure had to be exerted, and it was better than war.

November: I reported to my constituency party that at a meeting of the PLP Gerald Kaufman, Shadow Foreign Secretary, had said party policy remained the same: no blank cheque to the Tory Government, give sanctions time to work, if force to be considered should only be with UN backing.

December: Shadow Cabinet team leaders told to inform their front-benchers that they were to vote in the same lobby as the Government if a vote were called. I immediately informed Jo Richardson that I would refuse to vote for any motion which expressed or even implied support for war when sanctions had not yet had enough time to succeed.

In the debate, the speeches of both Douglas Hurd and Gerald Kaufman made it quite clear they would both prefer a peaceful solution, but they accepted the authority for war was contained in UN Resolution 678. Considering the USA had now sent more forces to the area than they had in Germany at the height of the Cold War, I did not believe we should support the UN in all its decisions, when it was so strongly dominated by the USA. At the PLP meeting on 6 December, I said I would not vote as directed.

12 January 1991: A massive demonstration in Glasgow's George Square, calling for a peaceful solution.

14 January 1991: Early Day Motion tabled by Dawn Primarolo and signed immediately by 36 others, including myself. This was by no means the 'usual suspects'. Other signatories included David Blunkett, Bruce Grocott and John Prescott. It urged that UN authorised forces should not take military action before sanctions had been in operation long enough to have the maximum impact, and every effort should be made to achieve

a solution through diplomacy and other peaceful means consistent with Security Council Resolution 660.

15 January: I wrote to Neil Kinnock to offer my resignation from the front bench. John McFall was the only other frontbencher to resign. I argued for sanctions to be continued, considering Iraq's foreign currency was draining away, and its exports of oil could be completely stopped. Denis Healey – no trendy lefty he – had condemned going to war as a stupefying lack of proportion. I added that I felt particularly critical of the role of the US Government within the United Nations, and its control of our troops. What about its own defiance of UN resolutions, funding of tortures, disappearances and killings in Central America, and destabilising of democratically-elected governments? I quoted Hamish Henderson's anthem:

> Nae mair will oor bonnie callants merch tae war
> when oor braggarts crousely craw.

I went on, 'While the statesmen are sending others to their deaths, in most of the countries concerned the wives and mothers do not even have a vote.' I ended up thanking him for appointing me to work with Jo Richardson, and said I would continue such work from the back benches. Neil sent me a warm, friendly letter in return. He thanked me for the typical courtesy and candour with which I expressed my views, and said he knew I would continue energetically and effectively to work for the objectives we shared. Interestingly, he also wrote:

> ... given the great limitations of Opposition, I will continue to make the case for change without further use of force whilst recognising that, in the very nature of his regime and actions, it may not be possible ultimately to get that change without force.

On the same day we had the vote. It was not a straightforward matter of a substantive motion to say Yes or No to war. It was whether the House should adjourn. This device left no possibility of amendments on such issues as whether sanctions should be given more time to work, or whether we should support a French initiative that the Americans had rejected. Earlier on Adam Ingram, who was in Neil's leadership team, had tried to persuade me that this adjournment device did not really matter. How could I make a principle of whether or not the House should stop talking about it? But I dismissed this as nonsense. To vote with the Government on the adjournment would be seen by the general public as meaning we would side with them on going to war. It was strongly denied by Neil that this adjournment vote was a device cooked up by both front benches: in which case, why try to argue it did not signify? Why not publicly protest to the Speaker that this was not wanted by the Opposition? I can only imagine the answer is that our front bench knew war was imminent, that sanctions were simply not going to be allowed more time to work, and Neil did not want any confusion or misrepresentation about supporting our troops once they were committed to battle.

In the debate Neil argued the case he had argued with me – that sanctions would be best if possible, but a war in the Gulf may ultimately have to be fought. Then he said that considering Saddam Hussein's record, sanctions alone could never be enough to prevent his further aggression. At a later point in his speech he said:

> 15 January should not be regarded as the date of ultimatum... all efforts short of war should be exploited for as long as possible, before force is used... until it can be shown beyond doubt that the only means of securing the objectives of the United Nations is by resort to force.

I found all this confusing. If that was his thinking, why were we being asked to go into the same lobby as the Government, who were clearly gung-ho for going in without delay?

Edward Heath got up to ask an awkward question: 'If we were to go to war because we were impatient, our forces could say: "We are being sacrificed because you are too impatient to pursue the alternative course".' He went on to argue for persistence with sanctions. It is not comfortable to agree more with a former Tory Prime Minister than with your own party leader.

Dennis Skinner mentioned that when the UN proposed that a vote should be held on 15 January, America was so far behind with its subscriptions to that body that it had to hurry to pay them before the vote was held, and told Egypt that the United States would bail it out with $3.5 billion.

As far as I was concerned, Denis Healey made the clincher speech:

> This is the third time in my nearly 60 years in the House in which I have watched a great nation sleepwalking to disaster with its eyes open and its mind closed. Suez... Vietnam... now the Gulf. In all three cases the central problem has been the inability of governments to accept the facts about the consequences of their actions that have been put to them by their own advisers, allied with quite a stupefying lack of proportion... it

is surely madness to embark on war if any alternative is available. Is war necessary to achieve the objectives agreed by the UN resolution that was passed a month or so ago? We are assured by the head of the CIA, no less, that it is not. He told the US Congress in great detail that sanctions were already having a major effect on the civilian economy of Iraq and that within three to nine months they would have a major effect in crippling Iraq's military capability.

Despite such sound common sense being spoken, in the end the vote was 57 Ayes, 534 Noes.

16 January: Maryhill Labour Party put out a press release to say I had their unconditional and unreserved support for my stance. They went on: 'We are delighted to be represented by an MP who places peace before war and principle before preferment.' It was marvellous getting such strong support, given at the earliest moment possible.

17 January: Allied commanders launched a military offensive in the small hours. Who, I wondered, in our corridors of power knew two days ago that we would be at war immediately? I asked the Prime Minister, John Major, if the debate on the coming Monday was to be yet another Adjournment debate, or would the Government make a clear statement of the position? He replied that would be discussed between the usual channels in the usual way.

When we went to war I wrote an article, in answer to a challenge from the *Sunday Times*, in which I raised a few points I had no opportunity to bring up in the debate. Ex-President Nixon had declared the USA was right to be in the Gulf, defending their economic interests. At least he was learning honesty in his old age. It was utterly right to condemn the inhumanity of Hussein's regime, but as Edward Heath had pointed out, all these things were known throughout the eight years in which he was attacking Iran, built up by the USA, the Soviet Union, and our own Government. If the US Government cared so much about human rights, why was it even now funding torturers and murderers in Central America? In Nicaragua it was applying a trade embargo, so rigorous not even wheelchair spare parts for the disabled could get through. There were Conservative MPs whose care for human rights was such they had invited a Contra leader to their party conference. My final point was this: if this war is genuinely on behalf of the UN, why did the Secretary-General, Perez de Cuellar, not know it had begun until he switched on his TV set? I should have known better. My article had been clearly typed up in my office and double-checked, there could have been no possibility of misreading the text, but they made changes that distorted what I said.

21 January: Sure enough, we had another debate but no opportunity to vote on a substantive amendment tabled by John Cryer, which fully supported our brave men and women in the Gulf, but also called for a peaceful settlement. The Speaker had simply decided not to select his amendment to be debated, and he had the last word. Tony Benn, Alice Mahon, John McAllion, Audrey Wise and I made the point that this injustice did nothing at all for the reputation of Parliament. Since I had voted the week before, I had received over a hundred letters from people in Scotland and elsewhere, all but two in support. Apart from many that could be expected, I also had a handwritten note from, of all people, someone as eminent as the Bishop of Salisbury. I concluded by asking how was it that, in the name of the United Nations, only a tiny minority of countries were at war. The vast majority of UN members, who always pay their dues, were not at war.

The motion was finally agreed:

> That this House expresses its full support for British forces in the Gulf and their contribution to the implementation of United Nations resolutions by the multinational force, as authorised by UN Security Council Resolution 678; commends the instructions to minimise civilian casualties wherever possible; and expresses its determination that, once the aggression in Kuwait is reversed, the United Nations and the international community must return with renewed vigour to resolving the wider problems in the Middle East.

I remember thinking *I'll believe that last bit when I see it*. Here we are, over 20 years on, and still no nearer to achieving a just settlement.

Each time I spoke, Tory backbenchers kept trying to shout me down, and the Speaker didn't do anything effective to shut them up. To my delight and surprise, Roy Hattersley wrote in his *Guardian* column:

> The cliché describes bone-headed intolerance as saloon bar behaviour. But many bars of my acquaintance would be ashamed to behave as Tory backbenchers often behave these days. Sometimes they dress up their hooligan conduct as respect for the rules of the House of Commons. When Denis Healey, limited by standing orders to a speech of ten minutes, overran his allotted time by a second or two, they began to chant and point at the clock. Mrs Maria Fyfe was howled down on the pretext that her

question lasted too long. There would have been no howls if she had been demanding total war.

This kind of behaviour was not limited to the Chamber. In those days Members did not have TV sets in their offices, and the only way you could catch up on the news was to visit one of the four rooms in an upstairs corridor that had a TV set, each permanently on one channel. I could not bear to be in the same room as the Tory backbenchers. They were worse than wee boys watching a war film at the Saturday matinee, whooping and yelling with rapturous glee at the sight of every bomb caught on camera as it landed.

8 February: My local weekly, the *Glasgow Guardian*, ran a survey. Seventy-one per cent of respondents opposed the war at all costs, and of that number 95 per cent said they believed sanctions were not given enough time.

9 February: The Labour Party Scottish Executive called for a ceasefire.

12 February: A nuisance I had to deal with. The *Sun* alleged that I said 'The party's behind me, not Neil Kinnock.' So I wrote to Bob Bird, the editor, to tell him these words were not spoken by me, nor could anything I said be reasonably interpreted as such. They were a fabrication. In fact, I had been asked that question, and I said no, that is not what I am saying. I had about 20 witnesses to the truth of my account, and I was considering legal action. He phoned me to say the reporter in question was not one of the paper's regular staff, and he would print a correction. I told Neil about it, and he just laughed, saying he knew perfectly well, without my telling him, I would not turn this difficult issue into a me versus him story.

On the same day we had another debate that had been secured by Tam Dalyell. I got in to put on the record some of the facts that had been unfolding. The war, allegedly in the name of the United Nations, had been going on for three weeks, during which time the UN had not even met. In his fairly frequent press interviews, General Schwarzkopf had referred to his political masters in the United States. He had never made any reference to the United Nations. Well down a lengthy article in the *Evening Standard*, he was asked whether it was possible that if Saddam Hussein used chemical weapons the west would respond with nuclear weapons. He replied there had been no consultation with the allies. He did not even mention the UN. He said President Bush would not be able to rule anything out. I went on to mention that Canon Kenyon Wright had drawn attention to information sent to him by church relief workers in Jordan: three cargoes of baby milk powder had failed to reach babies in Jordan because the American forces were not letting them through.

When the Minister Lennox-Boyd replied to the debate, he did not mention this matter. So I wrote to Douglas Hurd, the FCO Secretary of State. It took him months to send me a reply. War caused confusion. He hoped the matter had been resolved.

15 February: The Iraqi Revolutionary Council sued for peace, but Britain and America were unwilling to consider the peace proposals they had put on the table. The reason given for rebutting were the conditions attached. Free elections in Kuwait (er, weren't we supposed to be defending democracy?), an end to the Israeli occupation of Palestinian lands (precisely what UN resolutions had called for), and a ceasefire and removal of all troops from the Middle East (but if the war aims were limited to liberation of Kuwait, then why would we want to continue with a military presence when that had been achieved?). Many of us thought that, no matter what anyone thought of these conditions, it should have been seen as a bargaining counter that was worth discussing at least.

Harry Ewing and I co-chaired a new organisation, Scottish Labour Against War in the Gulf. Bill Speirs (who died too young a few years ago) was its secretary. The STUC itself had moved swiftly to adopt an anti-Gulf War stance. We did not want to replace the broad campaigns against the Gulf War, we wanted to ensure that the voices within the party against the war were heard loud and clear and often. We made it clear we opposed Saddam Hussein's occupation of Kuwait, called for negotiations under UN auspices, and an international conference to tackle the key problems of the Middle East, including an Israeli-Palestinian settlement.

17 February: Bill Michie and Terry Davis tabled a motion to the PLP calling for an immediate halt to offensive action to allow a new round of diplomatic initiatives. The motion called for a negotiated settlement that would include withdrawal of all Iraqi forces from Kuwait and a peace conference. I supported this move, arguing that many of my colleagues had accepted the war through a desire to back up the United Nations, but here was an offer by Iraq made to the UN and rejected out of hand by the United States, as if they had the right to call the shots.

I was a speaker the same day at a meeting of retired members of the Transport and General Workers' Union, whose national executive had come out against the war. In opening, I made the point that over the years the Government had protested it did not have enough money for a number of things they were campaigning for, yet for the Gulf War there was an open cheque book. I was heckled, 'Cut out the war stuff', and a number of people (including Adam Ingram's dad) left the hall. However, the majority stayed and we went on to discuss other topics, which had been my stated intention.

John McFall and I were speakers at a 1,000-strong rally in George Square. John called for Labour to end its backing for 'operation double standards'. I told the rally that I had two sons, and would not want them to fight in this war. So I was not going to vote to send anyone else's sons to the Gulf.

March 1991: The Labour Party Scottish Conference unanimously adopted a statement that unequivocally condemned the Iraqi invasion of Kuwait, regretted the decision to commence military action before sanctions had been fully exhausted, welcomed the end of hostilities and liberation of Kuwait, and called for peace negotiations to commence immediately under the auspices of the General Assembly of the United Nations. It went on to call for constitutional democracy in Kuwait, and concluded that if the UN was to perform its function, it must be seen as the architect of justice for all nations of the world, and not just those supported by the superpowers for strategic or economic reasons. In the debate, general revulsion was expressed at what US airmen had described as a turkey shoot, shooting rabbits in a bag or rats in a trap: the slaughter of the retreating Iraqi soldiers on the Basra road. I myself had been sickened at being in the company of Tory MPs watching the news, cheering the needless and barbaric killing of the Iraqi conscripts, who had no say whatsoever in Hussein's actions, as they trudged their way home.

When I was called in the debate I wanted the Party to reunite, but also recognise what needed to be done. I said as follows:

> We recognise we have been through a difficult time in the recent past in the Labour movement. All of us know we must win peace and justice in the Middle East and there must be a conference including the Kurds and the Palestinians.

Since then there have been further Gulf crises. I marched against the 2003 war, like so many others. I was glad to see, on 26 February that year, no fewer than 122 Labour backbenchers voting against supporting America once again. It was the beginning of the end for Tony Blair.

CHAPTER EIGHT

On the Scottish Front Bench

1992–1993

IN APRIL 1992 we had a General Election. In the run up to polling day, a letter from Ian Lang to John Major was leaked, in which he wrote: 'It is almost as important for us to keep the SNP at bay as it is to use them to split the Socialist vote.' There were no denials of its authenticity, merely bleats that it was unfair to expose its contents to the Scottish electorate. This was proof that the Tories, having given up any hope of beating Labour in Scotland, therefore hoped the Nationalists would do well, and were trying to use them to divert voters from Labour. It was 'Buy Salmond, get Forsyth free'.

With incredible effrontery, considering their sustained and bitter opposition to Labour's national minimum wage policy, the Tories started to present themselves as the friends of the poor. As one constituent said to me, 'I had to rub my eyes and pinch myself. Was this the same Michael Howard, the pusher of the Poll Tax, the destroyer of trade union rights? Who does he think we are, Red Riding Hood?'

The hustings threw up some memorable moments. One was run by local churches, billed as being about moral issues in the General Election. Elspeth Attwooll, the Liberal candidate, and I were the only candidates who stood up unequivocally for equal rights for gays against some in the audience who were very hostile. Gays were spoken about as if they were enemies of society. I had to point out that we could be talking about the sons or daughters of people in that very audience, even if it was true – as one person claimed – that not a single one of those present was gay. Then someone raised abortion law. Then stem cell research. Again neither Elspeth nor I would placate or equivocate. While most of the audience were silent, some guys – and they were all men – were laying it on thick. Everything they said was backed up, according to them, by the Bible.

Was anyone, I wondered, going to get around to other aspects of morality – like Jesus clearing the moneylenders out of the Temple? I was beginning to think I had somehow wandered into the American Bible Belt. Then one man stood up, and I could have hugged him. Looking around the hall and very directly into everyone's eyes, he declared he had come along that night thinking we would be talking about moral issues that mattered to him. Like what would the political parties do about countries that cannot afford schools and doctors? Indeed, what about unequal access to education and health in our own society? Like money not buying power. Like decent housing for all. He changed the tone of the whole meeting. Some of those who had until then been sitting quiet strongly applauded him, and began talking about their church's involvement in development work overseas.

The Muslim community held their own meetings. One particular mosque had very strict views on hand shaking between men and women. On no account, I was advised, should I offer my hand when I met any of the men. I was there with the other Glasgow Labour MPs, and as a female MP was regarded as an honorary man. The meeting was for male members of the mosque only. The women were downstairs with the children. I wasn't having this. I asked if I could meet the women instead, to talk about election issues with them. No-one as far as I could see was thinking of doing anything to involve the women in the democratic process. So I had my meeting with the women, and all of us struggling to be heard above the racket of the children playing and running around, we talked about housing, education and health.

At a larger mosque one night, in a room above filled to standing room only with hundreds of men and teenage boys, but no women present except myself, I was asked from the floor if I agreed public money should not be wasted protecting Salman Rushdie. I replied that the money could indeed be saved, if the fatwa was lifted. I would never support banning his book. I thought it was appalling that Rushdie had to live in hiding, in terror of losing his life to some fanatic. I thought to myself, I'd rather not be a MP than fail to challenge death threats against an author of whom religious leaders, whoever they were, disapproved. I went on to say that if people didn't like what they had heard about Rushdie's book, they were under no compulsion to read it, and others were perfectly free to write opposing views.

I was asked at the same meeting if I would support Muslims being amongst the Lords Spiritual in the House of Lords, like the Christian bishops. They had not known, until I told them, that only the Church of England bishops were admitted, and other Christian denominations were not. Catholics most particularly not. They knew I had been happy to support Muslim members of the Labour Party seeking election to the Council, Westminster, and our Scottish Parliament when it came into being. But, I told them, I would really like to get rid of the Lords Spiritual altogether, as I thought the upper chamber should be a wholly secular body. In spite of all that, they stayed loyal to Labour. I was able to tell them I fully supported the provision of halal food in hospitals, a matter of some controversy at the time, and indeed had taken it up with the local health board. I couldn't understand why anyone would object. It was stating the bleeding obvious that people who were sick were more likely to get well if they got the food they regarded as comfort food, and not stuff that was strange to them. And considering how awful hospital food could be, I would be tempted if I were a patient to pretend I was a Muslim myself if I could get a scrumptious chicken bhuna that way.

One of the men told me that they approved of me because of my modest dress. They noticed I always wore trousers or skirts down to my knees or even my feet. In truth this had little to do with modesty, and more to do with realising I was past the age for miniskirts.

The local bingo hall manager invited all the candidates to speak briefly when his customers were enjoying a short break. The SNP candidate, a young man, unwittingly put his foot in it with the women. He urged them to take a gamble on the SNP, just like when they played bingo. But bingo players do not think of their pastime as gambling, and that did not go down well at all. You could hear the mutters of indignation all around the hall. He had come along mob-handed to pass out leaflets, but I was on my own, having thought I did not need any help and there was other work for the Labour campaigners to do. But two of the women in the hall came up to me as I was leaving the platform, and asked if I had any leaflets. Whereupon they quickly placed them on every seat in the hall, telling everyone to vote for the Labour woman.

We did not just rely on getting the vote out from our diehard supporters in the housing schemes. We loaned canvassers to knock doors in one of the wealthier areas of town. So one night one of our stalwarts walked up a lengthy drive to an imposing house, rang the doorbell and asked the man who answered what issues he was concerned about. At once the man began holding forth about the crime rate and anti-social behaviour. 'You seem to be strongly into law and order issues,' our canvasser remarked. 'Of course I am,' said the man. 'I'm the Assistant Chief Constable.'

We did well in Scotland once again, but Labour lost its fourth General

Election in a row. Neil Kinnock looked so utterly stricken I thought he was ill, and my heart went out to him. John Smith was shortly afterwards elected leader with 91 per cent support. Some thought John would lack Neil's passion as a speaker. They felt he had too dry a manner, too much like a Scottish bank manager looking at you over his glasses and telling you he wouldn't allow an overdraft. But that was not John at all. If you ever spent any time in his company, you would know him as a raconteur who could make you sore laughing, especially with his tales of the Scottish courts. Personally – maybe oddly for a politician – I am not keen on rhetoric and prefer to read to obtain information rather than listen to speeches. John turned out to be the best Prime Minister we never had, and I have lost count of the number of people who have stopped me in the street to say so, even to this day.

I was still working with Jo Richardson informally, and we decided something had to be done about one issue that might in some eyes be considered a minor point of annoyance. Women rightly felt it was unfair: the imposition of VAT on sanitary towels and tampons. These were necessities, and as such should be free of VAT, just as food was. When I pursued this I discovered that VAT, then imposed at 17.5 per cent, could be reduced to five per cent in the UK without our having to raise the issue in the EC, but outright abolition of VAT would require an EC decision. So in May I put down an Early Day Motion proposing a reduction to five per cent VAT and hoped that the then Chancellor of the Exchequer would respond. Jo Richardson had tried and failed in 1979, when the Commons voted against, with a Government vote of 263 and those supporting her motion 206. A supporting letter was sent to me by someone who had heard me on the radio, enclosing a copy of a letter she had sent to Margaret Thatcher, who was Prime Minister in 1979. No joy from that quarter.

Defeat in the general election meant once again hundreds of small improvements in people's lives like this one would be delayed.

I tried again in March 1993, when over a hundred Members signed my EDM, and again in July of the same year.

Letters poured in after I was interviewed on *Woman's Hour*. One such wrote, 'I don't know which party you are in, but it's about time that the Commons were used for practical, helpful policy formation'. Another wrote:

> In these so-called days of equality, why should women have to pay this tax? If my memory serves me correctly, the VAT was first imposed during a Heath Government. He is still a bachelor, is he not?

In April I received a welcome letter from a Co-op supporter, telling me about developments in that body's campaign on the same issue. They were happy to note that although we had not succeeded, we had achieved a raising of consciousness of the issue, and there had been coverage on the *Jimmy Young Show*, on numerous local radio stations, and widely in regional newspapers. Further, a confidential source at the Consumers' Association had advised that the removal of VAT was given very serious consideration by the Government prior to the Budget. But still no go.

I returned to the fray in November 1997, when we now had a Labour Government. More to the point, Gordon Brown had put more women on his Treasury team than there had ever been before. It took until January 2001, but we finally won and got the VAT reduced to five per cent.

On holiday with my chums in Turkey in July 1992, I returned one day to our hotel, where I was told there was a phone message from a Mr Smith. Could that possibly be John Smith, I wondered? Yes, it was. His office had been trying to get me all day, to tell me he wished to appoint me to the Scottish front bench. Tom Clarke was the team leader, and the other members were John McFall and Henry McLeish. I was told my remit would cover Health, Housing, Arts, Environment, Women and Fisheries. This gave me a problem. Having had nothing but the occasional cold all my life, except for whatever it was I had caught in Nicaragua, I knew practically nothing about Health issues. The way to my GP's surgery just about covered it. I did know about Education, having worked in it for 16 years, but in politics it is not at all unusual to be given a job that does not even come close to matching one's previous experience. Then they wonder how civil servants run rings round them.

And as for Fisheries! I knew zilch about that, and I remembered vividly the fishermen's delegation to the House of Commons who complained vehemently about Tory Ministers' lack of attention and ignorance of their needs. They were not likely to take kindly to a Labour spokeswoman who was a city dweller, and whose knowledge was limited to what she could identify on the fishmonger's slab. So I said to Tom Clarke that I did not want to do that. I had a great deal on my plate without it. It was not as if any of us got extra paid help for research. At this point Tom said he had given me Arts as well, not because I had any particular expertise to offer, but because I went to Royal Scottish National Orchestra concerts and the occasional opera, which was more than he or the rest of the team did. I was so determined not to do Fisheries I said to Tom I would rather return to the backbenches than have to do it. He realised I was serious and kindly let me have my way.

Then, in September 1992, we had Black Wednesday, when Norman Lamont, the Chancellor of the Exchequer, announced that Britain was forced to withdraw Sterling from the European Exchange Rate Mechanism. I saw this on the news while sitting with my son Stephen in the BA lounge at Heathrow. We were returning home from visiting my younger son Chris, who was working for two years with Voluntary Service Overseas in Guyana. Interest rates were rising fast and had reached 13 per cent. The Treasury was spending £27 billion to shore up the pound, and John Major, who was Prime Minister by then, recalled Parliament. There goes the Tories' reputation for being good at economic and financial affairs...

In November the Government knew what to do to keep businesses happy. They moved to abolish all the wages councils. I tabled an Early Day Motion that gathered dozens of signatures calling on all those who voted for this to live for just one week on any wage council rate they cared to choose, and report their experiences to the House. None took me up on it. I also asked Peter Lilley, the Social Security Secretary, to ensure that when he tried to save money by claimants' benefits being paid into bank accounts, instead of using payment books, the banks would be made to co-operate. The banks were being extremely unhelpful by refusing to open accounts for people who wanted to cash benefit cheques. Lilley was actually responsive, to my surprise. He replied that he would be happy to discuss the matter with the banks, and tell them they should not refuse, because social security payments are reliable, good money, and if people wish to receive their benefits that way that is better than benefits being paid by more expensive means. But the banks remained obdurate.

Came the day we were due to go on our Christmas break. Some of my colleagues had been reading their Order Paper for the day's business before I was even awake, and lost no time in telling me that Phil Gallie, the Tory Member for Ayr, had that morning put down a question. He had asked the Secretary of State for Scotland when he intended to announce the outcome of the current applications for NHS trust status, and whether he would make a statement. We then learned that a written answer was to be given to the question later that day and that there would be no public announcement. I raised a point of order with the Deputy Speaker, informing him that the Scottish media were already aware that no fewer than eight of those hospitals were to be announced that day, with a further announcement the following week on another six. I went on to say how unpopular the whole idea of trusts was in Scotland. The Government was too gutless to come to the Chamber. Could we demand that a Minister comes to the Chamber at 12 o'clock to answer questions on the matter?

The Deputy Speaker replied, perfectly correctly, that matters of state are nothing to do with the Chair, but he hoped the Treasury Bench would have heard and listened attentively, because it was obviously important. Other Members chipped in with points of order. The Deputy Speaker repeatedly said the matter had been dealt with, and pleaded:

'I ask Hon. Members to recognise that this is the season of goodwill.'
Hon. Members: 'Not for these hospitals.'

John McFall got in to tell the Deputy Speaker that attempts were being made through our Chief Whip to arrange for a Minister to come to the House that afternoon. Yet more points of order, and George Galloway tried to pull the 'I spy strangers' trick, to no avail. We waited until our next opportunity came. Forty-five minutes later I raised a further point of order, to ask if any progress had been made. No, there had not. Alastair Darling pointed out that Madam Speaker and before her, Mr Speaker Weatherill, deprecated the practice of Ministers making press statements but not statements to the House. Further, when hospitals in England went through the same process, the Minister did come to the Despatch Box. Why not for Scotland?

Several more Labour Members raised points of order about their constituents phoning them about their own local hospitals when they had read their newspapers that morning. Here we were, in late morning, still not knowing anything further. Then I spoke again, to tell the Deputy Speaker that I had just learnt that no Minister would be coming to the House to make a statement. This was, as my Hon. Friends behind me were loudly proclaiming, disgraceful. We would have to continue to press the issue outside the Chamber. I closed by saying, 'We have used this opportunity to put our points and it is a pity that no Minister has had the guts to come here to discuss the matter with us.'

I really thought that was the end of it for that day. But at once some of my colleagues left the green benches to stand in front of the Mace, which meant no business could be conducted while that was going on. I was tempted to join them, but George Foulkes and John Maxton urgently whispered to me not to do so. Front benchers were supposed to uphold the dignity of the House, not subvert it. Then it occurred to me that those of my colleagues who were carrying out the action had not forewarned me, or sought my participation, so presumably they did not expect me to join in.

Betty Boothroyd was now in the Chair. Ernie Ross tried to explain to her, making it clear they intended no insult to her or her deputies. His point was that we had become aware the Leader of the House was in the building, and if a Minister was not present, he could make a statement instead. Yet more points of order were made. The Labour Members were in full flood, and fuming. The Speaker's patience was wearing thin when she let me in again. I asked her to clarify further what she had said a moment ago when she said she believed negotiations were continuing. We understood just a few minutes ago that there was to be no ministerial statement. Was it her understanding that negotiations were still continuing? She replied that she was only saying what she had seen on the Annunciator (TV screens placed around numerous locations in the building to let people know what business was afoot). Clearly no-one had updated the message.

John Home Robertson came in with another point. By this time Betty was on the point of explosion. It seems to me, looking back on it, that she should have made it her business to be fully informed before she took over the chair that day, or at least before making any pronouncements. I could tell she was not as much in sympathy with our cause as her deputy had been. But then, to be fair, she was not long in the top job and this kind of action was unprecedented.

With a tight-lipped pronouncement, she suspended the House until 3pm. Well, we didn't get our Ministerial statement, but my colleagues who stood in front of the Mace certainly made sure our anger was made known by the media throughout Scotland. And here's what amuses me. When I looked at Betty's memoirs in a bookshop, I was intrigued to see my name unexpectedly in the index. What had I done, I wondered, to get this mention? It turned out she blamed me for the Mace incident and thought my behaviour was disgraceful. She seemed to think I had been pulling my colleagues' strings. As if. But then Brian Wilson got one solitary mention, too, for the unforgivable sin of letting his mobile phone ring when he was in the Chamber. Really, if this was the most important thing she thought worth recording about Brian, it does not say much for her sense of proportion.

We were soon to learn who would sit on the boards of these trusts. Many of them had Tory connections. It was not unusual to have no connection whatsoever with the area the board served. Greater Glasgow's new chairman, Bill Fyfe (no relation), was a one-time Tory activist, and a leading right wing businessman was a newly appointed member. But no voluntary body was represented, nor any trade union. None of the names of these new board members were known to people who worked in the health service. And this was what they had the nerve to tell the public was a great step forward. There was no democratic accountability from these people. It was one man, one vote, and the man with the vote was Ian Lang.

My son Stephen – a whiz with statistics and computers, unlike his mother – put together an audit of the state of the health service in Scotland, which I entitled 'Time for a Check-Up' and repeated the exercise the following year, entitling it 'Taking the Temperature'. By this time we were getting a flavour of what the new regime was creating. In Dumfries and Galloway, Government-appointed NHS managers were demanding that only old people with less than £3,000 savings should qualify for automatic free health care. Waiting lists for in-patient and day case treatments had soared during the previous five years from under 60,000 to over 80,000.

Numbers of nurses and midwives in training had been slashed. Salaries of trust board managers and hospital administrators had spiralled, while ancillary workers suffered substantial wage cuts in real terms.

There were 15 councillors on health boards and trusts: six Conservatives, six Independents, one Labour and one SNP. Scotland's regional councils made 51 nominations. Only one was successful. So unpopular with GPs was the idea of fund-holding, there were only three in the whole of Glasgow.

I had my greatest fun with answers to Parliamentary questions. In the first audit I used them to reveal that the Scottish Office could tell us that 320,000 people visited the Loch Ness Monster exhibition in 1991, and they had gathered statistics on how much we spent on hats, gloves and haberdashery. But they could not tell us how many consultant posts were vacant for mental illness, or what was the average waiting time at A&E departments, or what was the number of vacancies for anaesthetists. For each of these questions and more, the answer was: 'This information is not held centrally.' But I did find out, from the answer to a PQ, that the increased expenditure on administration cost the Health Service £192 million in 1992/3, an increase of 48 per cent from 1989/90.

1993

The anti-blacklisting campaign had a final meeting and decided to wind it up. We put its funds into the Campaign for Freedom of Information, which seemed the organisation that most closely matched what we had been about. We thought, too optimistically as it turned out, that we were a highly unusual campaign: we had actually succeeded in our objective, so there was no point in continued existence.

That summer the Secretary of State for Scotland announced plans to reorganise local Government services, including water. They knew perfectly well that there was no support amongst the public for water privatisation: in fact they were up in arms at the very idea. The stuff fell from the sky, with a frequency and in quantities greater than any of us would wish, and now we were being asked to hand it over to private companies to let them profit from it! No way!

Quite cheekily, Maryhill Labour Party asked people to support Maryhill Conservatives in their motion to the Scottish Conservative Conference opposing any privatisation by direct sell-off or franchise. We set up a stall outside the local shopping centre to seek support for their motion. The response was magnificent. People queued up to sign even before we had our stall set up.

The Labour Party and the STUC held a highly successful rally in Glasgow's George Square, which saw over 10,000 men, women and children take to the streets in protest. The rally heard Labour leader John Smith, to loud cheers, promise that a future Labour Government would return every last drop to public ownership.

Tom Clarke sent a letter to John Major, signed by Scottish Labour front benchers, demanding the resignation of Ian Lang, the Secretary of State for Scotland. This was to be followed by the magnificent action of Strathclyde Regional Council, who held a referendum to which the public responded in strength and made their feelings clear. This campaign remains a shining example of Labour campaigning at its most effective. People banded together. Their workmates and neighbours were enthused to cast their vote. Did they give up in the face of the mantra 'There Is No Alternative'? Not for a moment. And they won a famous victory: 70 per cent turnout, with 97 per cent voting against. The privatisation plan was binned.

The battle for women's seats went on. In 1993 we argued that we needed a new approach to solving the problem of the under-representation of women. 'A woman on every shortlist' was simply not working. Some crafty opponents had worked out that all they needed to do was allow a woman on the shortlist, but vote as usual for the favourite son. Somehow, there never seemed to be a favourite daughter. To keep within the rules, they had even been known in some cases to nominate a female collaborator who had not the slightest intention of seeking selection. Conference that year decided that 50 per cent of selection conferences for new candidates in safe and marginal seats should have women-only shortlists. When John Smith backed it, he told the conference, 'for far too long the Parliamentary party has been dominated by men, and women have been grossly under-represented'. Two of our male MPs sitting in the hall were heard to say, 'rubbish, complete bloody rubbish'. So you can imagine the reaction when some of the women party members in Scotland argued that all selections for new candidates should be women-only, and not just 50 per cent. We still had only three women (Irene Adams, Rachel Squire and myself) out of 49 Labour MPs, compared with England and Wales where 34 of 222 MPs were women. This, of course, caused uproar. Johann Lamont, chair of the Executive, made short work of their complaints. She commented:

> We've been sidelined for 70 years and we believe now it is the men's turn... that may block the aspirations of younger men in the party but that's not our fault. If anyone is to blame it's their older male colleagues who were too greedy. Women hold only six per cent of the seats. Why don't they take up their problem with the 94 per cent?

She went on: 'Women believed the party was male-oriented, but women candidates would be able to present Labour's policies for women better.' The columnist Gerald Warner offered a chilling thought on the matter. 'Forty-nine Maria Fyfes in the House of Commons will convert Scotland into a Tory heartland within five years.'

I don't recall if he ever criticised Sir Nicholas Fairbairn, then MP for Perth. This eccentric character habitually wore tartan trews and a matching jacket he had designed himself, but he was always so dishevelled he looked as if he slept in them. I first became aware of his peculiar views in a committee meeting one day, when we were discussing children's access to pubs. I made the point that too many pubs' toilets left a lot to be desired. No hot running water. No soap. Often a roller towel in a grubby state. Or no means to dry your hands at all. So, I argued, before anyone was permitted to have children on their premises they should be required to have decent standards. Fairbairn commented that he could never understand this working-class obsession with cleanliness! When I told this to Neil Carmichael he said it was true there was a class difference. He had seen upper-class women dressed up for functions, but with bra straps peeking out that had gone grey, something you would never see on a working-class woman. Once, when Fairbairn had obviously been imbibing too well, Brian Wilson got around the rule that a Member cannot accuse another one of being drunk in the Chamber, by observing he was 'swaying gently in the non-existent breeze'. Fairbairn was so full of himself he even listed 'making love' as one of his recreations in *Who's Who*. I was baffled that any woman would want to.

Whatever prowess he may have had in that regard, he was noted as a portrait painter. In Annie's Bar one night, he caught sight of me as I chatted with a group nearby, and asked if I would sit for him. He seemed quite astonished when I refused politely but firmly, and asked me why I was turning down such an exceptional offer. I explained to him that while he was correct in saying this was most probably the only chance I would ever have of having my portrait painted in oils at no cost to myself, the best piece of advice I ever received was not to do anything that could have you on the front page of the *Daily Record*, and not in a good way.

But he utterly appalled me one day in the Scottish Grand Committee. We were debating sentencing in rape cases. Fairbairn stood up to speak and told us that women could never be victims in any situation. They were participants. He claimed that, as a former advocate, every rape case when he had defended the accused had stemmed from a false accusation brought out of 'remorse, contrition or bitterness'. He attacked the proposal women MPs had put forward that victims should be anonymous. 'Why should they be protected because they're women?' he asked. 'Are women some feebleness, that they have to be protected? Not at all, they are the tauntresses.' I have to admit that I was lost for words. I was so utterly taken aback by anyone genuinely believing there was no such thing as rape, I only listened wondering if I was hearing right. It was partly that word, 'tauntresses'. Had he really said that? Not a word I had ever heard before, or since. Could he really believe all his clients had genuinely been not guilty? What planet was this guy on? At last I got my act together and said what I should have said earlier. As usual, the media asked Labour women MPs for quotes, and they certainly got them. But why on earth do they never ask any of the men what they think of such remarks? And why did the Tory hierarchy not pull him up? Did none of the Tory women have anything to say?

Then we had an aspect of Tory attitudes at their worst: the Peterken affair. Mr Laurence Peterken was the General Manager of Greater Glasgow Health Board, and one day he was summarily dismissed with immediate effect in his absence by the then Chairman, Mr Bill Fyfe. To explain it all I can do no better than quote the words of George Robertson, who was now Shadow Secretary of State for Scotland:

> He had, allegedly, questioned the level of expenses claimed by Mr Fyfe, who happened to be Ian Lang, the Secretary of State's, golfing friend. The dismissal of the chief executive reached the ears of Ministers not through any formal channel but by means of a press release from GGHB. Two weeks later, that top official, who was so bad and so useless in his job that he had to be instantly dismissed in his absence, is found a new, unadvertised, senior and extremely well-paid job with the Minister's own national health service executive. Then the very man who dismissed him, and who will now not face the legal action that the dismissed official said that he intended to take, tells us all how wonderful the original chief executive was and how complimented he is that he has been found a job inside the national health service.

He went on:

> Nobody answers questions. Not the chairman of GGHB, not the Minister, not even the Secretary of State. Public money is spent; jobs are lost and suddenly found, reputations are damned and then resurrected. 'Back to basics', the Government say, their tongues in their cheeks and their hands in their wallets.

I certainly knew all about the unanswered questions. George had asked me, as the deputy in his team with the health remit, to table as many awkward questions to the Secretary of State as I could come up with, and he was delighted when I managed around 40. George put down yet more questions. At one point I put down a question to ask why there were no replies to my questions in a space of over five weeks. George certainly taught me how to milk such a situation to the utmost, and we both thoroughly enjoyed discomfiting all those involved in this shabby affair.

George had everyone in the team in knots one day when he showed us his reply to a woman who had written a testy letter to him, criticising him on a number of counts. She concluded by telling him to 'get rid of that silly wig'. His elaborately courteous reply answered all her points, concluding with, 'and may I assure you, madam, that if I did buy a wig, it would not be one with a hole in it'.

Housing was an important part of my remit, and at least I had past experience from my days on Glasgow District Council. In December 1990 I had organised a visit by Glasgow MPs to soup kitchens and homeless day centres in London, because Shelter had alerted me to the fact that hundreds of young Scots had travelled south, with no job or accommodation lined up, little money in their pockets, and found themselves in a Catch 22: they could not get a job without an address, and they could not get accommodation without money to pay the rent. So they ended up sleeping in shop doorways. We tried to get the railways to bring those who wanted to get back to Scotland on overnight trains, as the seated accommodation often had places to spare, but nothing doing.

Every year we had the debate on the housing support grant. Lord James Douglas-Hamilton was the Housing Minister when I was opposition spokesperson for Housing. It has to be said he was a thorough gentleman, but shall we say his class background may have clouded his judgement. In that year alone, spending on council housing had been cut by £56 million. Lord James commented to the *Evening Times*, 'on the plus side, virtually everyone now has an inside toilet'. This, in 1993! Were we supposed to be grateful? In one such debate I argued that, listening to him, you would never think that thousands of Scottish houses were unfit to live in, that children in bed and breakfast accommodation were more likely than others to suffer from ill health, and that amongst these children, gastro-enteritis and chest infections were normal. Listening to him, you would not think that people with disabilities waited years for suitably adapted housing, that overcrowded families could not be housed because their council did not have the right size of housing for their needs, or that single men and women could wait years just to get a small flat. Nor would you think that refuges for women were lacking compared to the level of need. The Government knew that thousands of excess winter deaths occurred every year. Scottish Homes had carried out a survey revealing widespread damp and condensation. Over half a million households with one or both problems. One in 20 – 95,000 – were below the tolerable standard. The total bill for putting all this right would be £3,711 million. But the government did not plan to ensure that everyone could afford to heat a well-insulated house. In fact they were planning to introduce VAT on fuel bills. Glasgow's Director of Public Health had only recently reported that half of all households with children had problems with dampness or condensation. There were houses lying empty because they were in an unlettable condition and the councils had no money to improve them. Despite all that, housing support grant was to fall from £47.5 million in 1993 to £36 million in 1994, and eventually be withdrawn altogether. Talk about swingeing cuts! The Minister had tried to argue that Housing Benefit made up the shortfall, but it did nothing of the kind. Further, the incomes of Housing Association tenants had fallen over the previous two years by 3.6 per cent, but their rents rose by 16.5 per cent.

Glasgow had a huge problem of housing debt: no less than £176.8 million by September 1996. A crazy situation had developed, in that when a sitting tenant bought his home, or the house was sold to a housing association or bulldozed to the ground, the outstanding debt on the capital for the building of that house remained with the council. The remaining tenants were having more and more of such debt loaded onto their rents, when those houses had nothing to do with them. Subsidy from the rates had been abolished. In that year alone over £19 million taken out of the council's housing revenue (income from rents) was servicing that debt. Taking this to its logical conclusion, if Margaret Thatcher had her way and more and more tenants bought their homes, the last tenant left would have the entire city's housing debt paid from his sky-high rent book. Nor was there any subsidy for tenants, while new owner-occupied housing benefited from tax relief on the mortgage. Far from being subsidised, each tenant was paying nearly £4 extra every week to service a debt that was no responsibility of theirs. This had been drawn to the attention of the Glasgow MPs by the city's outstandingly able housing convener, Councillor Jim McCarron. He had repeatedly tried to get the Tory Housing Minister, Raymond Robertson, to deal with the problem, to no avail. In fact, Robertson instructed the Council to get rid of a further 1,000 properties, which would have resulted in a further debt of over £10 million being imposed on council tenants. A solution to this problem had to wait until Labour's General Election victory in 1997.

In August a White Paper was published, with proposals for a Children's Bill that would legislate on children in need, disability, those leaving care, carers themselves, child protection orders, exclusion of alleged abusers, adoption, responsibilities and rights of parents, and limiting physical punishment. We had such a large number of issues to be resolved, simply because there had been no legislation for children in Scotland for decades. There had been an Act recently passed for England and Wales, so it was recognised it was high time to catch up. When the Bill went into committee I led on it for the Party. I was hugely helped by all my male colleagues, who were not slow to condemn men who abused children mentally or physically, and fathers who dodged paying for their children's keep. If the media thought I was intimidating, they should have heard Sam Galbraith on the subject of 'wasters'. We also sought to give rights to good fathers, whether they were married or not.

Most of the men were hesitant about taking part in the committee at first, saying they knew nothing about it. I told them, of course they did. They were fathers. Did that mean they could make a useful contribution? Of course!

That committee did something that was in the Parliamentary rules but seldom acted upon. At my request, James Douglas-Hamilton, the Minister in charge of the Bill, asked relevant organisations such as Children in Scotland, children's panels, Barnardo's and others to meet the committee and make any suggestions they wished before we began looking line by line at the clauses in the Bill. We therefore had much better legislation passed than it might otherwise have been – and it had been 25 years since last there had been any law affecting children in Scotland, when the children's panels had been created. Another reason for wanting a devolved Scottish Parliament.

In October Janet Andrews, who had worked for me in my constituency office, decided to retire. She had been a lecturer for several years at Jordanhill College of Education, but later on she wanted to do a political job. In that she was absolutely superb, and she became a highly-regarded councillor in due course. I was very lucky with the women who worked for me in my local office, doing casework and research: Catriona Burness, who earned a doctorate in history and is widely known as an authority on women in politics around the globe; Pat Rice, who had been a medical secretary, very handily, and went on to gain a good honours degree in English; Emma McCrae, the daughter of Rosina, the renowned women's activist, who tackled casework in a way that left some officials wondering what hit them. The general public do not know how much a MP depends on the quality of their staff.

On steps of Keir Hardie House, celebrating 1987 General Election wins with our successful candidates. Maria is in the third row. *Herald*, 17 June 1987.
© *Herald and Times.*

Self with late husband, Jim, on holiday in East Neuk.

Campaigning with sons Chris, left, and Stephen, right. *Evening Times*, 25 March 1992.
© *Herald and Times*

With Daniel Ortega, President of Nicaragua, May Day in Glasgow, 1989.
© *Alan Wylie*

A VOTE AGAINST ALTON
IS A VOTE FOR WOMEN AND CHOICE

The rally against the Alton Bill in City Halls, Glasgow. Maria in chair, Jo Richardson MP, Labour Shadow Secretary of State for Women, speaking.

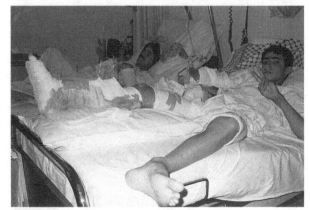

Palestine, 1988. Boys – a few of several – in hospital, wounded by Israeli soldiers.

With Mo Mowlam MP and Clare Short MP, meeting a Palestinian trade unionist.

With Alice Mahon MP,
Audrey Wise MP and
Sandinista reps in
Nicaragua.

First meeting of the
Scottish Constitutional
Convention.

Gwyneth Dunwoody,
Harriet Harman,
Mo Mowlam, Maria Fyfe,
Jo Richardson, Diana Jeuda
and Joan Ruddock,
presenting programme
for women.

Joan Lestor, Janey Buchan, Glenys Kinnock, Maria Fyfe, campaigning for Janey in Euro elections.
© *Murdo MacLeod.*

Scottish Labour Party conference.

Scottish Labour Party conference.

British-Irish Parliamentary Body. Maria is in the front row.

Speaking in Chamber of House of Commons.
© *UK Parliament – Parliamentary Recording Unit*

Speaking in Council of Europe debate, Strasbourg.
© *Conseil de l'Europe.*

Campaigning in Maryhill.

Campaigning in Maryhill.

With election agent
John Gray, 1992.

Scottish Labour front bench team, Gordon McMaster, Henry McLeish, Maria Fyfe, George Robertson, Jack McConnell, John McFall. *Herald* 8 January 1994.
© *Herald and Times.*

Celebrating award of Doctorate from Glasgow University.

As above, with son Stephen.

Receiving award from STUC Women's Committee.

POLL TAX REVOLT OFF WITH A BANG

Branson sells off condom firm

By ALAN WALLACE

WORKMEN hammering and banging turned the launch of non-payment campaign against the Poll Tax into a near shambles.

The choice of the People's Palace in Glasgow Green was explained by Labour MP John McAllion, chairman of the initial Committee of 100.

"For most of this century," the Dundee East MP said, "Glasgow Green has been one of the places where Scots people have launched campaigns against injustices from conscription to nuclear disarmament."

PERSONAL

It had been thought that workmen on scaffolding would stop for the 30-minute news conference.

The clattering swelled at times to a a crescendo that made the speakers virtually inaudible at times to the rows of newspaper, radio and television journalists, some of whom had travelled from London for the launch.

Cameraman quit filming the conference to climb vantage points for shots of the men at work.

Finally, Mrs Maria Fyfe, MP for Glasgow Maryhill, called a halt and suggested personal interviews.

Although eight Scots Labour MPs are among those who have signed a declara-

FORWARD LINE . . . Dennis Canavan, MP, Dick Douglas, MP, McAllion, MP, Rev. John Prescott, Benny McLaughlin and Maria Fyffe, MP

tion not to pay, Mr McAllion stressed it was a non-political body.

The conference was chaired by Dumfries minister, the Rev. John Prescott, who introduced himself as an "Anglo Scot Irish mongrel."

He claimed he knew Conservatives who were dissatisfied with the tax.

Academics, councillors, churchmen, a student leader, and entertainers were among those at the campaign launch.

The committee also includes ethnic

community leaders local government workers and union officials.

The Govan by-election delayed the original launch date as organisers wished to stress the committee was all-party and non-party.

Dr Una McLean-Mackintosh, widow of the late Labour MP John P. Mackintosh, said: "How he would have deplored our present state. I want to have my name alongside MPs Dick Douglas (Dunfermline West) and Dennis Canavan (Falkirk West).

"They are positively and openly opposing Maggie on this iniquitous matter of the poll tax."

Bill Speirs, Scottish TUC deputy general secretary, said: "It is important that those who are in a position to use non-payment as a form of moral and political protest do so in as effective a manner as possible.

"That is why I have agreed to join the Committee of 100 and why I hope that similar committees are set up all over Scotland."

RICHARD BRANSON is selling his Mates condom business to an Australian rubber company, Pacific Dunlop.

The deal will net £1 million initially for the Healthcare Foundation, the charity set up by the music-to-airlines millionaire.

Pacific Dunlop, through its subsidiary Ansell International, has supplied condoms to Mates since the brand was launched a year ago.

They have since captured around 20-25% of the condom market.

OWNERS

As well as the first payment, Pacific Dunlop will pay an annual royalty on sales to the foundation. The charity was set up to promote safer sex and Aids information.

Mates has a 75% stake in Mates Vending, the country's largest vending machine operator.

Philip Brass, managing director of Pacific Dunlop, said the new owners planned to take the Mates brand into the European market.

"We believe there are excellent growth opportunities in these markets and our objective is to increase sales and market share," he added.

Launch of Committees of 100 Against Poll Tax.
© *Tribune magazine*

LABOUR IN BLACKPO

AS EVERY year, Tribune
of the pictures from Lab
where better to begin th
Todd delivering his deva
Tribune rally? No sho
women in sharp suits h
really dated thing in th
Tribune banner, which
masthead the paper g
Photo: Stefano Cagnoni.

Moving clockwise, we
looking mean and made
ence emblem behind hi
suits your values"?; an
dynamic modernisers
guaranteed him many v
men in shiny suits fro
Engineering Union. P
(IFL).

Next, it's a case of "
didn't have one in your
consoles Michael Meach
way around?? after she
lost his in the electio
Executive Committee. F
noni.

On the left (yes, you c
suit) and at the bottom (
top as far as NEC electi
Dennis Skinner contem
of another year's deba
ilateralist defence policy
(IFL).

Which brings us to an
suits lost. Jubilation a
(Alice Mahon, Maria Fy
MEP, Joan Walley and Jo
applause from Norman
disdain from male front
Donald Dewar and Geor
the news that conference
women on every par
list.   Photo: Stefano Ca

Alice Mahon and self
celebrating one
woman on every
shortlist at Labour
Conference.
© *Tribune magazine*

Members' Cloakroom: the pink ribbons are for holding swords that no-one possesses.

CHAPTER NINE

'New'. But is it Labour?

1994–1996

THE HERALD PUBLISHED a picture in January of the Scottish Labour Front Bench team, taken at Loch Lomond because of its beautiful snowy background. There we were, one woman and five men, not wearing coats, scarves or gloves at George Robertson's insistence and trying not to look chilled to the bone as we walked towards the photographer. Male politicians think wearing coats when having your photo taken outdoors is for softies. They think being coatless in freezing weather makes them look strong. Personally, I'm sure people just thought we are mad, walking about in our indoor clothes when everyone else, if they went out at all, was kitted out for the North Pole.

I was no longer the sole woman in the Scottish Labour Group. Irene Adams had joined us in a by-election in 1990 following the death of her husband, Allen, who had been the Member for Paisley North. There had been a campaign earlier on to get Irene onto the Scottish front bench team, whether alongside or instead of me, but George Robertson told John Smith he was content with the line-up as it was. The fact was, Irene was never going to be put on the Scottish front bench by either George or John, in the light of her support for Scotland United, a now defunct attempt at an alliance between Labour and SNP members against the Tories, and calling for a multi-option (status quo, a devolved Parliament, or independence) referendum on Scotland's form of government.

Jo Richardson died in February 1994. She had suffered terribly from arthritis for many years, her fingers twisted so badly she could not straighten them out. She had to take huge dozes of painkillers every day, and had latterly needed a wheelchair. I was furious with the House of Commons authorities over their failure to provide an office for her on the ground floor. They shrugged and said there were lifts all over the place. Yes, there were, but they were crowded when the division bell rang, and Jo did not want to take up nearly all the space in a lift and make others wait or take to the stairs. What they refused to do for Jo, they did manage to do for Anne Begg when she was elected three years later, possibly because as a brand new member she stood out and rightly had immense public admiration for the way she tackled what must be huge difficulties getting up and down from Aberdeen to London every week.

Jo was also convinced that Peter Mandelson was keeping her off platforms, given that she was an older woman in a wheelchair, and thus did not suit the image he wanted to portray of Labour being new and shiny. She never got the publicity she should have had, considering her remit. If so, he was profoundly mistaken. Jo was admired by thousands of women up and down the country, who saw her as their champion. And wouldn't voters recognise our platform as representative of the people? She won a degree of affection that I don't see Peter ever winning.

At our Scottish Conference we had yet another debate on all-women shortlists. We were determined, but so were our opponents. The argument was being put about that women would feel patronised if they were on an all-women shortlist. Speaking at the rostrum, I recalled many an all-male shortlist. Party members had a choice: they could pick any bloke they wanted, left winger or right winger, old or young, fat or thin, with or without a trade union card, with a nice grey suit or a woolly jumper, a moderniser or a traditionalist. Varied as they were, I did not recall one ever complaining that he felt patronised at being on an all-male shortlist. Of course not. And why? Because the job was seen as a man's job, and it was high time that changed. I went on to say that, 25 years ago, the Church of Scotland had ordained its first woman Minister, and they now had over 100. Not a single thunderbolt had struck any kirk where these women preached, so we must conclude God is not opposed to this, and She may even be quite pleased. Could this Party, the Labour Party, the Party that exists because it recognises the inequalities of class, recognise there are other inequalities, and try to be as radical as any one of 100 kirk sessions?

Then, in April 1994, surprise of all surprises. Hospital workers at Glasgow Royal Infirmary were supported by our Tory councillors in their plea against their wages being slashed. The hospital board had brought in private contractors to do the work of the porters and cleaners. Cleaners would now be paid only £3.15 an hour, and porters £3.20. They had awarded the contract only days before the Royal became a Trust hospital, and the Tory Government had created these trusts precisely in order to run hospitals as if they were commercial enterprises. The Tory councillors in Glasgow rightly attacked this onslaught on low paid workers as immoral, and demanded Scottish Office action to protect them. Councillor Bill Aitken, for so many years the opponent of all our moves to improve the lot of workers, declared:

> It is not Tory philosophy to grind people into the ground on the basis of their salary and conditions. We have written to Scottish health minister Lord Fraser of Carmylie... highlighting what we consider to be a totally outrageous abuse of people who are already on very marginal incomes.

Had something been put in their tea? Had they not known these workers' wages had not kept up with inflation since 1989? Well, I said, let us welcome this change of heart. Susan Baird, a Labour councillor and former Lord Provost, stepped into the battle. She had been appointed to the hospital board earlier that month, and asked the chairman for an extraordinary meeting to discuss the situation. And if that was not successful, she would seek one third of the board members to back the call. A vigorous campaign was waged by the trade unions, other members of the Trust itself and senior medical staff. I had a lump in my throat when I read about the cheers ringing down the hospital wards when they heard of the workforce's victory, when the in-house bid was won, and I am sure I was not the only one.

John Smith died in May 1994. I was in bed at home in Glasgow that morning, feeling run down and fluey, and when I woke up I turned on the radio to hear the news. It was announced he had suffered a heart attack, and then shortly afterwards that he had died. I was stunned. It was hard to take in. I remember thinking, 'Can this Party not have any luck?' He had only been in office a few years, but he was clearly on track to winning the voters' confidence. They liked him. We were going to win. And now this. When he had his previous heart attack and was off sick I got a 'get well' card and passed it round the rest of the Scottish Group of Labour MPs to collect signatures. When I spotted the card in the shop I was amused by the message on the front. Above a cartoon of various wild animals running around dementedly were the words: 'Get well soon. We can't menagerie without you.' That summed up exactly what I thought. As the card went round, Sam Galbraith said to me, 'that's a wifey thing to do'. He was the one who invented my nickname: Wifey Fyfey. I just replied that the party could do with more wifey things being done. That was the trouble with it.

I attended John's funeral. I have forgotten what was said in the tributes to John, but Kenna Campbell's beautiful singing of a psalm in Gaelic – a language I do not even know – will remain in my memory for ever. Colleagues from down south, attending the service in this well-to-do part of Edinburgh, were astonished that such an area should vote Labour.

The manoeuvring to succeed John began the very day he died, much to my distaste and annoyance. The *Evening Standard*'s front page called for Tony Blair to succeed, before John was even buried. Yet more distasteful things were to occur. I was told by two prominent Tony Blair supporters that we could not have Gordon Brown, because he was gay. The country would never vote for a gay Prime Minister. This was based on nothing more than the fact that at his age he was still single, although he had in his past had a romance with some princess or other. I didn't care whether he was gay or not, though I didn't believe so, and I preferred him to Tony Blair. And I was even less likely to vote for Tony when he allowed his supporters to campaign in this way. Donald Dewar suggested that perhaps Tony wasn't aware of it. I replied that he must know by now, could tell them to stop it, but he had not.

Then, later, we began to hear about a mysterious 'Bobby' who was on Tony Blair's team. 'Bobby' said this, and 'Bobby' did that. Who on earth was Bobby? I for one assumed it must be someone from his constituency party, or a staffer in Westminster. It was only much later we learned that this was Peter Mandelson, who was so unpopular in the party Tony did not want us all to realise he was at the heart of his campaign to be elected leader. His efforts were rewarded when he was made Minister Without Portfolio later on in the year. Tony once said on television, famously, that he thought people knew he was a straight kind of guy. I can only say his moral compass should be thrown in the bin if he thought this kind of deception was straight.

I knew perfectly well how far apart in his attitudes Tony sat from the mass membership of the party. It was the major reason I would not vote for him. I really do think he won votes because, obviously, he was good-looking, charming and personable, and many people are too influenced by a pretty face and a winning smile. Witness Nick Clegg's popularity, before the public knew him better...

Labour Party members simply did not believe Tony could be that much adrift from traditional Labour thinking. It was even believed by some that all his right wing speeches were a pose to get past the *Daily Mail* and the *Sun*, and he would reveal his true colours as a Labour man when he got elected. To be fair to him, he told us again and again he meant every word of his 'New Labour' mantra. Yet he knew how far he could go. He admits himself he hid his intention to get rid of Clause 4 while he campaigned to win the leadership. But a major influence on party members' thinking, that people are inclined to forget, was that by then we had lost no less than four General Elections in a row, and a fifth defeat was to be avoided at all costs. Many felt we had to get back into power if we were to survive as a party. If that meant pandering to right wing attitudes in the south of England, so be it. And any Labour Government had to be better than any Tory Government. That was the doubters. He had, of course, plenty of committed supporters, true believers in the Third Way, whatever that meant, not to mention the ones who would always back the leadership because it was the leadership. If someone else with completely contrary views became the next leader, they would follow him too.

There were some women hopefuls, dubbed the Blair Babes when they were duly elected, who saw a way to gaining a seat in Parliament that caused much hilarity amongst the sisters. The STUC women's committee put it in a nutshell with their song to the tune of 'Clementine':

In a ward in Glasgow somewhere, she's been turned down once before.
Now she thinks she has the answer, now she thinks she knows the score.

CHORUS: Oh my darling, oh my darling, oh my darling Tony Blair,
Politics are oot the windae – got the image, got big hair.

With a nose job, with a hairstyle, I could be a candidate.
Send me to the Labour charm school. I'll not disappoint you, mate.
With the help of Barbara Follett, I could look the very part.
Shoulder pads and fancy briefcase, gleaming teeth – that's just the start!

Now that Bambi will accept me, I'm assured a Labour seat.
With my Gucci umberella and my new designer chic.
Don't you ask me our position. I've been told – Prevaricate.
Till a policy commission can decide – you'll have to wait.

No! Our story isn't ended, for again she's seen the light.
She's a woman, not a hairdo. Underneath she knows what's right.
So she fights for equal status. Helps her sisters in distress.
'Cause she knows that women's power is much more than power dress!

Tony Blair's leadership had undoubtedly brought something unfamiliar to Labour politics. He wanted Labour MPs to smarten themselves up and make a better impression, and Barbara Follett was put in charge of this campaign. Strenuous efforts were made to 'Follett' us all. The men were urged to pay attention to how they knotted their ties, the style of their shirt collar, whether the colour of their shirt went well with their suit, what kind of shoes to wear for each occasion, and so forth. This was a culture shock to those who spent their days in shiny-bottomed suits, the trouser waistband nestling under the beer belly. As for me, I hadn't even known before that the knot in a tie was held to send some kind of signal. I am still mystified. Barbara asked us all to take advice on whether we were winter, spring, summer or autumn people, so as to choose the right colours for our ensembles. Some actually did, while praying fervently this never got into their local paper.

I personally found clothes shopping so tedious I would give it ten minutes in Marks and Spencers and then head for the nearest bookshop. I was not being purist, it was just the age-old problem of the garment trade being uninterested in attractive clothing for sizes 16 and upwards, and I had been putting on a lot of weight, what with no exercise and a sedentary occupation. However, it has to be admitted that Barbara had an unexpected success when she persuaded Donald Dewar to stop wearing jumpers with holes in the elbows. Donald had led a demonstration against unemployment through the streets of Glasgow in just such a state. I had to tell him his constituents would be having a giggle over their well-paid MP not having a decent jumper to his name. He could at least do his bit to help overcome unemployment in the knitwear trades. I was, of course, remembering – as he did too – the famous crack made by a heckler to James Maxton about his long hair and unemployed barbers. Leading party women like Helen Liddell and Wendy Alexander asked me to get Donald to brush off his dandruff before meeting VIPs or going on a public platform. I, in turn, protested I couldn't. I wasn't his wife or his mammy. Nevertheless, I ended up doing so. Then one day he strolled into the Members' Tearoom wearing a tie with the letters 'YSL' emblazoned on it. People stared in stupefaction. Had Donald actually gone and bought an Yves St Laurent tie? If so, this was a Damascene conversion indeed. No. The letters stood for the name of a major employer in his constituency, Yarrows Shipbuilders Ltd., where he was well known to the shop stewards and management and had been given a gift of this tie. But people loved Donald because they could see past the lack of 'presentation' and knew how genuine he was.

To give Barbara her proper due, anyone who thought she was an airhead just interested in clothes could not have been more mistaken. When she had lived in South Africa she had, with her first husband, been an active opponent of Apartheid. He was killed by a government death squad. When people talked of being 'brave' politically, when all they were doing was throwing away a chance of promotion, or being criticised, I would always think of people like him, who really knew what 'brave' meant.

Barbara laughed when I told her about one unfortunate soul I had been helping. When I was the minder one day for a female candidate in Kensington, not a seat we had a hope in hell of winning, she was going to give a press conference, and as she headed towards the room where the media were assembled I noticed that her underskirt was hanging down below her hemline. I called her back into the toilet, where we solved the problem with the time honoured method of rolling up the underskirt's waistband. She told me that party officials had told her she dressed too drably, there was too much black and navy in her wardrobe, and she would have to get some new, brighter clothes. But, she protested, she could not afford to buy all that. Get them somehow, anyhow, we don't care how, they replied. She borrowed skirts from her friends, who were shorter than her, and so her own underskirt was too long. She spent the entire by-election campaign trying to concentrate on getting Labour's message across while worrying about her underskirt. I told her what happened to Jo Richardson many years before. As Jo said, 'whatever you do, it won't be worse than kicking your knickers into the face of the local reporter'. It was hearing stories like these that made Barbara and others create 'Emily's List', copying the idea from the United States. This was about identifying women who would work for women, and funding their travel and clothing for selection conferences if they could not afford it themselves.

Another Blairite innovation was our pagers. When we were first handed these things, many of us didn't even own a mobile phone. We were told to have our pagers on our persons at all times, because it would give us messages about imminent votes, and tell us how to vote. And so one of the most irritating ever phrases, 'on message', was coined.

At the regular Parliamentary Labour Party meeting one Wednesday morning, we were having the whole idea explained to us. The pager would ring, or it could be set to vibrate if we were somewhere we did not want any noise to disturb. But it had to be on at all times we were awake, one way or the other. We were told to fasten them to our belts. Audrey Wise rose to point out that while men commonly had belts around their trouser waistbands, women wearing skirts or dresses would usually not have any belt, or not one that would hold the pager securely. 'So,' she asked, 'where are the women supposed to put these vibrating thingies?' You could see faces all around trying desperately not to laugh, and finally exploding, while Audrey looked around in puzzlement, wondering what she had said that made us all fall about.

And so we were enslaved to our pagers. But human duplicity is hard to beat. We were becoming accustomed to being told to return to the Commons if we were outside the building, for a vote we had not suspected was coming up. One night, when one of my colleagues was on the way to the airport for the journey home, his pager had a message urging him to return for an unexpected vote. He phoned the whips' office to reply, saying he wasn't sure if he could make it back in time, as he was only ten minutes from Heathrow. What he didn't tell them was that he was still travelling towards Heathrow.

In November I was re-appointed as Scottish Affairs spokesperson, and while my new remit was Education instead of Health, otherwise it was the same as before. David Blunkett was Shadow Secretary of State for Education for England and Wales.

In December I ran into difficulties over funding of higher education. We needed to find a way forward, because the student loan system was a disaster. Students would often be paid weeks late, and when they phoned to protest they were told the computer would not allow it. Nobody seemed able to put the right information into the computer: it was as if the thing had a will of its own, like Hal in 2001: A Space Odyssey. Not quite as malevolent, to be fair. On top of that, there was a well known scam that better-off families used. Their student offspring would not need a loan, but they got one anyway, paying a lower interest rate than they would get anywhere else, to fund some other purpose that had nothing to do with their higher education.

Then Kim Howells, one of the English education team, put forward the idea of a graduate tax in the national media. He aired it as if it were an idea of his own he was putting up for consideration. I was a regular attendee at the English education team meetings, so that we could keep our respective teams in touch with one another, and no-one had ever mentioned this. I wrote an article at the request of the Glasgow *Herald* defending current policy, as far as Scotland was concerned, which was to restore grants. I argued that taxes should be paid proportionately to earnings, and I was concerned in case such a policy would deter youngsters from poorer families. Before sending it to them I showed it to George Robertson, my team leader, as was expected of junior spokespersons. To my complete surprise he told me I would have to withdraw it. But, I protested, Kim has gone to the press to argue against party policy, I'm the one who is defending it. Only then did I learn the plan had backing from the very top.

After arguing about it on the phone with George at great length, I confess I finally gave in. George's technique for dealing with rebellion was astute. He knew I could not, and would not, hang up on him. And he just kept on and on until I had nothing else to say.

It would be useful if somebody would do the sums and see what could be done for student funding today if we did not waste billions on Trident, and a crackdown on wealthy tax dodgers could only help too. But while we wait for that happy day to arrive, we still have to decide how to fund higher and further education from the resources we do have. There are far more young people in higher education today than there were back in the days when grants were taken for granted: that alone would make it highly unlikely that a full-scale grants system could be affordable any time in the foreseeable future. Especially considering the many whose wages are so low they need a benefits top-up, and the huge number of families relying on food banks, whose needs must surely take priority. What I most certainly do not agree with is massive cutting of further education funding, which is what our SNP Government is doing.

Then another educational controversy arose. Labour's plans to stop public subsidies to private sector education were being attacked, at a time when funding for the state sector was being cut. I commented that when you talk about charitable status being given to independent schools, it is the rest of the tax-paying population, whose sons and daughters go to state schools, who pay for it. Talk about the ragged-trousered philanthropists!

Then George and I did not see eye to eye on school league tables. He felt we could not oppose them, as they would be popular with parents, who had a right to know how their children's school compared with others. He did realise, of course, that such tables had to be treated with some caution, as it was hard to compare like with like. It would hardly be fair to compare the results of a school in a sink estate with one in a leafy suburb. It was also true that some teachers had a bad attitude to working-class youngsters, and simply did not expect them to achieve. So it was important to distinguish those schools that tried against all the odds from those that did not.

It seemed to me that Strathclyde Regional Council's quality assurance unit, producing reports running to several pages on each one of our local schools, was of far greater use to parents than crude tables of exam results, and that seemed to me the obvious way to go. While we were still pondering the best way forward, David Blunkett, Education Shadow Minister for England and Wales, made a statement supporting league tables, and sent George and me an apology for not making it clear the policy applied only to England and Wales. So both George's and my phones were ringing off the hook, with enquiries about when this would take effect in Scotland. But that's much of the media for you: they ought to have known that Scottish education has been a separate institution for centuries – way back into the mists of time. Roll on the Scottish Parliament!

1995

Most constituency casework is fairly routine. People have problems with public authorities or private sector businesses who just don't listen, until they receive a letter with the House of Commons portcullis logo at the top. You don't even have to threaten them with unwelcome publicity, usually. They know perfectly well this can result. But now I had something totally out of the ordinary. A man called Iain Gordon, a member of Maryhill Labour Party, told me he had been found guilty but insane of the murder of a young woman many years ago when he was a young airman serving in Northern Ireland. She had died of 37 stab wounds. He had been imprisoned at Her Majesty's Pleasure, but the doctors in the secure unit had been unanimous in their view that he was neither insane nor guilty. He wanted a fresh investigation to clear his name. The young woman was Patricia Curran, the 19 year old daughter of a Northern Ireland High Court judge, and Iain had been posted in the vicinity of where she lived. The circumstances of the investigation and trial were extraordinary. The Northern Ireland police, helped by Scotland Yard, did not think it relevant to question Patricia's parents or brother about their movements around the time of death. Nor did they ask why her body, with legs stiffening in rigor mortis, and therefore obviously beyond hope of medical attention, had been lifted by her brother and taken in his car to the local GP, who said she had been killed by shotgun wounds. She was buried only two days later. A family such as this – father a judge, brother a barrister – must have known not to disturb a crime scene. The police, in spite of such strange goings-on, did not examine the family home until two to three days after the discovery of the body in the driveway up to it. Nor was it investigated where she must have been murdered, which was not where she was found. There were too many stab wounds for the small amount of blood on the scene.

Iain, who knew the family slightly through attending the same church, confessed after three days' interrogation. It seems he was pressured about visits to prostitutes in Belfast and experiments with gay sex that he was afraid his mother would learn about: not too bright, I agree, to fail to realise that confessing to murder (especially in those days, when the judge could put on his black cap and sentence someone to death) was something his mother would presumably find more upsetting. His alleged confession contained a statement that he used his service knife, but at that time the RAF did not supply service knives. On top of all that, when it came to court, his senior defence counsel agreed to take his case provided he did not have to cross examine any of the victim's family!

There is much more detail to tell, which can be found in Ludovic Kennedy's account of his investigations published in 1970.

I took it up in Parliament, and Chris Mullin spoke to great effect when we had the chance of raising it one Friday morning, the day of the week for private Members' business. But before that we had to sit impatiently waiting while the Tory MP Eric Forth was talking at length in an effort to scupper another Labour Member's Bill coming after ours, and poor Iain was sitting up in the gallery not having a clue what was going on. In a fury I got to my feet and told Forth what he was doing. Wittingly or unwittingly, he was preventing an innocent man from getting justice. It was tight timing, but we succeeded in raising Iain's case. We sought and won a new, independent investigation, and in the fullness of time, it was declared that the Crown's case had not been proved. There has still been no attempt to find out who did commit the murder of an innocent young woman.

* * *

In October I resigned from the front bench, realising you can resign once and get back, but if you do it twice you've burned your boats. The time was approaching when there would be a General Election, and Labour was very likely to form the next Government. I simply did not want to be a Minister of junior rank, dogsbody to some Third Way enthusiast half my age – the best that would become of someone with my views, if I was lucky. Ministerial rank brings with it silence and conformity on all issues outside one's remit: I was finding that hard to bear as a mere Shadow Minister, when things had changed so much since John Smith's day. I had not been asked to stand down, but I could see it coming. Tony Blair would want new people in his coming reshuffle who were on message with his 'Project', not someone who regarded the whole thing as an assault on democratic socialism. It was good of both Tony and George Robertson, knowing my views, to send me handwritten letters regretting my decision. When I made my final front bench appearance at Scottish Questions, George said I had been invaluable in giving Labour the consistently high position it had with the Scottish people. Didn't know he thought that highly of me!

1996

On 13 March we were all set to have a Scottish Affairs debate in Glasgow City Chambers. Then the news came through that something dreadful had happened. A man had entered Dunblane Primary School and gunned down a large number of children. It later emerged that 16 had been killed, along with their class teacher. George's own children had attended that school. The ease with which Thomas Hamilton, the gunman, had gained access to guns was later revealed, to our intense horror. You would think there would be unanimity about changing the law, but that was not the case, as we later found out.

In May our attention was drawn to those who properly have authority to bear arms. Labour members had a free vote one night on the Armed Forces Bill, when the issue was an amendment tabled by Edwina Currie to allow gays in the armed forces, and I voted in support. The argument put up against it was that a soldier might put the life of a gay partner ahead of others. So he might, and likewise, like anyone else, his big brother, his wee cousin or his mates. By the same logic, a 'straight' soldier might reasonably want to preserve his own skin and get the hell out of it, home safely to his female partner. Edwina's amendment was lost by a large majority, as her own party were on a three line whip to vote against. I also voted for another amendment moved by Andrew McKinlay which attempted to secure a free pardon for men who were shot for 'desertion' in the First World War trenches. His point was that many of those men were suffering from shell shock, and in today's world they would be sent home for treatment, not accused of cowardice in the face of the enemy. This was also defeated.

Feeling fed up with the antics of Tony Blair's and Gordon Brown's spin doctors, forever briefing against their boss's rival and creating an atmosphere in which Labour MPs were cautious about being quoted saying anything critical, in case they too were briefed against clandestinely, I decided to tackle it head on. I submitted a motion for the following meeting of the Parliamentary Labour Party, which read:

> This PLP congratulates all spin doctors employed by any of its Members on the energy and ingenuity devoted to the victory of their masters, but feels that lately some have been overtaxing themselves and therefore proposes that a fund be set up to give those nominated a holiday, lasting at least one year, on a desert island, with no phones, faxes, email or any means of communication with the outside world, including carrier pigeons.

Donald Dewar asked me to see him. He told me that Tony was going to speak to the next meeting of the PLP, and if my motion appeared on the agenda that would be what the media fastened their attention on. We could not have that. Ok, fine – I told him I would withdraw it. At the subsequent meeting of the Parliamentary committee, Clive Soley, the Chair, reported that my motion had been withdrawn, but although written in jocular terms it nevertheless represented a serious message, and one that had been taken on board by the officers. Needless to say, the media manipulators did not remain chastened for long.

Yet more annoyance with New Labour. Stephen Byers, while dining with journalists in the middle of the TUC's annual conference, told them the party was planning to dump the unions. Apart from being such an unbelievably crass notion in itself: great timing, eh, Stephen? In a rage, I raised this with Donald Dewar. 'Isn't this guy supposed to be intelligent?' Donald confirmed that was indeed so. 'And when', I went on, 'did this become party policy? I only ask because I thought, being on the party's policy forum, I might have heard some mention of it. Would this have been considered too trivial to bring to our attention?' Donald then flabbergasted me when he told me that even he, a member of the Cabinet, knew nothing about it. Policy was being decided by a small clique.

Next Kim Howells, more Blairite than Blair himself, called for the humane phasing out of the word 'Socialism'. Tony Banks made the good point that front bench spokesmen were saying things which were not then denied by the leadership. I recalled the words of the late John Smith, who described himself as 'a democratic socialist who places equal emphasis on both words'. If that statement is too radical and extreme for some people in our Party, I went on, then I suggest they might care to consider whether they belong to the right party. But Tony Blair soon asserted that the business community was at least as important to us as the trade unions. So when was this historic change in attitude decided? Or even debated? At no time, of course. This was Tony 'leading', not listening.

* * *

Not long after this debacle, I had another unusual constituency casework experience. Constituents were coming to me with complaints about a local dentist, by the name of William Duff. They had multiple disastrous experiences in common, so I encouraged them to form a campaign group, chaired by the doughty Moanne Russell, who had been the first to tell me about all this. She had been inflicted with eight unnecessary crowns, root treatments, and part of a drill had been embedded in her mouth. Abscesses and tumours followed. She did not know it at the time, but he had been using unsterilised instruments. I heard more and more accounts of unnecessary fillings, cappings, bridgework and root canal treatment with unsterilised equipment, causing serious infections and abscesses, not to mention a great deal of pain. They needed all this work re-done. Some needed all their teeth removed. Many were told they could not have repairs carried out under the NHS. If they could afford it, the cost would run into hundreds or even thousands of pounds. Moanne herself faced a £40,000 bill to restore her dental health, which, as an assistant in a supermarket, she came nowhere near being able to afford.

When I wrote to Michael Forsyth, the Health Minister, he ordered that she be paid £325 for remedial work, the maximum payable under the existing rules, but that of course was only a fraction of what she needed. When patients tried to get the dental hospital to put matters right, they were in most cases refused and told to find another dentist. One was told he could see a consultant, but the wait this highly distressed person had to endure would be 20 weeks. One ended up in emergency hospital care when antibiotics did not work after unnecessary root canal work.

When any patient won a hearing with the Health Board, each one was on their own against seven members, accompanied by two admin and two observers, and in each and every case had their complaints dismissed. It was while all this was going on that I found out how complacent those in charge of this major service at that time could be. When I wrote to the Health Board to enquire how they explained Duff's unusually high earnings – £1 million between 1990–4 – they answered he must be more efficient than all the other dentists. He had been paid £450,000 in just one year. Even that did not make them investigate.

I obtained an adjournment debate to call into question GGHB's handling of this affair, and tabled a number of questions to the Health Minister when I did not get satisfaction from the local health management. At last things began to move. The Health Minister, the General Dental Council and the Fraud Squad all looked into it. A delegation of patients and myself had a meeting with Professor David Hamblen, the new chairman of Greater Glasgow Health Board, who was helpful and sympathetic to the patients' cause. He committed GGHB to repairing the damage and to examine claims for expenses incurred in remedial treatment. Duff was struck off, and banned from carrying out dental work anywhere in Britain a year later. A disciplinary tribunal of the General Dental Council had found him guilty of serious professional misconduct, having performed treatment on hundreds of patients who did not need it, including the fitting of 3,000 crowns. Then in February he pleaded guilty to fraud and using unsterilised instruments. He was given a jail sentence, but patients were still struggling on with their court cases. His admission of guilt meant that the whole story did not come out in the criminal court.

* * *

I had just been elected to the Council of Europe that November, in a ballot of the Labour MPs. Donald Dewar had urged me to stand for three reasons: he knew I would be interested in human rights work; I spoke a little French and German; and I would not treat the whole thing as a junket. He was trying to clean up British participation in this body, which had been seen as a 'jolly' and was rarely taken seriously. This was work I loved. We newcomers in the delegation got to know our counterparts in all the other European socialist groups, and we worked together on human rights, equality issues and children's welfare. To be a member state, it had to have no capital punishment. So my colleagues and I set about removing the last vestiges from British law. No longer would anyone be hanged for arson in a naval dockyard.

I was elected chair of the UK Labour delegation soon after I joined. My main activities were increased aid for poor countries, creation of an equality committee, protection of children from abuse and neglect, and a ban on asbestos. More and more nations signed up to membership while I was there. It is a body that is hardly noticed here, but I saw for myself that other nations reported on it more fully. Business there could make the front page on *Le Monde* but go completely unmentioned in our broadsheets. One member of the Socialist Group was a Spanish MP, who had been jailed for several years by Franco. He would never wear a tie, no matter how formal the event. This was because his prison guards, again and again, had garrotted him to an inch of his life. I was a champagne socialist for one night in my life, when we all went out and celebrated the Socialists' victory in the French general election.

Beavering away in our modest way, none of us expected to have anything to do with Silvio Berlusconi, the Italian Prime Minister. But one day the Socialist members of the Italian delegation sought a meeting with their fellow Socialists, to tell us Berlusconi had informed them that he wanted one of them to stand down, so that he could take his place. Why on earth did he want that? For the simple reason that membership of the Council of Europe brought with it protection from arrest anywhere in any of the nations signed up to it, and at that time Berlusconi was in great trouble with the law back home. We all told the Italians (and the other political groups, too, were of the same mind) that if that happened we would resign en masse. No more was heard from Signor B.

I was also elected chair of the Scottish all-party group on children, and remained so for three years. I wanted to ensure as much as possible was done for children while we had the opportunity, not knowing when our Scottish Parliament would be up and running.

In September the SNP were in the headlines, and not in a good way. Their Young Scots for Independence leaflet quoted lines spoken by Irvine Welsh's fictional character, Mark Renton:

> Some people hate the English... but I don't. They're just wankers. We, on the other hand, are colonised by wankers. We can't even pick a decent culture to be colonised by. We are ruled by effete arseholes. It's a shite

state of affairs and all the fresh air in the world will not make any fucking difference.

Renton, for those unfamiliar with the book, is a heroin addict. This fictional character's mind is not in a good state. What excuse had the publishers of this SNP leaflet and Alex Salmond concocted? I asked if the SNP thought this was appropriate language to recruit young people, and is this the case for independence that they wanted to make? It was grossly offensive to people who are our workmates, neighbours, friends and relations, and it was deplorable that a major political party had descended to this. Further, if anyone in England spoke of the Scots in such terms we would rightly be up in arms, and few noisier than himself. Can the Nats not love Scotland without making the absurd and ignorant claim that England does not have a decent culture? Now, years later, Salmond has been claiming an independent Scotland would be 'good neighbours' with England. If this is his idea of a good neighbour, I am glad I don't live next door to him.

CHAPTER TEN

Clause Four – A Battle Royal

NOWADAYS THE pundits don't feel satisfied until a new party leader has had his 'Clause 4 moment'. A day when he confronts his own party, leads by telling them they are wrong, wrong, wrong. What's more, not only does he knows best, but he must have his way, otherwise the hostile media will make mincemeat of both him and the party.

I was there, in Blackpool, in the hall at our party conference in October 1994 when Tony Blair sprang his famous speech upon us, rejecting Clause 4, Part 4 of our constitution. The Conference had spent years having major resolutions on issues of policy ignored by one leadership after another, but this was of a different order.

This was not merely an item of party policy – these were the words printed on every party membership card:

> To secure for the workers by hand or by brain the full fruits of their industry and the most equitable distribution thereof that may be possible upon the basis of the common ownership of the means of production, distribution and exchange and the best obtainable system of popular administration and control of each industry or service.

To show the extent to which things have changed, I have before me an official Labour Party document published in 1984, a mere ten years earlier, which quotes the Clause, and defines Socialism in the words of Clement Attlee:

> Socialism is an attitude towards life which recognises that the freedom and development of the individual personality can be secured only by harmonious co-operation with others in a society based on equality and fraternity. In the economic sphere this necessarily leads to a belief in the conscious organisation of the material resources of the world in the interests of all.

In a section on nationalisation, it points out that:

> Many people confuse socialism and nationalisation, but nationalisation is only a means towards socialism and neither necessarily involves socialism nor need necessarily be advocated by socialists for all industries and services. What socialists do hold is that at least the land, the minerals

under it, and the capital employed in industries and services which are of key importance and need to be conducted on a large scale ought to be publicly owned, in order to ensure their use for the benefit of the entire people.

In 1960, Aneurin Bevan made a statement, agreed by the National Executive Committee, on the need for sufficient public ownership to give the community power 'over the commanding heights of the economy'. A phrase Harold Wilson was fond of quoting, and both he and Clement Attlee had stood by Clause 4. Neither had interpreted it as advocating a command economy in which everything was nationalised, including the corner shop. Even Hugh Gaitskell, the most right wing party leader in decades, said in the same week:

> We emphasise that our social and economic objects can only be achieved by means of an extension of common ownership, in different terms, substantial enough to give power to the community over 'the commanding heights' – Mr Bevan's vivid phrase which I quoted with approval in just the same sense at Blackpool.

Of course, this was Gaitskell finally realising that he was getting nowhere with trying to ditch Clause 4. Instead he called for its retention – provided a new declaration of aims was placed alongside it. The draft affirmed that both public and private enterprise have a place in the economy, and that any further extension of common ownership should be decided from time to time in line with Labour's objectives. The party lived with this compromise for the ensuing years.

Now, on Tuesday afternoon at the tail end of his first Leader's speech to conference, Tony Blair was claiming it was a barrier to our electoral success, and pledging to drop it.

It appears no thought had been given to the fact that this very issue was due for debate two days later, in a composite motion (one that parcels up a number of points on a particular theme, composed by bringing together parts or all of original motions submitted) to be moved by Jim Mearns, the delegate from Glasgow Maryhill Constituency Labour Party. Trade unions and constituency Labour Parties had been mandated up to weeks before to support what had been seen as a routine, uncontroversial restatement of the Party's constitution, welcoming the previous year's conference decision to reaffirm Labour's commitment to Clause 4. Once the media realised there was a single motion on the conference agenda that actually mentioned Clause 4, Jim started to get their attention. Unison chief Rodney Bickerstaffe was quoted in The *Mirror* saying his delegation had agreed on the previous Sunday to back the Clause 4 resolution, 'because no idea had come to us that there was going to be anything in the leader's speech'. Maybe the leader's minions thought arms could be twisted, but in fact that did not happen. There were other ways, such as the infamous occasion in 1982, when Sid Weighell (then General Secretary of the National Union of Railwaymen), unblushingly switched his union's 170,000 block vote behind right wing Eric Hammond of the electricians' union for membership of the party's National Executive Committee, and not in favour of Eric Clarke, the Scottish miners' leader, who had been the choice of Weighell's own union and who had mandated him accordingly.

Now moves on both sides of the argument were being made. Jimmy Wray, at that time Convener of the Scottish Parliamentary Labour Party, advised Jim that the composite was the property of the delegates. It was not his to withdraw. But Jim was not inclined to withdraw anyway.

Jim and I phoned Maryhill party office bearers for their views. They did not offer instructions, but said the best thing to do was to seek consensus amongst those who had been involved in creating the composite. It boiled down to four choices: press it to a vote by show of hands, call for a card vote, which would show exactly who had voted and how, withdraw or remit to the National Executive for further consideration. Withdrawal would have meant Tony could claim he had already won the argument. It would have been capitulation, and none of us were in favour of that. Remission would mean the National Executive would be duty bound to consider it when formulating any new constitution for the party's approval. At that time the party's ruling body was not stuffed with Tony's yes men, so it would have received consideration. There were at least some members of the National Executive who would be sure to give it a good hearing. At least it wouldn't come across as outright defeat, and there might be some hope of building support across the movement in the meantime. It is only fair to record that Jim denied there had been any arm-twisting over the next two days to get him to withdraw or remit. Donald Dewar spoke to Jim on the Wednesday and asked him to remit. There was no mention of withdrawal. Donald's argument was that this was the Leader's first conference and it could be damaging if he were to face a big vote on a fundamental issue which might split the party so early in his leadership. Jim pointed out that Tony Blair was the one who had raised the issue, and Maryhill's motion simply reiterated our commitment to Clause 4 in a single sentence of a wider motion about redistribution and equality. It read in full:

> Conference welcomes the 1993 conference decision to reaffirm Labour's commitment to Clause 4 of the party constitution. Conference notes with concern that the electoral strategy currently being pursued by the shadow cabinet places little emphasis on this constitutional aim. Conference moves that the Parliamentary Labour Party adopts a firmer public line on issues of social justice. Conference believes that to achieve a fairer society, the redistribution of wealth must be a prime aim. To achieve this, the taxation system and public ownership should be used. Labour must present itself as a real and credible alternative. Conference strongly believes that to win, Labour must set out a positive and radical agenda which will unlock the great energies of the labour movement. Conference must recognise where core Labour support resides and be prepared to reinforce its strength. Conference believes that Labour must be presented as a far more distinctive party and should be demonstrating this by making use of MPs and members from all shades of party opinion. Accordingly, Conference resolves to reinstate into Labour's manifesto the commitment to bring about a fundamental and irreversible shift in the balance of wealth and power in favour of working people, and instructs that the popular objective of public ownership be fully incorporated into the party's policies. Conference calls on the National Executive Committee to draw up a socialist economic, industrial and social strategy which will give effect to this priority, give credibility to our pledges to bring about high levels of employment and a better welfare state, enable minority groups (disabled, gays, ethnic minorities) to benefit to the same extent as all other working men and women, and make Labour a clear alternative to the other parties.

Jim agreed, however, to ask the other six delegates who had been at the compositing meeting if they wanted to remit, as he viewed it as a shared motion. He managed to contact five of them. All five felt there was little point in having a debate if we weren't going to have a vote, and this information was duly passed on to Donald. Donald had spoken to me too, earlier the same day, to ask me what Maryhill would do. He was in no way trying to browbeat me or Jim. Donald simply did not operate that way. At that time nothing had been decided definitively, but I told Donald that if this was an embarrassment for Tony, then too bad. He should not go about changing things in that way. Maybe the words of Clause 4 could be put in more contemporary language, but that wasn't what this was really all about, was it?

As we discussed the issue amongst our supporters, and heard news from around the delegations, we felt suspicious that enough union leaderships had been squared to ensure its defeat if Jim did press it to a card vote. So, for that reason, my own view was that he should remit. I thought we would be defeated if it came to a vote. On top of that, it was only Jim's second time at conference, and he had never spoken at the rostrum before. He might be caught out by some chicanery or other. But I got it wrong, as was shortly to be shown.

With no sign of nerves whatsoever (even described by Peter Jones of *The Scotsman* the next day as looking 'cool and purposeful as he walked up to the rostrum, with a dozen TV cameras, a hundred photographers' lenses, and the eyes of an entire party on him'), Jim delivered what Patrick Wintour of the *Guardian* described as a powerful and articulate speech. Jim said Labour should stand for a fundamental and irreversible shift of power in favour of working people. He argued the clause was a succinct statement of our party's core philosophy, saying 'it didn't stop us winning elections in the past and it won't stop us winning elections in the future'. Nick Comfort in the *Daily Record* wrote:

> To loud cheers he told the Conference he was sick of political commentators saying that Socialism was dying. 'Socialism is very much alive and well, and striding forward to victory in sight. Fifteen years of Tory rule have certainly convinced me that unfettered capitalism is evil. We must use the power of office in the interest of our supporters as the Tories have done for theirs. Let's be tough on Capitalism and tough on the causes of Capitalism.'

That of course was a slightly mischievous mimicry of Tony's much repeated 'Tough on crime and tough on the causes of crime'. He ended with: 'Do more than sing about it. Let's do it. Raise the scarlet standard high and keep the Red Flag flying here!' Finally, having called for a card vote, he strode off the platform to thunderous applause. As he left the rostrum Dennis Skinner, MP for Bolsover, leant down from his seat on the platform and shook his hand, and Diane Abbott, MP for Hackney North and Stoke Newington slapped him on the back. Both had been elected to our party's National Executive that week.

In the course of the debate the party's General Secretary, Larry Whitty, bemused delegates by describing the drafting of the clause at the 1918 party conference as a fix:

> The two Fabian intellectuals, Beatrice and Sidney Webb, who drafted it, had to reconcile wide differences of opinion among different delegations. Representatives included supporters of the Bolshevik Revolution, Syndicalists, reactionary and cautious trade unionists, Fabian gradualists, and people well to the right of today's party. So the conference needed a lot of pulling together.

According to him, we had all been committed, all these decades that had gone by, to words that in his eyes clearly meant little, while we regarded the same words as the very heart of what we were about. Another thought occurred to me: how can anyone portray holding to Clause 4 as ultra-leftism, when it was the work of two Fabians, supported by, as Larry himself admitted, people who would find today's party a bit too left wing for them?

Denis MacShane, recently elected MP for Rotherham, urged delegates to support Tony, saying 'we are a party of the people, not a cult of Clause 4'. David Winnick, MP for Walsall North, supported the motion. He asked:

> Why should we spend the next twelve months going through the agony and the nightmare on Clause 4? What sense is there? The Clause had not stopped Labour winning in 1964, 1966, and twice in 1974. When you go on the doorstep, do people talk about Clause 4? No, they talk about poverty and unemployment. When the Tories gather at Bournemouth they won't be saying they need to apologise for their wholehearted belief in Capitalism. I say we need not apologise for our Socialism.

The National Communications Union's Maria Exall was called to the rostrum. In support of the motion, she pointed out that Tory privatisations had left behind poverty, squalor, unemployment and wage cuts. Then Alan Johnson, General Secretary of the Communication Workers' Union, welcomed the conference vote to oppose Post Office privatisation, but said his members:

> ... worried not one jot about words written by two middle-class Fabians in 1918. We – the Post Office – have been publicly owned for 300 years and we are still waiting for our members who work by hand and by brain to get the full fruits of their labour.

He went on to say it was 20 years since Labour last won a General Election and in that time the command economy had been discredited. I sat there thinking those who were opposing the motion seemed not to have read the party's own interpretation of the clause. It specifically did not commit ourselves to large state monopolies running everything. So why kick up a fuss now?

It was an extremely close result that followed. There were at least four recounts of the card vote, ending in favour of the composite 50.9 per cent, against 49.1 per cent. The unions voted 36.6 per cent in favour of Blair, 33.3 per cent for the motion. Constituencies voted 17.4 per cent for the motion, and 12.5 per cent against. Two hundred delegates from Unison, TGWU, ASLEF, NUM, UCATT, GPMU, FBU, and NCU voted to support Clause 4, and 241 delegates from AEEU, GMB, UCW, ISTC, USDAW, MSF, TSSA, and NCU (clerical) voted against.

Later on, Blair's media managers claimed the vote – which clearly rejected what he had said the previous Tuesday – was really a victory for the leadership, because a number of delegates were committed to support the composite by the body that sent them, whereas others with a free hand had decided to ditch Clause 4. The London media predictably started surmising Jim was some kind of loony Trotskyist. Jim said to interviewers: 'I'm no red-hot screeching Trot. I'm only a delegate who came here to do a job and I did it.' In response to media accusations of Militant involvement, he added, 'That is just total nonsense. I have never been in Militant. As a civil servant, I was in no party until four years ago.'

I was in a Radio Scotland studio early in the morning being interviewed by the redoubtable Kenny McAskill along with Peter Mandelson. Before we went on air, I warned Peter not to make that kind of claim against Jim or my constituency party, or we would sue. He disclaimed any such intention, and to be fair, in my hearing anyway, he stuck to the script of Tony's move being a necessary change. For my part, I told the radio listeners and the press that Maryhill was saying nothing more controversial than Aneurin Bevan's famous 'commanding heights of the economy' that had been quoted with approval often enough in the past by previous party leaders. Interviewed by several press reporters, I told them that if any of the media tried to tag the people in my constituency party with the stigma of being in Militant I would take legal action all the way. I added:

> None of them has had the courtesy to ask me what sort of constituency party is Maryhill. I will tell them it is responsible, hard-working, sensible and committed. The London media are talking rubbish and it shows they know nothing about us when they attack our members.

I went on to say:

> I expect the implied criticism in the composite to be taken into account
> in the constitutional review. The CLP has a long-standing commitment to
> public ownership and I share it. I think it is very clear that the great mass
> of people in the hall shared that when you saw the stupendous support
> for Robin Cook over keeping the Post Office in the public sector and for
> the NHS to be brought back into public hands.

Jim recalls that my son Stephen, who was minding the constituency office
for a few days while I was away, did a great job answering calls about him
from the media. The Scottish media took my point that they knew Maryhill
and the London-based Tory media did not. They knew which local parties
had been infiltrated by Trotskyists and they knew Maryhill had not. In
what became one of my treasured possessions, *The Herald* published a
cartoon depicting Tony Blair in a toga, with a stone tablet shattered at his
feet and the caption: 'Clause 1. Thou shalt consult Maryhill.'

With some rage, however, I realised that this is what we have come to.
That views expressed by former Labour Prime Ministers, no less, were
now being represented as off the wall ultra-leftism. Tony had worried
conference delegates when they read the following day's newspapers by
saying the vote 'had absolutely no significance'. Eh? So, having been won,
it would not even feature in any consideration of how to word a new
version of our aims and values?

By now there was such uproar amongst delegates, troubled by what
might be in store, that John Prescott had to reassure them when he made
his closing conference speech on the Friday. Tony Blair commented:

> I really don't think I have ever heard such a pathetic kerfuffle about a
> vote whose outcome was surprising only in that it was so close. To have a
> 50:50 vote indicates how far the party has travelled in forty-eight hours.

Geoffrey Parkhouse, in *The Herald*, wrote:

> It could have appeared to have travelled further if it had not been for Mr
> Jim Mearns, the Glasgow Maryhill delegate, who moved the motion at
> the start of a passionate debate.

Comment was made that it was ironic the block vote had been abolished.
The unions' share of the vote had been cut from 90 per cent to 70 per
cent. If still working on the old percentage, that would most likely have
delivered victory to the leadership. But having lost the vote, history was

subject to some revision. In the ensuing years I have often read that Tony Blair won that vote. In reality, his supporters had to go around telling anyone who would listen that the vote did not matter, and he would win in the end. Meanwhile, all the shadow cabinet were being asked where they stood on common ownership.

The following November there was an article in *Tribune* by David Winnick. In it he pointed out that Clause 4 was not, and had never been, about wholesale nationalisation. It was indeed the party's left wing that was critical of Morrisonian post-1945 nationalisation in so far as top management were remote and had much more in common with the way the private sector was run. Employees had no real say, and socialists have always been keen to involve both the employee and the consumer, hence the reference in the clause to popular administration. But, he went on, Clause 4 is not just something for the future, a goal for which we have a little prayer now and again. It is about the here and now like the NHS, local authority services and the way in which millions of people had their first decent housing as a result of council (not state) ownership. Then he came to the killer point:

> It will be argued that all that the arch modernisers want to do is simply update Clause 4 and make the whole thing more relevant to present times. Really? Does anyone seriously believe that to be the case? Surely, the whole purpose of the exercise is to signal that the party has dropped the whole idea of substantially extending public ownership. You can rest assured that those who least desire a Labour victory next time, particularly in the City and big business, will be the first to cheer if Clause 4 goes. If there has to be an electoral alternative to the Tories far better, as far as they are concerned, that the alternative party will not be particularly radical.

He made another telling point. 'Where is the evidence,' he asked, 'that the electoral misfortunes suffered since 1979 have been due to this clause? Some of the blame undoubtedly for continued Tory rule must lie with those ex-Gaitskellites who formed the SDP and then did their best to try to destroy the party in which they had made their political careers.' He concluded that the party was showing scant sign of wanting to become an SDP Mark 2.

Yet it was deeply uneasy about having lost in 1979, 1983, 1987 and 1992. Four in a row. Could the party survive a fifth defeat? And, they were asking themselves, didn't Tony seem like a vote winner? Could he just be trying to fox the Tory press? Maybe, some argued, he would revert to being a Labour leader as normally understood once he was safely elected.

In the months that followed, preparations went ahead for the Scottish Labour Conference in March 1995. This being the Labour Party, our Red Review people who entertained us with songs and skits at our conferences naturally wrote a song about it.

> When you walk down Lambeth Way
> Any evening, any day
> You'll see us all, writing the new Clause 4.
> Tony puts in 'tough on crime',
> Helen wants the Clause to rhyme
> We're having fun, writing the new Clause 4.
>
> CHORUS
>
> Everything's hunky-dory,
> Winning votes that were Tory,
> New Labour is the fashion
> That's our passion.
> Tony really has to win
> Railways out? No, put them in
> We're having fun, writing the new Clause 4.
> Commanding heights had quite a ring
> Now that's much too much left wing
>
> We're having fun, writing the new Clause 4.
>
> CHORUS
>
> Colleagues who hold Clause 4 fast
> Are just living in the past
> We're having fun, writing the new Clause 4.
> Nineteen-eighteen's long ago
> Capital ruled then, you know
> We're having fun, writing the new Clause 4.

A new draft of Clause 4 was written by Brian Wilson. It pledged Labour to 'nurture enterprise and promote common ownership' and 'cast out poverty'. His words appeared as an amendment to a motion from the Co-operative Party. But when the Co-op people said they wanted to withdraw their motion, the amendment did not fall, as it normally would under time-hallowed rules for the conduct of debate. Brian's words were deemed 'the property of conference' and would be voted on. I cannot recall the precise words that were eventually agreed, but the leadership did win the vote and further discussion ensued at a special conference on 29 April 1995 in the Methodist Central Hall in Westminster. Tony Blair addressed the conference, and when I re-read the speech today I am struck by how much it sounds like Alastair Campbell, who has always been much more of the Labour tribe than Tony ever was. The speech set out to reassure that our principles and values are still held dear. He noted that no-one in the widespread consultation disputed the need for some public ownership.

> That is why we fought the privatisation of the Post Office. That is why we will fight to keep our railways as a proper public service, publicly owned and accountable to the people.

Yet, not very many years later on, Peter Mandelson was telling us the Post Office had to be privatised. He went on: 'Strong public services – let me tell you this. I will re-nationalise the National Health Service to make it once more a service run for the whole nation.' (Yet Patricia Hewitt, in England and Wales, allowed market forces to enter in a way we managed to resist in Scotland.) 'Justice at work' was the next theme he mentioned. After affirming the right to be a member of a trade union and to be represented by it (which, incidentally, not even the Tories in umpteen Employment Bills had attempted to end totally) he won applause for pledging to restore trade union rights to the workers at GCHQ. But I remain disappointed at the way Peter Mandelson, as Business Secretary, influenced an approach that left British workers with fewer rights than many of our fellow members of the European Union or in the USA. It was not noticed at the time, but a paragraph in New Labour's legislation allowed an employer not to recognise a trade union where there was a pre-existing 'sweetheart' union. And so Rupert Murdoch got away with continuing to keep real trade unions at bay.

Tony Blair's speech, interestingly, went on to say, 'Never think that I lack pride in our past,' and praised the achievements of 1945. Why did he say that? Precisely because that was the impression being provided. New Labour was seen as ditching our history. If there was one thing notable about the Blairistas, it was their acting as if history began in 1994. Nothing was of any interest to them if it happened BT – Before Tony. The change in culture was notable. I well recall the first meeting of the PLP women's group after the 1997 General Election, when we were welcoming many new faces amongst the so-called 'Blair Babes'. One of them told us that she had been advised by a party official, when fighting her seat, to avoid banging on about poverty. He explained it made middle-class people feel left out of our considerations. I believe it was this lack of class empathy, never mind any question of class analysis, that made it possible for some Labour MPs to actually support the cut in lone parent benefit that followed soon after. Likewise there were other men and women who felt that empathy, usually from their own direct experience, and voted against.

So where are we now, today? No-one back in 1994 would have guessed that we would be nationalising banks to save the economy from going into freefall. Are people content with a society in which market forces have dictated high house prices, and there is not enough decent public sector housing available? One in which disabled people can be evicted from their homes because of the bedroom tax? In which hundreds of thousands have been made redundant in the public sector, including, incredibly, tax inspectors who could be raking in billions from tax dodgers? A society in which those whose greed and irresponsibility caused the crisis get away with their bonuses, and amass wealth they could never live long enough to spend?

If, in such circumstances, the Labour Party was still in thrall to Blairism, I would despair. Fortunately, we are not.

Perhaps it would be fitting to end with the words of the Clause 4, Part 1, that was eventually agreed. It goes:

> The Labour Party is a democratic socialist party. It believes that by the strength of our common endeavour, we achieve more than we achieve alone so as to create for each of us the means to realise our true potential and for all of us a community in which power, wealth and opportunity are in the hands of the many not the few, where the rights we enjoy reflect the duties we owe, and where we live together, freely, in a spirit of solidarity, tolerance and respect.

There is something of the King James Bible versus modern versions going on here, it seems to me. Our 1918 version, like the King James, has more poetry and succinctness in its language. The modernisers in religion as well as politics don't seem able to stir the soul. Fortunately, our voters remain uninterested in such matters. They just wanted their Labour Party back.

CHAPTER ELEVEN

1997: A New Dawn?

AT LONG LAST, the General Election. As I went campaigning around my constituency I always liked to have a tape of 'Maryland', the trad jazz tune, belting out from my car's loudhailer. It would be recognised as 'The Red Flag'. People warmed to it, as they never did to any official party election music. Not 'Things Can Only Get Better', and certainly not the tuneless few bars of Brahms that had been Neil Kinnock's choice. When they heard 'Maryland' in Maryhill, they waved back at me. They even danced a few steps on the pavement.

But on polling day itself, as I drove along Liddesdale Road in Milton, what was this coming towards me? Can I be hearing right? It's another Labour car and it's blaring out, of all things, 'Don't Cry for Me, Argentina'.

'Stop! Stop!' I called to them. 'Why on earth are you playing that?'

'Why, don't you like it?' our supporter replied. 'It was just that Eva Peron was another female politician, so we thought you'd like it.'

I explained I did not think it a good idea to associate me in any way with a woman who had worked her way to the top on her back.

'Eh? Oh!'

Campaigning can certainly throw up hilarious moments. Norman Buchan, in one of his election campaigns, had gone around with his loudhailer calling out VOTE BUCHAN LABOUR! A woman phoned the campaign rooms to complain. 'Was it too loud?' his agent asked. 'No, it's not that,' she replied. 'It's just that there's no need to swear, is there?'

Hustings, too, were great value entertainment. They are less well attended than they used to be, yet the hall was well filled on the night the Natural Law Party candidate assured everyone they could bring about world peace by meditation and levitation.

'So,' one of the audience members reasonably asked, 'can we see you levitate just now?' He was answered that they could only do it in a quiet, calm, receptive and unchallenging atmosphere.

'So, it wouldn't work against a tank coming along the road, then?'

That year their Maryhill candidate's surname was Blair, and they achieved a vote three times as many as any of their other candidates in the city. With a hefty majority like ours in Maryhill, Labour could afford to be nonchalant. Still rankles with me, though.

That year, too, there were an unusually high number of Trots not so much expecting to be elected as competing to see which of them could save their deposit. At a hustings in Lansdowne Parish Church, one of the Trots proclaimed that Labour's promise of the introduction of a National Minimum Wage at what might be £3.60 an hour for an adult should be set at a higher amount. Vote for him and £7 an hour. '£7!' the next scoffed. His party would make it £8. 'Any advance on £8?' the Minister chairing the meeting languidly enquired. The third man trumped the lot. 'What a bunch of class traitors! Everyone should get the same pay.'

At another hustings, the room had a number of Scottish Nationalists present, claiming that Tony Blair had earlier that day compared the planned Scottish Parliament to a parish council in England. And what did I have to say to that? I had been out and about, and not seen the teatime news, but I was sure this could not be true. Tony was never enamoured of the idea of devolution, but I was certain he just wouldn't say anything as daft as that. So I told the assembled multitude of a dozen or so, all there on behalf of their parties, that I did not know what he had said, but there was no way I would rely on SNP supporters' version of whatever he had said, and would find out for myself. Then we could return to it at the following night's hustings. Sure enough, it turned out that, when he was asked by a reporter why the Parliament should have tax-raising powers, he said in support of that plan that if even a parish council can, why shouldn't the Scottish Parliament? And so went the headline, 'Blair Compares Parliament to Parish Council'. This distortion is still repeated on some websites.

There is no excuse for that. There are only three possible explanations: either a degree of stupidity, or illiteracy, that should disbar those journalists concerned from this kind of paid employment, or plain dishonesty. And I don't think it was stupidity.

On polling day I was standing outside Dunard Street Primary School in the heart of my constituency, when a Channel Four reporter asked me if he could speak to a Labour voter. Of course he could. Soon afterwards there appeared, walking slowly along the pavement to the school gates, a little white haired old lady, leaning on the arm of a younger man who looked as if he might be her son. She looked the very picture of a sweet faced wee granny. She gave me a big, beaming smile when she spotted me, and then told me she would not miss voting Labour today although her legs were sore. I asked her, would she be willing to take a moment to tell this TV reporter why she was voting Labour? She would. The reporter got her to stand where he wanted, and held out the large, furry mike to her to say her piece. With no hesitation, she spoke clearly and firmly. 'Ah'm votin' Labour because I hate thae fuckin' Tories, Mister.' No doubt about it, she spoke for Maryhill.

What joy it was when, as the night went on, we realised we were winning a huge majority. Labour scored no less than 13,517,911 votes. We now had a record 418 MPs to the Conservatives' 165 and the Liberal Democrats' 46 (as a matter of historical interest, we had even more votes in 1951, our highest ever tally, yet we lost that year because it's seats that count, not votes). Now we had 101 Labour women MPs, the largest number for any party in British history. Tony Blair was Prime Minister.

As for Maryhill, once again we had a huge majority. My vote was 19,301 and the nearest was the Scottish Nationalist candidate with 5,037. There were a few spoiled ballot papers, as usual. One had no cross against any candidate, but it had a few lines of handwriting which read: 'They are all bampots but at least Maria Fyfe helped me.' Another simply read, 'I love Maria'. The other candidates' agents generously proposed that their intentions were clear, but the returning officer was inclined to disagree. We had all been up for hours and were dying to get to bed, so I said to everyone let's not waste any time on this. Let's get some sleep.

I was awakened by the *Daily Record* phoning me at home when I had had about three hours' sleep, to ask me if I would meet one of their photographers in Maryhill Road to get a picture of public reaction to the result of the election. I got dressed hurriedly and raced up the road, thinking the best that was likely to happen was a picture of some smiling faces. It could hardly have turned out better. As the photographer and I stood outside the public library, where my constituency office was on the floor above, a guy I didn't even know came strolling along towards us, beamed from ear to ear when he spotted me, and holding out his arms to hug me, called out joyfully, 'Maria, my flower!' Then he pulled me into a waltz right there on the pavement, the photographer snapping away for dear life. What a contrast to 1992, when I saw stricken faces everywhere I went on the streets of Glasgow.

Now let's see what Labour would do. Give any seats in the Cabinet to the Liberal Democrats? Were they having a laugh? Tony had wanted to do that because he had remained unconvinced we would win after all those years in Opposition. But as the Greek newsagent near my London flat put it, the dogs in the street knew this was Labour's year.

After being in opposition for ten years in my own case, enjoying my job so much the time had flown in, I was now to find out what it was like sitting on the other side of the Chamber. Peter Mandelson began to irritate me by standing at the side of the Speaker's chair and looking out over the ranks of Labour back benchers as if he was keeping an eye on us all. Hadn't he enough to do, in his job as minister without portfolio? He wasn't a whip, and the whips did their job more discreetly than that.

Labour ministers were getting used to sitting opposite where they had been for so long, and seeing the Tories now on the opposition benches. For the first few days it was quite easy to wander in absentmindedly and sit on the wrong side of the Chamber. Then be poked fun at for allegedly crossing the floor. We were soon to realise that the Conservative back benchers were not much good at opposing. They didn't turn up in any great numbers, maybe because they were spending more time with their business interests. They didn't tackle us the way we had tackled them. It was as if, after so many years in power, too few of them had any idea how. There was another side to this coin: I realised that the expertise that my chums and I had developed over the years in giving Ministers a hard time would hardly be welcomed by the new Labour Ministers. Would we find day in, day out, simple acquiescence boring? Not that we had acquiesced all the time with our front bench when we had been in opposition – the first Gulf War particularly came to mind – but we would not be Labour MPs in the first place if we did not anticipate that quite a lot of the time we would actually agree with our own front bench.

But now wrongs could be righted. I immediately applied for an Adjournment Debate to raise the Glasgow housing finance issue, and was given 8 July as the first available date. North Edinburgh and Leith MP Malcolm Chisholm was the newly appointed Housing Minister, and in his reply to my plea he stated that the debt could be paid from the Council's general fund, instead of the Housing Revenue Account (the income from rents), something of which Glasgow officials had been unaware. The civil servants had revealed there was a seventeen year old Scottish Office circular which allowed both the debt from borrowing capital for house building and the cost of demolishing old properties to be transferred to the Council's general fund. I got hold of this circular and presented it to

Councillor McCarron, the Chair of the Council's housing committee. The following year he was able to announce that £26 million a year would be released to refurbish the city's housing, and the tenants would no longer have to pay this completely unjustified charge that took up a large slice of their rent. And of course it freed up a lot of money for carrying out much neglected work. I still feel angry that such a blunder should have been allowed to continue for so very long, at great cost to the living standards of thousands of people. It would not have happened if even one individual at governmental level had been motivated by any sense of justice.

More good news for Glasgow's housing stock was to follow. When Gordon Brown became Chancellor he decided to pay off our city's entire housing debt of over £900 million. This made it possible for the new not-for-profit Glasgow Housing Association to carry out the long-delayed repair and refurbishment of the housing stock. Donald Dewar asked me to join the GHA Board, and I did so because I had a longstanding interest in bringing our housing up to a standard fit for the late 20th century. It did not seem to me too much to ask, in one of the wealthiest countries in the world, that everyone should have accommodation they were happy to call home.

At the Board's first meeting, seconded by Liberal Councillor Christopher Mason, I moved that our standing orders should require that a tenant should always be the Chair. We both also put forward the idea that consensual decisions should be sought. It was better to work together to find solutions, and not just have one lot outvoting another lot. These moves were intended to counter the propaganda being put about by the SNP and others hostile to the stock transfer that the tenants were being taken for mugs, and would be outvoted by the politicians. Which was in itself an insult to the Glasgow tenants, who had been running effective tenants' associations for many years. They might lack political guile, but they were not stupid.

*   *   *

The new women MPs certainly won attention. The Chamber looked utterly different, with all the brightly coloured jackets, whether Follett-inspired or not. They were shocked to find themselves sometimes treated in the Chamber with an incivility they had never experienced in any previous occupation, but we found an answer: doughnutting. Now, if a Labour woman was speaking, if she wished she could be surrounded by some of the sisters, ensuring she did not appear isolated and without support. The older ones amongst us, experienced in the ways of sin, showed the new ones how to retaliate against hecklers. It's always good to have a crack or two up your sleeve, in case you don't think of a crushing put down off the top of your head. I recalled being a fairly new Member, and being heckled by a drunken Tory back bencher one night. I couldn't make out what he was saying, his speech was so slurred, but as he had a self-satisfied grin on his face I realised he thought he had said something devastating. I responded, 'The Honourable Gentleman thinks he's a wit, but he's only half right.' The *Evening Times* reporter, Ian Hernon, loved that and for ever after sought quotes from me. I didn't confess until I saw him as a friend that it wasn't original. I had remembered it from the days when the Young Socialists stood on soapboxes in Sauchiehall Street, speaking on world affairs to an audience that was not always friendly.

Some thought the way to deal with rudeness and bad behaviour was to complain to the Speaker, but Betty Boothroyd pooh-poohed their complaints, feeling no sympathy for them whatsoever. She had battled her way to the top, regarded those selected as candidates on all-women short-lists as inferior to those who had made it through an open selection, and vehemently asserted that if they weren't hard enough, they should stay off the battlefield. But Michael Martin, one of her deputy speakers, did listen, sympathise, and advise, thus making him a popular candidate for Speaker when the vacancy next arose.

The sheer number of new women meant some changes around the House. Realising they needed exercise, some organised tap dancing sessions and became so good they went on to entertain under the name of The Division Belles. Unwisely I tried to give this a go for an hour one night. Returning to the dinner table to meet my chums, panting and red-faced, I met Lewis Moonie (a doctor in his previous life), who enquired what I had been doing. 'For Christ's sake, Maria,' he went on, 'are you trying to kill yourself?'

In June some of my friends back home exploded when Donald Dewar, putting together his Scottish front bench team, appointed Henry McLeish as Minister for Women. A man! When there were now no less than eight Labour women elected in Scotland! Henry also had to deal with devolution and home affairs. John Penman wrote in *The Scotsman*, 'Maria Fyfe left the Scottish front bench around 18 months ago. New Labour does not seem to have room for the occasionally rebellious Ms Fyfe at the top of the tree'. Which showed he was unaware I had made it clear when I left the front bench that I did not want to go back. But what about the other women? Helen Liddell had taken my place when I stepped down, but now she was off to higher things as Economic Secretary to the Treasury. Rachel Squire was PPS to Education ministers Stephen Byers and Estelle Morris. Irene Adams, as a Scotland United supporter, would know she would not be joining the Scottish front bench team. The others, Lynda Clark, Anne McGuire, Rosemary McKenna and Sandra Osborne were, I was told at the time, thought too new to be promoted. Things have changed since then in Westminster. It used to be a Member would serve many years on the back benches before being considered for junior ministerial rank, but now I see people in the Cabinet who don't seem that long out of school. Indeed, when the Scottish Parliament was finally up and running, there was no help for it but to throw quite a few beginners in at the deep end.

However, Donald pleased women activists more when in July we had a row in the party about whether abortion law should come under the devolved Parliament or be reserved to Westminster. Not once had this come up during the years of the Scottish Constitutional Convention's work. But now George Galloway argued:

> It may be the importance of the Catholic and Protestant Churches in Scotland would lead to a tighter administration of abortion policy. If so, that is our right, and not one which can be taken away from us by any English lobby.

In reply, I pointed out that it had nothing to do with any English lobby. It was women throughout the UK uniting in defence of women. It was obvious that the new Scottish Parliament would be under a great deal of pressure from those who opposed abortion on any grounds to tighten abortion law in Scotland. Look at Northern Ireland, where Unionists and Nationalists were united on at least one thing: their assumption of the right to forbid abortion even in the most dreadful circumstances. As a result, many women had to travel to clinics in England or Scotland to obtain a termination that was perfectly legal on the mainland. So it would not be a good idea to land ourselves with a similar problem, and create cross-border traffic between England and Scotland, which was sure to happen if Scotland had markedly tighter legislation. Donald came down on the side of making this a UK-wide matter.

* * *

Sunday, 31 August 1997. I was staying with my son Chris and his partner Rosie in Oxford, woke early and put on the radio. They were saying Princess Diana had died in a car accident in Paris. When I returned home George Square, the main square in Glasgow opposite the City Chambers, was filled with flowers.

* * *

It was not long before the first major division of opinion in the Parliamentary Labour Party. It was in November 1997, and Gordon Brown as Chancellor of the Exchequer was holding fast to his undertaking before the General Election to keep to Kenneth Clark's Tory Budget for the first two years. I had thought at first he must surely mean he intended to stick to the overall total of spend, but make adjustments up and down to fit in with our own priorities. Within that huge amount of income at his disposal, running into billions, it should surely be possible to make decisions to spend more on some items and less on others, and still add up to the same overall total. That was precisely what local authorities did – on a much smaller scale of course – when drawing up their budgets, year on year: making adjustments up and down on a huge list of items. But no, he meant each and every item would stay with the same level of spend as Kenneth Clark had laid down.

I can understand why, in a way. If he did allow, say, Social Security some extra spending on some item, or even merely save it from a particular cut, in no time the Ministers for Health, Education, Defence and so on would be knocking on his door making their cases for a higher spend on their own priorities. And no-one would be happy to have to find cuts elsewhere to pay for them. He was a brand new Chancellor, he had never done the job before, and he had plenty on his plate without inviting a deluge of demands from one and all.

And yet. I never thought I would see a Labour Government cutting benefits for lone parents and their children. Labour MPs were now being told it was inevitable. We were reminded we were elected on a promise to stick to the Tory budget, and that meant making hard choices. (I hate that phrase, 'hard choices'. It's uttered by people who are making decisions which rarely impact on themselves, but that leave other people with really hard choices: like whether to put more money in the meter or buy some bread and margarine.) The Tories had been planning to carry this out because in their view, lone parents did not need or deserve any extra help. The New Labour Government was carrying out this cut, not because it thought it was right, but because we had 'inherited' the Tory budget. I could only think of the single parent who had come to my advice surgery one night, telling me that because her former partner had once again failed to keep to his arrangement to pay his share of the children's needs, she had lived on nothing but bread and margarine all week until her benefit was due, in order to ensure the children were fed as well as she could.

The argument from the Treasury was nonsense. The sums involved were a tiny proportion of the gigantic social security budget. And I did not meet many people who would want us to stick to these targets at the expense of impoverished children. How would we promote 'education, education, education' if Mum could not buy books? How would we keep children from running wild in the streets when home was cold, bare and unwelcoming? The whole analysis behind these cuts assumed that all lone parents needed carrots and sticks to get them to work, and that the jobs were there to be found.

The cut was due to come into effect in June 1998, when 'new' lone parents would no longer get a level of benefit created by a former Labour Government precisely so as to help with the difficulty of not having a partner's time or income. No-one would dream of telling 'new' pensioners that they would get a smaller pension, or telling 'new' jobless people they would get £10.25 a week less in Jobseeker's Allowance. So why were 'new' lone parents being singled out?

We were told it was because the New Deal for Lone Parents, helping them to get jobs and training and finding childcare, was to come into effect in October 1998. But the entire cost of that package was only half the amount saved in three years of these cuts. It was lone parents themselves who were paying for the New Deal. A lone parent would count as 'new' if he or she took up a job and subsequently lost it, even if it was through no fault of their own. Then that parent's family income would be down by an average of £10.25 less than the pittance they had at the time.

Such a parent would be very careful not to lose that job. Extra unpaid hours? She would be wise to remain silent and unprotesting. Unfair treatment? No industrial tribunal would be open to her if she were working less than a year in that job. Stingy pay packet? More than likely no trade union, no national minimum wage yet, and no wages inspectorate yet.

When Labour MPs discussed this at a heated meeting of the Parliamentary Labour Party, we were given a rosy picture of the New Deal. Lone parents, we were assured by Harriet Harman, could be so much better off in their new job, they could plan to take the children to Disneyland. I put it to the meeting that if any of us told that to our constituents, they would think it was we who were living in Disneyland. There was an assumption that a lone parent would actually get a job under the New Deal measures. But the areas with the highest unemployment also had the most lone parents. Unemployment causes family breakdown. Glasgow would be likely to lose heavily from lone parent benefit cuts because of the large number of lone parents. But we would be likely to benefit less than other parts of the country from the New Deal measures to get unemployed people into work simply because there were not enough jobs.

It seemed to have been forgotten that, following divorce or separation, young children especially may feel very insecure. This was perhaps not that great a problem for those who employed nannies, but we were supposed to be aware of how most people lived their lives. My view was that a mother was likely to know better than the social security officer whether, right now, her children needed her presence and her care. But no matter how justified her view might be, if she was a 'new' lone parent, she would lose benefit. Already she would get a cut of £19 weekly in benefit if the Child Support Agency did not accept her reason for refusing to give information about the father's whereabouts: often it would be the threat of violence that made her prefer to take the cut.

Some of us felt all the more angry about this because it was being imposed without a chance to discuss it in the party's National Policy Forum – the body which, we had all been told, was the great step forward in involving party members in policy making. The party conference had not debated it: it was removed from the timetable. We were told there was no commitment to lone parents in the manifesto. But nor did it say we would cut the benefits bill by making lone parents poorer.

Efforts in the PLP to raise it met with hints that consequences would follow for those individuals who openly disagreed. Newly elected MPs were being told that disloyalty would be remembered, and so would loyalty. All this just made me feel the more enraged, and all the more determined to rebel, and if that meant being expelled from the Parliamentary Labour Party – as was threatened – then so be it. It had happened before, to better people than me. I would still be in a job, and much better paid than most. And Maryhill Labour Party were backing me to the hilt.

There were plenty more of us who felt the same, and so the umbrella Save Lone Parent Benefit Campaign was born at a meeting on 11 November. Along with Audrey Wise and Lynne Jones, I spoke from the platform, and 25 other MPs, mostly Labour, attended. I was particularly struck by the support we got from a good number of male Labour MPs, some of whom were usually considered right wing, and certainly had not shown before any interest whatsoever in women's issues. But the crux of the matter was, quite a number of them had been brought up by their mothers on her own. Either their fathers had died young, sometime during the war years, or the marriage had broken up, or their mother had always been a single parent. So their mothers had taken low paid cleaning jobs, at difficult hours, to keep the family fed and clothed fit for school. These guys had first-hand experience of poverty, and knew better than some of our other colleagues how hard it must be for mothers like their own.

I made this point with some vehemence at the PLP meeting, making the barbed remark that this was the kind of thing that turned you into a socialist. Unlike some of the new women, who felt neither bound by class loyalty nor by feminist sympathies, or just human fellow feeling, to do the right thing by women in need. Donna Covey of the GMB commented that, 'Labour women MPs who supported the cut had no right to get elected on the back of women-only shortlists, and then vote for anti-women policies.' She was referring to the fact that, on the Standing Committee considering the Bill, there were six Labour women who failed to mount the slightest objection. And it was surprising to find a few left wing men failing to support us. When George Galloway was asked by Hillhead Labour Party why he had not backed the rebellion, he replied that, as he had a record of voting against the official Labour line, he had to choose his issues carefully, and not jump to support every cause. But then it is not unknown for supposedly left wing leaders of men to have scant regard for the female half of the human race.

One of the participating bodies in the campaign was Grannies for Lone Parents, founded by a group of Labour women MPs including myself, ranging on the political spectrum from Gwyneth Dunwoody, renowned for years past for her old school right wing views, to Audrey Wise, one of the most left wing women ever to sit on the Labour benches. Gwyneth was scathing when she tore into the case the Government was making.

Audrey's eye for detail made her exceptionally good at briefing people on the proposed legislation. When Audrey briefed you, you stayed briefed. There was a hilarious moment in the Chamber during the debate on 10 December when Audrey offered advice to women who thought their old man was going to leave them. 'Tell him to hurry up,' she said, 'and do it before the legislation kicks in and makes you worse off than you have to be.' This was such a contrast to the usual advice to women to keep their marriage together at all costs, and avoid ending up a single parent, it made some mouths fall open.

The PLP had met on 19 November, and the main business had been an effort to get this proposed legislation thrown out. Harriet Harman was attacked for supporting a cut she had opposed in November 1996 when we were in opposition. She has since come to realise that was a mistake on her part, and has certainly done plenty for women in the years since, more than making up for it. I realised what we were up against when Stephen Pound was supported by some when he chided the Bill's opponents in terms that made me unable to believe I was listening to a *Labour* MP: 'What was all the fuss about?' He asked. 'It's no more than the price of a couple of packets of cigarettes.' It was revealed that the savings from the combined cutting of Income Support and Child Benefit for lone parents was estimated at £60 million in the first year, rising to £195 million in the third year, out of a total social security budget of £100 billion. Meanwhile, incredibly, £828 million (well over £1 billion at today's prices) was being spent on, of all things, the Millenium Dome! Oh, yes, it must be really necessary to deliver on that. And what had happened to the sense of proportion of anyone who would rather raise money for that white elephant than help out poorer parents?

On the night of the vote, 47 Labour MPs voted against and there were about 100 abstentions, many of them pointedly sitting in their seats while the vote was taken. During the debate only a handful of MPs spoke to support the measure, and had their arguments torn to shreds by Members who had been well briefed by Audrey. It was reported that some of the new women Members were crying as they went through the voting lobby in support of the Government. At the time I felt no sympathy for their distress, only anger and contempt. But now looking back on it all I can see how these 'newbies' were pulled in different directions. They had only been elected a few months before, some without much political experience, and had not anticipated ever, or at any rate so soon, finding difficulty in supporting our newly elected Labour Government. They were torn between what their heart told them and their fear of getting on the wrong side of the whips. A threat of being expelled from the PLP is a frightening one for those who have barely set foot in Parliament. They were not all just careerists. They had also been told that if they signed a letter, not for publication, to Gordon Brown then in that way they could make their protest and seek an amendment to the Bill without voting against the government. Around 120 MPs, including parliamentary private secretaries, signed.

Innocent souls they were. The news of this leaked out, and so the media knew that support for the government on this issue was a lot flakier than the spin doctors were trying to tell them.

As I saw it, Labour voters rightly expected their Labour MP to be loyal to the party line, in the general way of things. But we were not robots, and the whips were not Daleks. For the pay we received, we were surely expected to be more than voting fodder. The dimmest, least politically minded amongst our population could manage to walk into one voting lobby or the other as directed by a whip. But should anyone be paid a substantial salary just for that? Shouldn't a Member engage brain before starting feet? If after careful thought it seems necessary to depart from the 'line', it should be possible to explain to anyone, whether the whips, your local party, the media, or the constituents. And take any consequences that might ensue if any of them don't like it.

The leadership should have paid attention to the range of opinion against the cuts in Lone Parent Benefit. In Scotland alone we had a line up of Cardinal Winning, the Church of Scotland, the STUC, Save the Children, the lone parents' group One Plus and others, all begging MPs to reject targeting such vulnerable people. But they remained obdurate, saying they had been told by their focus groups that people did not care. I said they should sack the focus groups.

Our New Labour Prime Minister insisted yet again that the proposals to cut benefits for lone parents were necessary to keep tight control of public spending. He argued:

> We were elected as a government because people believed we would keep a tight control on public finance and because we said clearly before the election – and I repeat again now – that what is important is to get as many people as possible off benefit and into work.

Audrey Wise put it succinctly when she said in response:

> I do criticise the attitude that says that all parents of small children should be willing to go to work – cleaning, shelf filling and leaving their children with somebody else. Lone parents are mostly the result of marriage breakdowns, not mostly the young, reckless or foolish. But if there is such a mother, is she going to be a better mother by making her poorer?

Alice Mahon got sacked for voting against. She argued:

> Lone parent families are only just surviving and now the first Labour Government for eighteen years was planning cuts for the most disadvantaged. Where in the manifesto did it say we were going to make cuts to lone parents? 'Things Can Only Get Better', we all sang on 1 May. I think I missed the verse excluding lone parents.

Malcolm Chisholm, the Local Government Minister for Scotland, resigned rather than vote for this. Disgracefully, the spin from Number Ten was 'Malcolm who?' There were hints he had gone, not because he was against this cut, but because he could not do the job. That kind of thing was one of the most unpleasant features of the Blair regime. I had not known it under either Kinnock or Smith, but now I knew colleagues who were reluctant to put their heads above the parapet for fear of what might be said in anonymous briefings against them.

Three days after the vote, *The Economist* warned Blair against providing an issue which aligned left MPs with the centre and right against the Blairite modernisers. It went on to say, 'the sight of a Labour Government scuttling around the television studios justifying cuts in social security for lone parent families sickens members across a wide range of views'. In a *Guardian* poll the day before the vote, public opinion was against the Government by a factor of three to one. The whips found themselves in an impossible position. The size of the revolt was so large, and public opinion so overwhelmingly with us, they were unable to withdraw the whip, despite the new PLP standing orders making it a disciplinary offence to vote against the Government. But five holders of office either resigned or were sacked from their posts (Alice Mahon, Malcolm Chisholm, Gordon Prentice, Michael Clapham and Neil Gerrard). Single mothers had demonstrated outside Parliament, travelling by overnight bus from as far away as Scotland. Thousands phoned to express their anger to radio call-in shows and to constituency offices of MPs.

After all this, years later, Kenneth Clark admitted he had not seriously thought Labour would stick to his cuts programme. He had deliberately designed a severe budget that he himself had no intention of implementing, in order to make life difficult for what everyone knew would be an incoming Labour Government. He certainly succeeded. It may be clever politics, but it makes me feel disappointed with someone who generally comes across as a decent bloke that he would treat lone parents as pawns in his game, or possibly be so far above such considerations he was not even aware of that outcome.

It is also fair to say that Gordon Brown went on to bring in the National Minimum Wage against bitter and sustained Tory propaganda, hugely increase Child Benefit, create tax credits that helped working parents with childcare costs, and generally do more than any previous government had ever done to substantially reduce child poverty, both here and in developing countries.

I find it curious that neither Tony Blair, Peter Mandelson nor Alastair Campbell mention any of this, an issue that had the Parliamentary Labour Party in ructions, in their own memoirs. I don't think it is because they are avoiding unpleasantness. Their memoirs deal largely with interpersonal relationships at the top of the tree. We foot soldiers in the PLP didn't matter that much to them.

I only ever had one face to face contact with Alastair. I was first on the list for Prime Minister's Questions, and Labour Members knew they should go and see Alastair beforehand, so that he could let Tony know what questions the Labour back benchers were going to raise and could prepare a knowledgeable and helpful answer. So I told Alastair I was going to raise an item in the news about Glasgow hospitals. He then told me he would like me to raise instead an issue affecting St Thomas's Hospital on the other side of the Thames. So I then said:

> But Alastair, if people back home watching Parliament on the telly see me going on about St Thomas's, and not the Glasgow hospitals, they'll wonder what on earth I am doing.

'OK, but could you try to get in a mention of St Thomas's at the end of your question?' I replied, 'I will try, but you know what the Speaker is like. If he thinks I'm going on too long he'll stop me.' Alastair concluded our interview by saying, 'I'll leave it to you to get it over as succinctly as possible.'

I headed back to the Members' Tearoom, where some of my chums were having a lunchtime snack. Ian Davidson remarked, 'You seem to still be all in one piece. Did that go ok?'

'Perfectly', I said. 'I don't know how he gets the reputation of being so aggressive and threatening. He was perfectly nice and reasonable.'

'Well,' said Ian, 'He wouldn't be horrible to *you*, would he?'

'Why not?'

'It would be like giving cheek to your mammy!'

CHAPTER TWELVE

Steps on the Road to Devolution

FOLLOWING OUR fourth consecutive defeat at the General Election in April 1992, we had a meeting of the Scottish Group of Labour MPs at Keir Hardie House, the party's Scottish headquarters. We now held 49 seats in Scotland. Sadly, Frank Doran, a good comrade, had been defeated. There were six new members: Malcolm Chisholm, Eric Clarke, Mike Connarty, Ian Davidson, Brian Donohoe and Rachel Squire. Now the female contingent were up to a whole three out of the 49, Irene Adams having won a by-election in 1990 caused by the death of her husband. Wow – at this rate we'd be up to equal representation by 2100.

The meeting affirmed its support of a multi-option referendum on Scotland's future government: status quo, devolution, or independence. In retrospect, I don't think we gave enough thought to the possibility of a confusing result, with three choices resulting in no clear majority for any one of them. First Past the Post would hardly be seen as a good way to settle the matter if a majority were against the winning option. But devolution was gaining in popularity and likely to win.

A short while before that the Glasgow MPs had been at a meeting. When we left, George Galloway and I were standing outside the King's Theatre when he surprised me by asking me to join a newly formed organisation to promote the fact that three quarters of Scottish voters had voted for parties that did not want the status quo, to be called 'Scotland United'. Jim Sillars was one of its co-founders, and it was Dennis Canavan who had come up with the name. I told George that, after my experiences back in the mid-'70s with Sillars' Scottish Labour Party and that man's autocratic notions of how to run a political party, my answer was that I could be stupid once in a particular way, but not twice. Later George came back to me, telling me that Jim Sillars had not meant to expel me. True, he closed down the branch that I chaired, with no discussion and no appeal, but he would have reinstated me later. Well, thanks for nothing. He could keep his Scotland United.

Not that I had any intention anyway of uniting with the Nats, even if Sillars had not been involved. When a few constituents asked me why I had not joined, I told them I was hardly likely to join forces with a party that had spent the last five years dubbing Scottish Labour MPs 'the feeble fifty' because we could not stop the Tories, with their large majority, from winning votes on Bills. What we could do was force them to achieve less of their agenda than they would wish by being prepared to stay up all night again and again to breakfast time, fighting Tory Bills line by line, and I did not recall Alex Salmond putting in shifts like that. Even Margaret Ewing, who woman-to-woman had occasional frank conversations with me, told me one day she carried an unfair workload compared to her colleagues. Added to that, the Nationalists had expressed no interest whatsoever in women's representation in the Scottish Parliament, professed support for a Scottish Parliament but had played no part in the three years of work to date in the Scottish Constitutional Convention, and in any case had a prescription for Scotland's future that I regarded as poison.

A few weeks later, on 27 April, Betty Boothroyd was elected Speaker, to my great delight. At last a woman had broken through that particular glass ceiling. Later the same day we had another meeting of the Scottish Group, where we had further discussions on what we needed to do now that we were in Opposition once more. The Scotland United supporters raised their dissatisfactions with John Smith at UK level and Donald Dewar at Scottish level. George Galloway made an impassioned speech, describing with his customary eloquence what he found to criticise in a wide range of themes. Then he sat down to thunderous applause from his supporters. I was convener of the Scottish Group at that time, and as I listened carefully to what he had to say, I realised that he had not actually suggested doing anything specific as an alternative. So when the applause died down, I asked him if he was moving something. He had been so intent on opposing, he had given no thought to proposing. He looked a little deflated and at a loss, unusually for our George. But it must have been even worse when I suggested we move on to next business so that he could have time to think up something and we would return to that item later, and Donald Dewar offered to help him word his motion. John Smith had been in the room, and left with a barely hidden smile on his face.

After some minutes George was ready to move that the Scottish Labour MPs should have a strategy conference, to which we would all be able to submit papers, and that was agreed unanimously, although some people in senior positions were worried that the media would be negative and treated this development as a split. My own view was that we ought to do this, whether the media were for it or not. But I was also concerned about our acting amongst ourselves, and not involving the Scottish Executive of the party, grassroots members or the trade unions in our deliberations.

All of us felt we needed to thrash out our views on where we went from here. We needed to take more time over it than in an evening meeting in the House, interrupted by the Division Bell, which wasted 15 minutes every time it rang, so I supported George's proposal that we have an away day, and the meeting agreed. We could then ask the Scottish Executive of the Party to consider whatever we came up with.

Two days later the *Sun* ran a story about our meeting. One unnamed Labour MP had told them our 'closed doors session' (it was always closed to outsiders) was 'absolutely brutal – like a bear pit'. I wondered which of our lot – if he or she really existed – had led such a sheltered life. Scottish politics has always been described as 'not for the fainthearted'. At the next meeting of our Group's executive committee I drew attention to this report. No possible good could come of such malicious reporting, which had obviously been done on the basis of an unauthorised briefing, and I intended to raise it at our forthcoming AGM.

We agreed to take up our desire for a multi-option referendum through the channels of the Parliamentary Labour Party, to benefit from the declared support of all our Labour MPs, not just those in Scotland alone.

On 12 May we had the ballot for election of our Convener. The rules laid down that the existing Convener before a General Election could stand for re-election – a point George Galloway had shown some interest in having elucidated – and I was glad to win decisively.

We also decided who would represent us for the coming year on the Scottish Constitutional Convention, and as Convener I would remain one of them. This was how we were really going to make our breakthrough to achieving devolution.

George, however, had other thoughts. In late June I was shown a SNP News Release that announced a joint statement between Scotland United and the SNP, following a meeting in the SNP headquarters in Edinburgh. The statement said they were both committed to the holding of a multi-option referendum. Scots of high public standing would be sought to ensure a scrupulously fair wording. It concluded:

Following the recent invitation to a Scotland United representative to address the SNP's annual Bannockburn Rally, SNP Leader Mr Alex Salmond

MP has been invited to address Scotland United's mass meeting in the City Halls, Glasgow on Sunday 19 July.

This was the last straw for me. We had not even had our away day yet to discuss policy and strategy, which George himself had urged upon us, planned for 10 July. But while a few of us wanted no change, the vast majority supported devolution and had no wish to work with the SNP, who had a very different agenda. Donald Dewar immediately condemned George's actions. He had to make it clear that George was not speaking on behalf of the Group. He pointed out that only this month the SNP 'had made it brutally clear that its top political priority was the destruction of the Labour Party'. Absolutely right. How else could anyone interpret Salmond's words to delegates at his party's national council: 'One of our major Unionist opponents is disintegrating before our eyes. Let's get the lever in and prise them apart.' Donald went on to point out that we were to review policy and tactics on 10 July, which was the obvious opportunity for George to make any proposals he wanted. Donald refrained – I wouldn't have – from pointing out that our strategy meeting was being held at none other than George's own initiative. So what was George playing at, collaborating, as Donald said, with people who were out to destroy our party? Why couldn't he wait another couple of weeks to see how things at our planned meeting transpired? 'Collaboration' was a word George took offence at. I don't know what else anyone would call that behaviour.

In somewhat tense circumstances, we held our strategy conference as planned. If George had done nothing else, he had certainly created great media interest in our deliberations. I told them I was looking for specifics and not interested in striking poses. I wanted a programme for parliamentary activity and campaigning around Scotland. It was all very well to call for disruption, but Scotland United supporters had to say doing what, precisely, and what could it be expected to achieve? George came up with boycotting Scottish Questions and ambushing Commons business by parliamentary device. I thought, if Ian Lang gives in to that, he's an idiot. And he isn't an idiot. It seemed to me that what we needed to do was to seek ways of arousing public opinion about how ill-served Scotland was being between the Nats and the Tories.

In his own submission, Dennis Canavan drew attention to the fact that although we had won 49 out of 72 seats, the Labour vote had fallen from 42 per cent to 39 per cent in Scotland and was now substantially below our votes in all but the south and east of England. He added it was only fair to point out that we did so well in 1987 it was difficult to improve on such a high base. But, drawing on a post election analysis by MORI, he noted that our share of the vote amongst 18–24 year olds dropped from 46 per cent in 1987 to 36 per cent in 1992. Less than half of the unemployed and less than half of trade union members now supported us in Scotland, and we should take warning from that. Our share of the vote amongst AB voters dropped from 23 per cent to 21 per cent, and amongst C2DE voters plummeted from 54 per cent to 47 per cent (the AB Tory vote, I noted, rose from 38 per cent to 46 per cent).

So Dennis went on to propose a much more vigorous campaign of opposition to the Government, both inside and outside Parliament, while at the same time projecting our alternative policies in a positive way. I agreed with him on that. I have always thought that some of my Parliamentary colleagues are too much given to thinking Parliament is the only place to conduct opposition. Those of a right wing bent can be highly dismissive about extra Parliamentary activity like sit-ins and sit-downs.

But when Dennis went on to air the 'no mandate from Scotland' argument I felt we needed to be careful about what we were actually saying. This was where he and some others in the Labour Group had come together with Nationalists in the Scotland United campaign. He was perfectly correct in pointing out that sectarian squabbling amongst anti-Tories was exactly what the Government wanted. However, that was precisely what the Nationalists had been doing, and viciously at that. They would try to use any Labour members who campaigned with them to promote the nationalist perspective, and we could not, and should not, try to out-Nat the Nats. We should be pointing out the pitfalls in separation, and the benefits of being in the Union. Dennis nevertheless advocated working together with them and anyone else that wanted to sign up for a multi-option referendum to win a Scottish Parliament. Labour, after all, had signed the Claim of Right, explicitly supporting the principle of the sovereignty of the people, and this principle, he argued, could unite all the Scottish opposition parties.

Why, therefore, did the Nationalists refuse to have anything to do with the Convention if they were so keen on working together? They had refused to join the Convention out of hand. They had not even had the courtesy to answer the Convention's invitation to an 'open conversation'.

So when Dennis urged that the door should be left open to them, I was less accommodating than that. I did agree with Dennis on other points, such as not waiting for the English regions to support regional assemblies (just as well. Only now is there a glimmer of it being considered for the future, there having been no desire for it in the intervening years). He was right about anger felt amongst the general public over decisions forced upon us that we did not vote for: the Poll Tax, hospital opt-outs, electricity privatisation, warrant sales, and so on. There were issues where Scotland had different systems, like education and local government funding, on which we could argue that the Government had no mandate. There were other issues, of UK-wide importance, where the Government could argue that their mandate came from all the nations of the United Kingdom. So I for one would feel happier if we kept the 'no mandate' argument for those issues that were of specific relevance to Scotland.

Neither was Dennis keen on the term, 'Devolution'. He suggested 'Scottish Home Rule' or 'an autonomous Scottish Parliament' would be better. I agreed with Donald Dewar that these wordings were a slippery slope towards breaking up the United Kingdom. After all, we had Irish history to draw on, when their Home Rule movement was really a cry for independence. That did not bother the more nationalistic amongst Labour members, but it certainly bothered me.

In my own paper I looked at the gender gap in voting results in Scotland. The nationalist vote amongst women had gone up by three per cent, but amongst men it went up far more, by 13 per cent. Could that be because the Nationalists were uninterested in low pay, women's rights, and equality in the Scottish Parliament? Jim Sillars had faced both ways on abortion. And generally speaking, women are less impressed by flag waving and patriotic posturing.

Then, look at the youth vote in support of the Nationalists: that was higher than older groups. One analysis simply had it that people grew out of nationalism as they got older, and adult concerns with their homes and their workplaces came to the fore. But some people would stay with the party they first voted for, and we had to investigate why we had lost so much support in the past five years amongst the young, and make plans to remedy this.

I looked at other aspects of voting behaviour. The higher the status, the less likely to vote SNP; the lower the status the more likely to vote SNP. Why were we appealing less successfully than before to working class and 'underclass' voters? We needed to know what policy issues we were losing them on. For example, council tenants' support for Labour was down four points, and Nationalists up 12 points. Should we not conclude from this that we need to campaign more on housing issues, and tackle the problems of variable quality in service to the public amongst Labour-controlled councils? I was thinking about how the majority of councillors were hard working and dedicated, but others were a disgrace, only managing to be selected as a Labour candidate because they could bring along a large number of friends and family to vote for them, never to be seen again until their man was up for re-selection. And some housing officials treated the general public with disdain when they were only making a perfectly reasonable request. I thought we needed to get a grip on that.

I find it exasperating to think, all these years on, that we still do not have a decent home for everyone to live in, although huge advances have been made. In Glasgow alone, Gordon Brown's writing off £1 billion housing debt meant it was possible to tackle dampness, carry out a gigantic programme of repairs, and fit new kitchens and bathrooms on a grand scale.

Rachel Squire, who was only in Parliament a few years before she developed a brain tumour from which, sadly, she subsequently died, developed an idea that I now hear Ed Miliband advocating. 'If we can,' she wrote, 'in commonsense language, set a political agenda about giving individuals and the community more say and more power, we'll get a response'. Her argument, boiled down, was that we came across as bureaucratic and no longer radical, and we needed to combine the radical and the common sense.

A range of other issues were considered. George Foulkes raised the West Lothian Question, and proposed that the answer was for Scottish MPs to no longer exercise a say in English matters once a devolved Parliament in Scotland was set up. I believe he was right, and English MPs have every right to be annoyed if they have a policy affecting England alone foisted upon them with Scottish votes, exactly as we railed against in Thatcher's day. Yet I once voted for the Church of England to have women priests. If they were daft enough to let me, with no connection with their church whatsoever, and an atheist at that, have a vote, then I was going to use it in support of women.

Calum MacDonald pointed out that the Tory strategy in Scotland worked that year. They were successful in getting attention away from the issues on which they were unpopular, such as the NHS, the Poll Tax, unemployment, etc, and focussed attention on a simplistic choice between union and separation. Their vote went up and stayed ahead of the SNP. 'The lesson for us', Calum wrote, 'is that there is no separate Scottish route to Socialism. If ever we allow a future election to become polarised over union versus separation we would play right into Tory hands'.

How things change in less than a couple of decades. The Tories went on in the following years, as we all know, to suffer a series of humiliating defeats, losing more and more MPs in Scottish seats, finally ending up with just one. And while Scottish Labour clearly avoided going down the separatist road, it is interesting to look back and remember that, in 1992, Calum and others felt strongly they had to argue with all their might for no change whatsoever. Interesting, too, that Calum alluded to 'the route to Socialism'. That became the unsayable 'S' word in Tony Blair's time. Calum wanted us to work more closely with the Liberal Democrats and identify all that we had in common. That was a common view amongst Labour's more social democratic tendency, who argued that a Lib-Lab pact could be in power virtually endlessly at UK level, and the Lib Dems would be useful ballast against Labour left wingers, trade unionists, or anyone else that dared to rock the boat. It will be remembered that Tony Blair was keen to bring Liberal Democrats into his Government, only to be frustrated by Labour MPs rejoicing in our huge majority in 1997 and seeing no reason to share any of the spoils with another party. I agreed with them. Not that I was expecting any promotion myself – I had too many disagreements with Tony for that to be a likely prospect. You can resign from the front bench once, and make a re-entry. I did it twice, and I recognise there is a limit to any party leader's toleration of that kind of thing.

Alastair Darling argued our main opponent in Scotland was the Conservative Party. It was not the SNP. Their fundamental demand of separation attracted less than 25 per cent of the vote. Their argument against us, he went on, only gains strength when we are seen to be losing the fight against Conservative ideology. He then put an argument I agreed with:

> The next months and years should be spent advancing our arguments for change and at the same time challenging the Conservatives. If we devote our time to fighting or, even worse, helping the nationalists, the Conservatives will be let off the hook and will start to make real progress in Scotland.

Gavin Strang's thesis was that three important conditions had to be met for Labour to move forward in Scotland: remain at the forefront of the campaign for constitutional change in Scotland; educate the Scottish people to understand there are no easy shortcuts to a Parliament or a Scottish Labour Government; campaign more effectively than ever on issues like employment, economic development, the environment, education, housing, health, and social justice. How right he was. The figures for subsequent elections in Scotland prove the sense of what he said.

John McFall noted that a BBC Exit Poll in Scotland on 9 April 1992 showed that voting intentions were influenced first and foremost by concern for the NHS, followed by unemployment, schools, and the economy in general. The future government of Scotland came fifth in the list. This confirmed our experience in doorstep campaigning and at public meetings. So he was right to say we should avoid making this the main focus of our endeavours. He was also right to say that the Scottish Question was the dominant theme in the political world. Here he took issue with Scotland United, and asked, *what is the objective of disruptive tactics?* He doubted the efficacy of disruption of Parliament, thinking the general public would regard such tactics as a waste of Parliamentary time, and there was no likelihood that the Tory Government would give in just because MPs sat down on committee floors, or bemused visitors up in the Gallery were forced to leave if a Member shouted 'I Spy Strangers!' I had to agree with him there. I had followed Dennis in that ploy when I was a brand new Member, and saw for myself that it had no impact whatsoever on the Government. But then again, I did not want to confine our activities to debates alone. Couldn't we think up campaigning methods that had imagination, which caught the attention of the public, and got over our point in a few well chosen words? John went on to give a hilarious account of some of the views expressed by some leading members of the Scotland United campaign. Apparently, someone had described Edinburgh as a city under occupation and compared it to Vilnius before the collapse of the Soviet Union.

This reminded me of one of my hustings meetings in Maryhill, when a Nationalist had declared that Scotland was every bit as oppressed as the people of Burma under the rule of the military junta. I had been in arguments where Nationalists stated that England would invade Scotland before it allowed it to be free. Worse, no-one in the SNP leadership ever seemed to try to damp down this kind of nonsense.

And it was seeping into our own debates. Mike Watson's paper described the Tory plans to privatise our water as 'Anglicisation of the Scottish landscape'. I had a comment in the margin: what do Socialists in England call privatisation of their water? Yet I shared with him his frustration at the lack of imaginative campaigning tactics. John McAlllion wanted the Scottish Constitutional Convention to transform itself into a different kind of body, committed only to campaigning for a multi-option referendum, so as to bring the SNP on board. He did not want the Convention to abandon its own Home Rule project, but develop a twin-track approach whereby it continued with its own project while having a separate campaigning arm in relation to the referendum. Personally, I could think of no reason to distract ourselves from our efforts to bring about a new kind of Parliament for Scotland for the sake of unity with the Nationalists. We would get a Scottish Parliament, and not bring about the breakup of the UK, when we had a Labour government.

John expressed the view in a piece in the STUC Review of April/June 1992 that Labour was unlikely to form a majority government when the next General Election came along. Well, I shared his gloom at the time. I thought we might make a lot of improvement in our vote, but not enough to win outright. That seemed an impossible dream. There was, too, the danger of the consequences of losing again and again and again. Yet we all know what happened in 1997. Labour won an incredible 179 seat majority, the largest in the Party's history. What had happened was that by that time people around the UK – not just in Scotland – were thoroughly fed up with the Tories and had worked out how to vote to get the most likely anti-Tory candidate elected in their own constituencies. It worked a treat. I do not, and never have believed, that this was entirely Tony Blair's doing. I am certain John Smith would have won handsomely if he had lived to be our Prime Minister in waiting.

George Galloway came up with an idea that year. Why not, he argued, boycott Scottish Questions until the Government comes to the negotiating table? The entire hour was a farce, with Ministers not answering questions and the Tory benches packed with Members who knew little or nothing of Scotland, and who were just there to make up the numbers and ensure they got called as often as Opposition Members who actually represented Scottish constituencies. He proposed a Shadow Scottish Parliament in Edinburgh. I was a bit more dubious about that. What would happen after it met a few times? Would media boredom set in? Wouldn't we need to first build public support for a Scottish Parliament? Or was George right, and it was the other way round? Would our Shadow Parliament build support for a Scottish Parliament? We will never know, because it did not happen. We did, however, create a shadow Scottish Grand Committee that allowed us more scope to publicise Labour policies on health, education, housing and so forth.

Typically of Donald Dewar, he submitted a much lengthier overview for our consideration than anyone else's. His view, contrary to some of the others, was that the SNP did badly in the recent General Election. They were reduced to three seats and 21 per cent of the vote. This was below their opinion poll ratings. In taking 49 seats, we had only one short of our record total. The result, he said, is certainly not an invitation to do nothing or a justification for negative politics. It should give urgency to analysis and policy development. He set out ideas for doing just that on health, local government, education and housing. On the national question, he argued Devolution and Nationalism are not two sides of the same coin. 'If this notion gains currency,' he went on, 'it will encourage the electorate to see Labour and SNP votes as interchangeable. The even more fundamental objection is that it would misrepresent our principled position.'

On Scotland United, his argument was spot on, as far as I was concerned. To quote it in full: 'There has been talk of 'holding out the hand of friend-ship to the SNP.' Apart from the fundamentally different vision of Scot-land's future, it is hard to treat with a Party driven by hatred of Labour. At their June National Council, former Tory turned Nationalist Ian Lawson's contribution to dialogue was blunt – 'We'll destroy Labour or they'll destroy us. There's no in-between. If you don't like confrontational poli-tics then that's tough…' Alex Salmond flagged up his party's intentions when, referring to Scotland United, he argued that 'one of our major Unionist opponents is disintegrating before our eyes. Let's get the lever in and prise them apart.' Donald went on:

> Constant press reports of dissent are damaging. The impression created is that whatever the Group decides it will be publicly attacked as timid and inadequate. The public values loyalty.

To my surprise, he also advocated a multi-option referendum, on the grounds that it would give the electorate the opportunity to endorse pos-itively our plans for a Scottish Parliament and, in doing so, to repudiate the very different position taken respectively by the Tories and the Nationalists. I was beginning to fear that such a referendum would open up opportunities for simplistic Nationalist slogans to gain ground. On disruptive tactics, his view was that disruption was at its most effective when it is linked to a specific situation with which the public can relate. Having point and uniting the Group were essential criteria.

Johann Lamont, who is now Labour Leader in Scotland and who was at that time chair of the Party's Organisation Subcommittee, pointed out that in May 1992 she had put together suggestions for activities and review of party structures, yet Scotland United pretended nothing had been done.

A general discussion ensued, along the lines of the papers that had been submitted. Willie McKelvey MP suggested the Labour Party ought to organise an all-party campaign against water privatisation. Others wanted it to be Labour and Trade Union only.

The Scottish Constitutional Convention continued its work, beavering away on all the issues involved, one of which was the number of members the Assembly (as it was then called) should have. Two per constituency, male and female, was winning support. Then it became clear that some of our party top brass thought that was too many, and it was proposed to our Scottish Executive that there should be 129 members. This arose from bargaining between George Robertson and Jim Wallace, Leader of the Scottish Liberal Democrats. George wanted 112. Jim argued for 145. So they compromised on 129. So much for democratic debate and consultation. There would be 73 elected on a constituency basis, Orkney and Shetland having one each, elected by First Past the Post, and 56 Top-Up seats elected from regional lists by a second vote, to achieve a rough equation between votes cast and number of seats held.

Just when we thought everything was done and dusted in legislating to create the Scottish Parliament, on 25 June Tony Blair dropped a bombshell. Scottish Labour Party members learned from the pages of a London-based newspaper that there would be a referendum with two questions on the ballot paper: (1) Do you support the setting up of a Scottish Parliament? (2) Do you support giving it tax-raising powers? This change of policy had not been discussed with the party at any level. It arose out of discussions between Tony Blair, George Robertson and a committee chaired by the Shadow Lord Chancellor, Lord Irvine of Lairg. These discussions had been so secret that even John McAllion, our front bencher whose remit was Scottish constitutional issues, knew nothing about the plan before it was announced. This was the kind of thing that New Labour engaged in that thoroughly got up my nose. In a supposedly democratic socialist party! No wonder members felt like cannon fodder. No wonder John chucked his front bench post.

It worried a lot of people who had put in a tremendous amount of work all these years planning for the creation of a Scottish Parliament. To me it smacked of arrogance, that all these years of effort and negotiation by those involved in the Convention could be so casually cast aside, on the say so of a few.

I was far from being the only one infuriated by this. Feelings of suspicion were rife, inside and outside the party, that the idea was to wreck the whole project. A pamphlet opposing the referendum, and particularly the tax question, was circulated by prominent activists: Margaret Curran, now Shadow Scottish Secretary, Bill Speirs, who became General Secretary of the STUC and, sadly, died far too young a few years ago, Ian Smart who became president of the Scottish Law Society and Bob Thomson, a well known trade union official.

Canon Kenyon Wright anxiously sought a meeting with Tony. It would have been polite if Tony had briefed him first, before going to the media. He was the chair of the Convention, after all. He has told the whole story of the Convention and its ups and downs, the assurances he received that there was absolutely no intention of reneging on what John Smith had described as 'the settled will' of the people of Scotland, in his own book, *The People Say Yes* – essential reading for any historian of these times.

Now, I am not arguing that having a referendum was not a good idea. If it was successful in gaining support from the voting public, then it would be virtually impossible for anyone in the Lords or the Commons to refuse it, or try to undo it later when the Parliament was in existence. But the way it was done was stupid in the extreme. It aroused widespread suspicion, even within the party, that Labour was finding a way to abandon its commitment to having a Scottish Parliament at all. No wonder party meetings were less and less well attended. Members felt there was no point. Nobody was listening. We were allowing the SNP to get away with their spin that Labour would not deliver, which, considering the fact that they had taken no part whatsoever in the work of the Scottish Constitutional Convention, was some brass neck.

Then, at last, the General Election in 1997. After all the gloomy predictions from some in the Scottish Labour Group, Labour had won a huge majority. The Nationalists had only six seats, and had won less than 22 per cent of the vote, a tiny improvement on their 1992 result. The referendum was held in September. Both questions won handsomely.

It was the work of the Scottish Constitutional Convention, in which the SNP refused to play any part, which led us towards the achievement of our Scottish Parliament. It was John Smith's and Donald Dewar's commitment above anyone else's saw us achieving so much in the first year of the Labour Government five years later.

CHAPTER THIRTEEN

The Fight for 50:50

BACK IN THE '70s and early to mid-'80s, the electoral reform debate was raging. Yet it was silent on one aspect crying out for reform: the extremely low number of women in Parliament and in our local authorities. Search through the literature, both pro- and anti-Proportional Representation, and you will spend a long time looking for the tiniest mention of any remedy for this imbalance in our elected bodies. It was as if the problem had gone completely unnoticed, or just didn't matter. Not surprising really, when, apart from Margaret Thatcher, women were rarely seen among the talking heads on politics programmes on TV, and even the lucky few failed to express any interest in advancing the cause of other women.

The story begins in August 1974, when Labour held a Special Conference which overwhelmingly supported maximum devolution consistent with remaining in the UK. In September the Labour Government published a Green Paper. This arose out of the Kilbrandon Report, which had been published the previous year. It drew attention to Scotland's role in the European Economic Community, and to the financial benefits of North Sea Oil, and rightly so.

A lot was going on. A discussion paper was published by Labour MPs Alex Eadie, Harry Ewing, John Robertson and Jim Sillars, criticising Kilbrandon because of its failure to push for economic powers, save only for the Highlands and Islands Development Board. Not a word to be read in any of all that on what devolution could do for 52 per cent of the population, that is, the women. It was alpha males slugging it out on the telly night after night, to the literal turning off of many women viewers.

But after the 1987 General Election, things began to change. Women in the Labour Party were feeling increasingly fed up with their lack of representation. The photograph of the newly elected Scottish Labour Group of MPs on the steps of Keir Hardie House, our party headquarters, with me in my red dress as the sole woman, amongst almost 50 men in their suits, illustrated the point all too well: talk about a picture being worth more than a thousand words. So women in the party got going (particularly Margaret Curran, Johann Lamont and Rosina MacRae) and fought year in year out, conference after conference, against the more benighted members of our movement.

Our Scottish Labour Group of MPs met regularly, and devolution was high on the agenda. Dick Douglas, who some years later defected to the Nationalists, was at that time our Chair. When I said during one of our discussions that I would not be interested in pursuing devolution if this was going to be yet another case of jobs for the boys, with little or no benefit for women, he could not believe his ears. His astonishment was comical, but fairly understandable. He and others in our Group had simply not heard this point of view before. But I told the meeting I was far from being the sole voice on this issue and they had better pay attention to it if they wanted to achieve the widest possible public support for their aims.

In November Donald Dewar presented a Scotland Bill. Dick Douglas was a co-signatory. There was general dissatisfaction with the way Scottish business was handled at Westminster – tacked on at the end of Bills largely dealing with issues affecting England, or a mixed bag of items stuffed into a compendium Scottish Bill every five years. All this was creating a degree of impetus for a Scottish Parliament. There was widespread dissatisfaction with having Tory policies imposed on Scotland when we had voted against them. The Press Brief for Donald's Bill made the first mention of women's participation in any of the official documents I have seen:

> [A Scottish Assembly] will widen the scope of democracy, giving a fuller role to all its members, especially women, who have not so far been adequately represented in our existing democratic institutions.

In July 1988 the Campaign for a Scottish Assembly published 'A Claim of Right for Scotland'. It stated that Scotland had a distinctive corpus of law and acknowledged rights to distinctive policies, but did not have anyone expressly elected to safeguard and supervise them. It called for a Constitutional Convention to be brought together in order to work on filling the democratic gap. The Claim set out the possible composition for such a Convention. It was decided that all of Scotland's MPs should be invited, along with councillors, individuals nominated by political parties, those representing the worlds of industry, commerce, the trade unions, churches, and women's, ethnic and voluntary organisations.

And so the Convention got together soon afterwards. It included 80 per cent of our MPs, the regional and district councillors, all the above-mentioned sectors and the political parties that chose to participate were Labour, the Scottish Democrats, the SDP, the Co-operative, Greens, the Communist Party and the Orkney and Shetland Movement.

When it was set up, the Convention published a discussion leaflet, 'A Parliament for Scotland', and under the heading 'Making the Scottish Parliament Truly Representative' it said:

> The Convention will therefore consider, for example, the means of ensuring that a fair representation of women are involved; how the Parliament is organised, such as when it will meet, and provision of child and dependent care.

This is how this great change in attitude came about. 30 March 1989 was a day that will always stay in my memory. The Convention gathered together for the first time in the Church of Scotland's Assembly Hall on The Mound in Edinburgh. Canon Kenyon Wright gave an address that has since gone down in history. He knew he had to take on strongly the argument that Margaret Thatcher's Government might simply ignore this gathering of Scotland's voices. She had gained some notoriety as the years went by for seldom being in listening mode. And he certainly achieved that aim, when he said: 'What happens if that other single voice we know so well responds by saying "We say no, and we are the State"? Well, we say yes, and we are the people.'

I have a second reason for remembering that day. John Smith, then Leader of the Labour Party, leaned forward from a few rows behind me and urged me to speak in the debate. I hadn't thought to do so, but my colleagues and I were becoming increasingly irritated by the nationalistic sentiments expressed by some speakers, especially considering the SNP had refused to take part in the formation of the Convention. If anyone present saw devolution as a stepping stone to breaking up Britain, that was certainly not why we were there.

Alan Armstrong in particular (as convener of the Campaign for a Scottish Assembly) as well as a few others had been holding forth about Scottish ancestors and the Declaration of Arbroath in 1320, linking that document to the newly established Convention. But that Declaration, which Scottish Nationalists like to fantasise matches the Magna Carta in historical importance, was slung in a drawer and forgotten about for all of subsequent history until recent times. The peasantry in Scotland, just as in England, continued with no say whatsoever for centuries to come.

It so happens that when I was trawling through boxes of papers I had kept from my Parliamentary days I found my hastily scribbled notes for what I said at the rostrum that day. I observed that when the Declaration of Arbroath was being signed, my own ancestors were running around a bog somewhere in Ireland. My ancestors were O'Neills, a clan of some significance in Ireland's history, but I refrained from mentioning that – there was quite enough harking back to irrelevant ancient history already. I went on to say:

> Speakers have harked back to 14th-century Scotland. But our population includes many others whose ancestry has nothing to do with Scotland in 1320 – Irish, as in my own case, Italians, Asians and others. We must not make it sound as if you have to have ancestors going back to Scotland in 1320 in order to be a true Scot.

I urged the meeting that we should hold three principles dear: democracy, internationalism and equal rights for all.

But my third reason for remembering that day so vividly was quite simply this. Everyone knew already that the leadership in politics, business, the trade unions and the churches were male dominated, if not indeed wholly male. But to see us all gathered together in that room, with only 22 women present and 173 men, really brought the message home. I drew attention to that in my speech, and so did many other speakers, calling for gender balance in our Scottish Parliament-to-be.

An Executive Committee was set up, and I was one of the ten Labour MPs, led by Donald Dewar, taking part. In April 1989 we began to consider measures to ensure women and ethnic minorities were better represented in the Assembly than was currently the case in Scottish politics. On 14 April the Executive Committee appointed me Convener of the working group on women's issues. Its members included John McAllion, Yvonne Strachan, and the Reverend Norman Shanks.

We met the following month to identify the issues we should be tackling, and at our first meeting we agreed to seek views on the working day and year of the Assembly, remuneration of its Members, child care allowances or facilities, and electoral systems and their implications for women. We met again in June and proposed a Scottish Equal Opportunities Commission that would consider patronage and appointments, and we urged positive action in the selection of candidates.

On 18 June 'A Woman's Claim of Right' was launched, with women from all political parties present, except the Conservatives. But then, Tory women are notorious for treating a selection conference to choose an election candidate as an opportunity to pick a nice young man who would make a suitable son-in-law, and for thinking a woman's place is in the home, but seldom the House. In the same month the Scottish Labour Women's Committee published a discussion paper, noting that:

> If the party is serious about representing women, it is imperative that it actively campaigns for an Assembly scheme which is conducive to the participation of women… The inevitable corollary of this is the establishment of an internal Party selection system which constitutionally recognises the need to select more women.

Later that month, academics offered help to the working parties. Alice Brown, Mary Buckley and Pippa Norris from Edinburgh University offered expert guidance on political representation.

In July 1989, the *New Statesman* took note. In a full page piece by Sarah Benton on our working party's first report, she commented that this:

> … is one of the potentially most interesting political documents to have been produced in the UK for a long time. For in grappling with why political institutions are so alien to women, it tried to get to the heart of what is wrong with the way political institutions in general work. It will give heart to all those who have despaired at making politics work for the people. Her working party has sought views on almost every aspect of political workings, from the hours an assembly sits, through the need for childcare, to voting systems which will encourage those who are not quasi-professional politicians to put themselves forward.

When our working group had a meeting on 9 August we identified some issues to go to Kenyon Wright for use in preparing the consultation document. These were:

1   The need to take appropriate steps to ensure a more reasonable and realistic proportion of women are elected (or appointed) to the Scottish Assembly.
2   The need for the administration and working arrangements of the Assembly to be such as to facilitate full participation for women.
3   The need for the establishment within the hierarchy of the Assembly of a Ministry for Women to be responsible for constant scrutiny and monitoring of proposals to ensure that women's interests are well to the fore.
4   The need to stress that the establishment of a Scottish Assembly represents the creation of a completely new constitutional system which in turn should clear the way for a new approach to the role of women both in the Assembly itself and in Scottish society.

And then the fur really started to fly. The STUC Women's Committee published *Equal Voice for Women*, with contributions from a large number of prominent women demanding an equal voice in our future Scottish Parliament. Professor Lalage Brown spoke for us all when she wrote:

> After seven decades of the vote which our great grandmothers strove for, male-dominated political decisions hold women back at work and in education... We need enough women in the political arena to transform the agendas – and I hope new agendas would include care for the liberation of women all over the world.

But how many women were enough? The STUC Women's Committee submitted a challenging argument: it had to be 50:50 from day one. Their solution was simple, but dynamite. Why not, they asked, have two-member seats, and let the electorate vote for their choice from a female list and a male list? Problem solved, we thought.

The STUC published a document in support, pointing out that the existing system had already produced a 'bank' of male potential candidates in all parties sufficient to dominate the Scottish Parliament well into the 21st century. In an article published in September 1989 in *The Scotsman*, I pointed out that since 1923 there had been a total of just 21 women MPs in Scotland: ten Labour, seven Conservative, three SNP and one SLD. We could, if we had the political will, stop repeating that. A new Parliament would have no sitting members who would resist being dislodged. I went on to argue a parliament evenly balanced between the sexes would be a different sort of parliament, concluding, 'If we have the will, we can design a parliament that is neither the best club in town nor the noisiest school playground.'

By this time Neil Kinnock, at Jo Richardson's request, had made me Deputy Shadow Minister for Women at UK level. They were both intrigued at what was going on in Scotland.

The battle for 50:50 went on apace. Labour's Scottish Conference at Dunoon in 1990 stated its support for an equal outcome while not committing the party to any system for achieving it. And that was won in the teeth of vehemently expressed hostility from some MPs and other speakers from the floor to the very idea of ensuring gender equality. One line of attack was that it was bringing the State into the business of the party. That was rich, coming from people who wanted to change the voting system, achieve a historic change in the formal relationships between Scotland

and England, and create an entirely new Parliament. But women's political equality – that was too radical a proposal. Then there was the 'Is it
practical?' line. Would enough women of appropriate calibre come forward?
'Not sure,' I answered. 'How bad do you have to be?'

Then on 27 April 1990, when the Convention met in Glasgow, I was
astonished to be given a Guard of Honour by a lobby of women as I
entered the City Halls. The women were members of the STUC Women's
Committee, accompanied by actresses from the Wildcat Theatre Company
dressed in suffragette costumes and re-enacting speeches from Glasgow's
1915 rent strike, which won rent control legislation against the greedy
landlords. Incidentally, it was one Mary Barbour who got the rent strike
going first of all in Govan, and in 1920 she was one of the first female
councillors in Glasgow, pursuing a strong welfare agenda and new thinking for her time. Are there any statues or memorials to her? No. Does she
get her story told in Labour movement histories, along with the heroes?
No. See what I mean?

In June, the Electoral Reform Society poured cold water on the whole
idea. They were much more concerned with Proportional Representation
than with addressing the lack of women's representation, but by this time
few of us on the side of women were being distracted by their arguments.

On 6 July the Convention met in Dundee and debated the desirability
of guaranteed equal representation. It was continued for further consideration.

On 27 July 1990 the final report of my Working Group was published,
supporting 50:50. On 8 August the new Working Group on Making the
Scottish Parliament Truly Representative (a body that had been set up to
consider electoral systems) agreed that, in the event of no consensus being
achieved by the Executive Committee on the principle of guaranteed equal
representation for women, a possible compromise position might exist
whereby the first elections to the Scottish Parliament would not be subject
to gender equality requirements, but political parties committed to this
principle would make it a manifesto commitment for subsequent elections.

When I read this I felt quite insulted. I asked myself: 'Do these people
really think I'm daft enough to fall for this? Who do they think they are
kidding?' I then spent hours on the phone, with some success. On 10
August the executive rejected this 'compromise' and told them to consider
it further.

It was agreed that one of the principles by which an electoral system should be assessed was that it:

> ... ensures, or at least takes effective positive action to bring about, equal representation of women and men, and encourage fair representation of ethnic and other minority groups.

On 27 August the Working Group on Making the Parliament Truly Representative concluded that:

> It was not possible at this stage to reach a clear-cut decision on the means of achieving gender equality in the Scottish Parliament. The Convention should emphasise that all the major participants are fully committed to the principle of gender equality, and that continuing discussion revolves simply around the means of achieving it.

Around this time the Campaign for a Scottish Assembly declared that political parties presenting candidates for election to the Scottish Parliament should be required BY STATUTE to ensure through their internal selection procedures that at least 40 per cent of all their candidates were women. Here was an interesting step forward, in that using the law to lay down the law was a good idea. But would it guarantee much? Not when you examined it. Parties could quite easily contrive that the women fight more than their fair share of the hopeless seats. The beauty of the STUC system was that men and women candidates would be equally placed by their political parties in each and every seat they chose to contest.

Came 1991, and in May the Convention set up a Working Group on Electoral Systems to seek consensus on a system that most closely met our six criteria. These were:

1 Seats won should broadly reflect votes cast.
2 The link between MP and constituency should be maintained.
3 Ensures or at least takes effective positive action to bring about equal representation of men and women and encourages representation of ethnic and other minorities.
4 Ensures adequate representation for less populous areas.
5 Is easy to understand.
6 Greatest possible power left in hands of electorate.

It was chaired by Norman Shanks and I was a member. There was no way I was going to miss out on this one. On 23 May Murray Elder, Scottish Secretary of the Labour Party, wrote to Bruce Black, the Secretary of the Convention, to tell him that Labour's Scottish Conference had agreed that whatever electoral system is agreed it must take account of the Party's support for equal representation of men and women in the Scottish Parliament. Conference, he went on, was insistent that the Party should only accept an electoral system that guaranteed equal representation.

On 3 June the Working Group noted that the Labour Party was considering the Alternative Vote (AV) and Additional Member System (AMS), and the Scottish Liberal Democrats preferred combining the Single Transferable Vote (STV) and AMS. Murray Elder wanted Labour to have more time to come to a final decision on its preferred electoral system, and asked me if I could find some way to get the Working Group to kick the issue into the long grass for a while. I suggested that the Working Group ask academics for their views. That would be a sensible move anyway. Worth a try, he thought. But how to get the Liberal Democrats to agree? We needn't have worried. One of their number actually proposed we should seek such help, following my musing aloud about how useful it would be if only we knew the views of such pundits as Vernon Bogdanor, John Curtice and David Butler. Not that some of the academics turned out to be all that useful. They mostly favoured multi-member seats as a way of getting closer to gender equality and minority representation, under the charmingly naïve delusion that people would be embarrassed to have all-male, all-white candidates. Nor did some see any way to deliver 50:50 except by the totally unacceptable method of party lists for the entire country, not constituencies, which would mean party leaderships having even more control than they did already over local parties' decisions. And multi-member seats bring about the loss of the link between a member of a Parliament and their constituents, which most of us who have actually served as MPs value highly. You are more grounded in reality, because you are helping people with their problems. You become attached to your own patch, and – not just of electoral necessity – want to look after its interests. You get to know its local organisations and people who are active in their communities: impossible to do when you share a constituency the size of three, four or more of what you represented before. I loved working as the Hon Member for Maryhill. Not so good being one of several in a constituency that could be as large as half the size of Glasgow.

On 9 July I had my first sight of the Liberal Democrats' case against 50:50. It was, they held, fundamentally illiberal to enforce any quota, to instruct local party branches, or – this was really choice – prevent the public from having 60 per cent women if they wanted. Two thoughts immediately occurred to me. First, I'd worry about women being over-represented when we came to it, but I'd probably be dead before then. Second, if this was against their principles, why had they not said so months ago?

By this time I was getting fed up with the Lib Dems' inability to stick to any line. Each substitute at a meeting said something different from his colleague the meeting before. Did they actually talk to each other, I wondered? On one occasion Moira Craig even argued that we couldn't ever have gender equality anyway, because what of the case of a candidate who was undecided which sex they were? I replied, with some sarcasm, I will admit, that I would advise anyone with such a dilemma to decide to be a man: that way selection as a candidate was more likely.

Early in December 1991 the Working Group on the Electoral System declared broad agreement had been reached on an electoral system involving (a) two-member constituencies (b) a legal requirement on political parties to put forward a male and a female candidate in each constituency, and (c) additional members added as a top-up to achieve a high degree of proportionality.

Now we were into 1992, and the Convention was still undecided. The Executive met on 17 January and agreed to establish a Subcommittee of the Executive, to examine further the issues within these remits: agreement on the need to move towards closer correspondence between seats and votes; acceptance of the Additional Member System (AMS) as the means of achieving this; a statutory or other obligation on parties to put forward equal numbers of men and women candidates; and acceptance also that AMS should be used to achieve gender equality if not achieved by the constituency elections.

The Scottish Grand Committee met and I took the opportunity to point out we now had four Labour women MPs in Scotland – the highest ever number at any one time – and to urge that the new Parliament should work to sensible hours and organise its year to match Scottish school holidays. A few days later the Convention met, and among the points discussed about the electoral system, it noted that:

> There is an acceptance that this [equal representation of men and women] cannot be left to political parties but that there is a requirement for some form of statutory obligation. The form this might take, and its relationship to voting arrangements and to the size of the parliament, are matters which Convention members will wish to consider.

In 1994 the Convention set up a Scottish Constitutional Commission which recommended that all political parties be asked to achieve 40 per cent women's representation in the first five years of the new Parliament. They were not in favour of any statutory mechanism. This was hopeless, I thought. It threw away the chance of getting equal representation on day one. Thereafter it would be a case of bums on seats, 'mainly manly' (to quote Emma Simpson, now a BBC television reporter), and probably a longer wait for seats becoming vacant than in Westminster, because it was anticipated that it would be a younger initial intake than the average age of Westminster members.

However, informal talks had been taking place between Labour and the Lib Dems about finding common cause, and at the same time the STUC women successfully argued that equal opportunities should be one of the founding principles of the Scottish Parliament. This all came together in the Convention's final report, entitled 'Scotland's Parliament: Scotland's Right'. The section entitled 'Making Scotland's Parliament Truly Representative' held:

> One of the key principles of the Convention's vision is that there should be equal representation of men and women in Scotland's Parliament. Locally and nationally, women have been persistently under-represented in all areas of public life in Scotland. We believe that a new Scottish Parliament is a great opportunity to improve radically the representation of women in Scottish politics. Scotland's Parliament should represent the whole community and reflect the priorities of the people of Scotland The Convention, therefore, endorses the cross-party Electoral Agreement which (a) accepts the principle that there should be an equal number of men and women as members of the first Scottish Parliament (b) commits the parties to take into account both the constituency and additional member list candidates to select and field an equal number of male and female candidates for election and (c) ensures that these candidates are fairly distributed with a view to the winnability of seats... The Convention calls upon all other Scottish political parties to implement the principles of the Electoral Contract.

In March 1995 the Scottish Labour Conference approved a report, 'A Parliament for Scotland', that said 'it is our resolve to have equal representation for men and women, and its sittings, working hours and conditions will be designed for the 21st century'. It went on:

> The Scottish Labour Party believes that the legislation to establish the Scottish Parliament should ensure that men and women are represented in equal measure. We urged the Commission to consider possible options to implement this objective. However, the proposals on achieving equality of representation between men and women in the Parliament are not in accordance with existing Labour policy. Whilst we recognise the efforts made by the Commission to seek a formula we do regret that the Commission was not able to find a statutory method to ensure that women will be equally represented.

In November 1995 a formal contract between the Lib Dems and Labour was signed. Rhona Brankin, Chair of the Scottish Labour Party, George Robertson, Shadow Scottish Secretary, Jim Wallace, leader of the Scottish Lib Dems, and Marilyne MacLaren, their Convener, presented the formal document with some fanfare. Thereafter the contract was handed over to Canon Kenyon Wright for safekeeping. It is held now by the Convention in trust. Later, in 1996, they said they would like a flexible zip system for the list seats.

May 1997, and a Labour Government elected at last. We lost no time getting down to work on the Scotland Bill. That same month we had debates on the floor of the House of Commons on gender balance and on the issue of abortion, which had never come up in all the years of the work in the Convention. It was 'pro-life' supporters who wanted it put in the legislation that abortion law should be devolved. Scots law was, in any case, different from English law, but they wanted it set down in the Act in the hope of restricting it further. They hadn't had a word to say about any aspect of women's lives until then, in all the years of representations received by the Convention. Supporters of women's rights wanted it reserved. Donald Dewar won the support of Parliament when he took the sensible view that the last thing we needed was to create traffic between Scotland and England, as was already noted in the case of Northern Ireland, from where women travelled to clinics in England and Scotland. A row broke out between the Catholic Church and the Labour Party. Labour women had objected to a 'pro-life' stall being set up at the party conference, and George Galloway took the side of the Church. Funny old world, politics. 'Right wing' Donald Dewar bravely stood up for a woman's right to choose from the time he first fought and won Garscadden, and 'left wing' men such as George and Alex Salmond voted in the Parliamentary lobbies to keep women in their place.

A White Paper, 'Scotland's Parliament', was published in July 1997. But worryingly, the Guide to the Scotland Bill said nothing whatsoever about equal representation.

In January 1998 I tabled amendments and new clauses to the Scotland Bill on equal representation. I had tabled them because Scottish Office officials had been taking advice from a variety of people and their own legal advisers, but had yet to come up with anything that Henry McLeish, Minister for Women, felt he could support putting in the Bill. I also tabled some equal opportunities amendments. They attracted some attention. I began to receive dozens of letters asking me to support amendments I myself had tabled. This gave me some clue about how much some campaigners needed to learn about lobbying. I was up to my ears in work, but could not just ignore such letters: their organisations might put me down as uncommitted or even hostile, when I needed all the support I could get.

By April, thanks to Donald Dewar's acceptance of my arguments, the Government had agreed to improve on its initial stance, and had widened the scope of the equal opportunities covered. On twinning, the Government gave me an undertaking it would continue to look for ways to protect twinning from legal challenge, so I would have withdrawn the relevant amendments when they arose in the course of debate in the Chamber. However, through an error in procedure, my main amendment was put to the vote by the Deputy Speaker and so I and several supporting colleagues decided to abstain. This may seem peculiar, but the reason was that it was bound to be defeated, and if we voted that would be taken by our whips as an indication we no longer wanted to pursue it through the party's own processes. 'Jumping the gun' on the issue would not go down well with party colleagues who had promised action. I remained very concerned about the whole issue, because the Welsh Labour Party had been told by the Lord Chancellor that twinning would be unlawful. Thankfully, the Party's Scottish Executive still pursued twinning, although they were under the impression that nothing could be done to protect it from legal challenge. This was not the case, and I could provide legal advice on this.

On 1 July I wrote to Derry Irvine, the Lord Chancellor, seeking a meeting to discuss the Law Lords' advice on the gender balance issue in the Scotland Bill, and their interpretation of the European Equal Treatment Directive on Employment, which had been transmitted by the Lord Chancellor to an ad hoc committee of Ministers. A spanner had been thrown in the works by a Welsh Labour councillor who was taking the Party to an Industrial Tribunal because he failed to get on the panel of approved Parliamentary candidates, and he also disagreed with twinning. I had been told that my amendments would be unlawful, as they would be in breach of the Directive. Strange, because my socialist colleague in the Council of Europe, Yvette Roudy, a member of the French National Assembly, had informed me that Monsieur Jospin was seeking an amendment to the French Constitution, no less, to achieve gender equality in their Parliament. When I asked her if anyone had raised the Directive as a difficulty, with impeccable French logic she raised her eyebrows and asked me what a Directive concerned with management of the labour market in the member states had to do with the selection of Parliamentary candidates. So I enclosed cuttings from the French press about this development in my letter to the Lord Chancellor. Further, Professor Noreen Burrows, who lectured in European law at Glasgow University, assured me with chapter and verse that Lord Irvine was quite simply wrong. I was given a date for a meeting with him, which was then withdrawn. Then I put down written questions to the Lord Chancellor, and after a few weeks had gone by I was told he had asked the Department of Education and Employment to write to me. Then my questions were referred to the Secretary of State for Scotland. Ever get the feeling someone is trying to avoid you?

Not having succeeded in having my meeting, I did a trawl through the Sex Discrimination Act, the Equal Treatment Directive, the relevant clauses of the Maastricht, Rome and Amsterdam treaties, the UN Convention and the Beijing Platform for Action. Not that anyone was paying any attention to the last two, but by this time I was feeling ratty. The result of my labours was to confirm in spades what I was already being told by Professor Burrows and others with expertise in these matters. At that time there simply was no specific legislation in Europe that affected political parties' selection of candidates, but there was a raft of legal Articles that promoted gender equality.

Then the Lord Chancellor was reported to object that one of my amendments, which sought to prevent discrimination against women members in the selection procedure, was an 'artificial and expedient' measure. The General Secretary of the Educational Institute of Scotland (of which I was a member, being a college lecturer before entering Parliament) wrote to him, pointing out that my amendment:

... did not promote discrimination against men. Far from being 'artificial and expedient,' it had been a central feature of the debate over a Scottish Parliament for at least the last ten years in Scotland; it was clearly stated in the Scottish Constitutional Convention's plans for the Parliament, and it was one of the ground-breaking democratic issues which led to non-party political organisations such as ours supporting the Convention and the fight for a double Yes vote in the previous year's referendum.

He went on to point out that:

In terms of international law, this measure is fully in line with the United Nations position in this area, which argues that until parity of gender can be demonstrated, it is not discriminatory for governments, where the opportunity occurs, to allow temporary measures to redress a consistent imbalance over a period of time.

To no avail. I can only conclude that there were those in the Government who, regardless of Scottish Labour Party policy, wanted to avoid any guarantee of equality written into statute. So they got the legal advice they wanted, regardless of the evidence to the contrary.

The pact between Labour and the Lib Dems then fell apart. The Lib Dems' conference in March 1998 rejected intervention or zipping – which they themselves had proposed – as inherently illiberal. But then, there is nothing new about Lib Dems not being sure what principles they actually have in common. The Nationalists also rejected it at their conference.

It was 1999, and the first elections to our brand new Scottish Parliament. There were 28 Labour women members elected – the same number as our men. Labour alone had delivered on 50:50. Adding up all the parties, there were 48 women out of a total of 129, or 37.2 per cent, meaning that worldwide we were only bettered by Sweden and Denmark, and by Wales – yes, Wales! – at 40 per cent. As for the SLD, 15 men and two women were elected. So much for their commitment to gender equality. The Liberal Democrats did manage to achieve gender balance in Wales, to everyone's surprise, and if you can do it there you can do it anywhere. In Scotland, there were three women out of 18 Conservatives, but then they had never, in those pre-Cameron days, found any merit in positive action anyway. The Nationalists had 15 women and 20 men, a remarkable result considering they had shown no interest in the issue of gender equality either in Parliament or in the campaign for a Scottish Parliament. There were three male 'Others', but no women, and it was not until the next elections that Tommy Sheridan was joined by Frances Curran, Rosie Kane and others who eventually turned out to be his Nemeses, and good on them.

We didn't win 50:50 for the Parliament as a whole, but at 37 per cent we did better than we had ever dared hope ten years before. We had changed the face of Scottish politics. Now it is taken for granted to see a large number of women seated in the Scottish Parliament's debating chamber. Women have shown what they can do. They have changed the agenda. People forget there could have been the 'same old, same old'. New female politicians have come under attack for being women: for having higher voices, for everything from their hair to their shoes, for being themselves and not clones of leading men.

Fourteen years on, and we are no further forward. Back in 1999, 43 per cent of Nationalist MSPs were women. Today it is only 26 per cent. Far from undertaking to improve, they excuse themselves on the grounds that they have some prominent women. So it is Labour, the Greens, and even – God help us! – the Tories with six women and nine men who are making our Scottish Parliament look and sound like the people they represent.

CHAPTER FOURTEEN

The Mike Tyson Battle

LIFE WAS GOING on peaceably and uneventfully. Then the Mike Tyson controversy suddenly blew up. It seemed at first a straightforward fight.

Boxing fans who wanted to see the world famous Mike Tyson in the ring in Glasgow sat in opposition to those who argued against letting a convicted rapist enter the UK.

There was a ban on entry against anyone who had served a year or more in prison. Compassionate grounds were the usual reason whenever the ban was overturned, but in this case the only compassion sought was for people who stood to make a lot of money and would lose that opportunity if the ban were enforced.

Supporters of the bout, planned for June 2000 in Glasgow, sought to make the best case they could: he had done his time, he knew no other way of earning a living, he would be guaranteed, with minders around him at all times, to behave himself and not break any laws while here, and anyway it would bring financial benefit to Glasgow through massive ticket sales and hotel bookings. Jack Straw, then Home Secretary, took the view we were to have economic good done to us whether we wanted it or not. George Galloway, MP for Glasgow Hillhead at the time, even argued with me one afternoon in the House of Commons Members' tearoom that it was racist to oppose his visit. When I pointed out that the rape victim was also black, he dismissed any possibility that the judge and jury had found correctly, it being an American court. An attitude I find incomprehensible, considering Tyson's record.

Those of us who campaigned against leave of entry were mainly focussed on two arguments. First: what kind of message was this to young men – with Tyson held up to them as a hero – concerning the crime of rape? Here was our country forbidding entry to anyone who had committed a crime serious enough to merit a year or more in jail, but our Home Secretary, Jack Straw, was prepared to override that? And not for any substantial reason. It was just so that some people could make a lot of money from it, Mike Tyson could clear some of his debts, and boxing fans would get to see him live at extortionate prices.

There had been an earlier protest that year against a match involving

Tyson in Manchester, when Straw argued it was too late to prevent it and local businesses were at risk of going bankrupt if the match were abandoned. Fair enough. But now everyone knew the law, so what excuse could there be this time? We feared that some young men, presented with this character held up for admiration, whose supporters could override the law of the land, might conclude rape was not really that serious a crime.

Our second reason was related to our constituency casework. Jenny Jones, MP for Wolverhampton South West, and I had similar stories to tell. Asian families would come to us for help when they couldn't get permission for family members to enter the UK for a short stay, usually to attend a family wedding or other celebration. Again and again they were refused because it was suspected this was merely an excuse to gain entry and then settle here illegally, working in the black economy or relying on the earnings of their relatives. This would be argued even when said families had prosperous businesses to run back in Pakistan or India, or had jobs in the professions to which they wanted to return. As far as anyone was aware, none of these people had committed any crime, let alone one that carried a jail sentence.

My own fury boiled over when a young father was denied entry to see his dying baby son in our local children's hospital. The young wife and mother, in great distress, could hardly speak when she visited me in my constituency office for the tears pouring down her face. I was stupefied that anyone could be so heartless as to refuse entry in such circumstances. I asked the immigration authorities if they would like to see the story splashed all over the *Daily Record* before they let him in. By the time I had succeeded, it was too late. The child was clinically dead, kept on life support until his dad could arrive. So why could Tyson get in, merely to take part in a boxing match? Because he would be sure to return to the United States? Or because there was money to be made from his visit, and this Pakistani villager had nothing to offer?

The Scottish Nationalists, like others across the political spectrum, were also opposed to letting Tyson in. They saw it as a constitutional matter. It was always perfectly clear that this was a reserved issue, and therefore not a matter for the Scottish Parliament to decide, but undoubtedly they had the right to comment. Jack Straw's failure to take into account the representations of the MSPs in all parties, and the opposition from the Scottish public generally, simply gave ammunition to the SNP. It came across as arrogant, and not a courteous relationship between the centuries-old

Parliament at Westminster with Labour in power, and the new one in Edinburgh led by a Labour-Lib Dem coalition.

Upon reflection now, I think we missed one vital part of the jigsaw. We were focussed on the boxing world, and paid no heed to Rupert Murdoch's benefit from all this. He had the monopoly of pay per view of the match on Sky TV. He was also selling it around the world to anyone interested. On the night of the match, the audience at Hampden sat through over four hours of bouts between boxers few had even heard of until ten minutes to midnight, so that the big match between Tyson and Lou Savarese, who no-one expected to win, would fit in with American TV schedules. Could it be that all that profit for Murdoch was a major reason why Tyson was let in? New Labour had been glad to win Murdoch's support and were not going to upset him. Tony Blair had even visited him in Australia, buttering him up, an event I found unsettling and nauseating. On the other hand, the Labour whips did nothing at all to try to quieten Jenny Jones and me, who were day after day embarrassing a Labour Home Secretary, and we had both experienced the whips' displeasure on other issues. How glad I am now that Ed Miliband, Tom Watson and others have had the guts to take Murdoch on. Jenny was, and remains, a great chum. I first got to know her when she too stood up for lone parents when their benefit was cut in the first year of the New Labour Government in 1997, and that was harder for a newcomer to do than for us veterans.

But now, on the issue of Mike Tyson's visa application, there was widespread unity. Labour MPs from Scotland, including Mike Connarty, Ian Davidson, Norman Godman, John Maxton, John Home Robertson, Ernie Ross, and Liberal Democrat Ray Michie threw themselves into the fray. Harriet Harman and Tony Benn likewise. In all, over 80 MPs actively supported us on Tyson.

This is how the story unfolded. In January 2000, shortly after Parliament resumed after the Christmas holidays, the Parliamentary Labour Party was told that a visa had been granted to allow Mike Tyson to enter the UK for a boxing match in Manchester, despite his record, because of exceptional circumstances. Jenny Jones and I put down an Early Day Motion (EDM), No 290, which stated that:

> This House regrets the admittance of Mike Tyson, a convicted rapist, into the United Kingdom; is concerned that his presence will signal that rape

and violence towards women is less important than commercial gain; and calls upon the Government to ensure that in future the current law on admission of foreigners is upheld in all cases, there being no excuse now for any boxing promoter or anyone else to plead ignorance of the law.

I wrote to Jack Straw on 11 February, drawing his attention to our EDM. Along with everyone else, we had reluctantly accepted that the Manchester bout would have to go ahead, as many people would be badly hit financially, and even suffer bankruptcy through no fault of their own, if the match was cancelled. My letter conceded this, but pointed out:

> You will appreciate that while the Government does a lot of very good things concerning violence against women, the publicity for Tyson's arrival sadly outweighed all this by far.

So it was with great surprise that we learned on 12 May that Jimmy Wray, Labour MP for Glasgow Provan, had met Jack Straw on 3 May, to request once again leave for Tyson to enter the country, and had succeeded in gaining entry for three weeks, this time for a match in Glasgow.

I phoned Jack Straw's office for an appointment, and was told that Barbara Roche, one of his junior ministers, would deal with it. Then an official in her office tried to persuade Jenny and me that it was actually a Foreign Office matter. Tyson had been advised to apply in his own country before flying to the UK, and therefore I should seek a meeting with Keith Vaz, a junior minister in that department. This was nonsense, and rejected by us firmly. If that was the case, why had Jimmy Wray and Llin Golding, MP for Newcastle-under-Lyme, been granted a meeting with Jack Straw to urge him to let Tyson in?

Late in the afternoon of 17 May, Jenny and I were told by Barbara that no decision had yet been made. The Secretary of State had not even read the papers yet. If that was indeed so, I can only conclude that Jack Straw caught up on his papers that evening very hurriedly indeed, because a Labour back bencher, Claire Ward, MP for Watford, who to the best of my knowledge had shown no previous interest in the matter of the proposed visit to Glasgow, tabled a Parliamentary question on the evening of that day, for written answer the next day at 12.30pm. We did not know a question had been tabled, and only knew of it when Norman Godman, MP for Greenock and Inverclyde, happened to read the answer in that day's collection of business papers and told us. The question read: 'To ask the Secretary of State for the Home Department when he will make a decision on Mr Mike Tyson's application for entry clearance.' The some-what lengthy answer stated that:

> I have today informed Mr Tyson that he will be granted entry clear-ance... bearing in mind the residual discretion which I have... My deci-sion took account of the following factors: that Mr Tyson's behaviour on his previous visit to the United Kingdom was satisfactory; that any risk to the public... would be minimised by... the presence of his trainers and other supporting entourage... and that a refusal... would result in a loss of economic benefit to the United Kingdom, and in particular to the areas in which engagements took place, and would not enhance the UK's stand-ing as a venue for major sporting events. I also took account of the fact that Rule 320 (18) currently operates in an inconsistent manner in that those in the public eye whose convictions are known are more likely to be caught by its provisions.

What a stupendously silly argument! Were we to accept, therefore, that Tyson was being unfairly targeted compared to other convicted rapists? Was this Be Kind to Rapists Week? Was the conclusion that we ought to let him off the hook, rather than be resolute in defence of our laws so as to deter other rapists with no public profile from even seeking entry?

I was infuriated that those seeking Tyson's entry to the UK were heard by the Home Secretary, but no-one opposed to it got a moment of his time. And irony of ironies, the day we heard of Tyson's planned next visit was a week after Tessa Jowell, the Minister for Women, had been telling the Parliamentary Labour Party about the importance of the female vote, yet we were not even consulted about this. Women up and down the country, with many a male columnist in support, were expressing their views and the message was clear. Then all of a sudden, it was brought home how little women really mattered, compared to Mike Tyson and all his money.

Jenny, Ian Davidson, Norman Godman and I threw ourselves into opposing this plan in every way we could. Ian hit the headlines when he said, 'the message we are sending out is that Labour is soft on rape and soft on rapists'.

While all this was going on, Jimmy Wray told anyone who would listen that Jenny and I were simply anti-boxing and knew nothing about it (we often disagreed, but remained on good terms for the ensuing years until his sad death). As for me, it is true I don't like boxing, and know practically nothing about it except what it does to boxers' brains, but that had nothing to do with the case. As far as I was concerned, if Tyson had not been a convicted rapist, he could have come here as often as he liked. Where Jenny was concerned, Jimmy could not have been more wrong. Although she is not a fan of the sport, her husband, John, is an Oxford boxing blue, and her father-in-law, a former major, was one of his regiment's boxing champions. She knew from the start that boxers all around Britain were disgusted by Tyson's behaviour.

Our next step was to get Parliamentary time for a debate. Jenny's application was successful, and in a well-attended session in Westminster Hall, numerous Members tore into the Home Secretary's decision.

In a hard-hitting speech in the debate, Jenny pointed out the discrepancy between the Government's widely welcomed actions, including a review of sexual offences law, and a high profile convicted rapist being allowed into the country for commercial gain. 'It really does send out the message,' she said, 'that tackling violence towards women may be less important than making as much money as quickly as possible'. She asked: 'Is rape to be taken seriously, or is it only to be taken seriously provided it doesn't cost too much?'

In my own contribution to the debate, I commented that many women and men would be stunned and sickened by the decision:

> They are already saying money talks, and the only way to convince people otherwise is to bring in fair legislation that lets people without wealth and influence enter this country for funerals and weddings and to visit the sick, because at present that seems a lot less important than a boxing match.

A large majority of back benchers across all parties in the Scottish Parliament were appalled, and took immediate action as soon as they heard Tyson was to be admitted. It only added fuel to the fire when they learned that Jack Straw had not had the courtesy to discuss the issue with anyone there. Not Jim Wallace, who was standing in as First Minister during the absence of Donald Dewar, who was very ill at that time. Not David Steel, the Presiding Officer. No-one, despite urgent phone calls, until it was too late.

The battle raged on the front pages of all the broadsheets and the tabloids. There were titbits about Tyson's violent and erratic behaviour, while the Home Secretary was assuring us all he was likely to behave acceptably. Tyson had been accused in the USA of assaulting a topless dancer – a matter of which the Home Secretary was aware but he did not see fit to delay a decision until the US court had ruled. Why, I cannot say. It is only fair to record that later on the charges were dropped for lack of sufficient evidence.

The Mirror's chief boxing writer was on our side. The *Daily Record* pointed out that 62 per cent of Scots were against. Their front page on 19 May was headed 'SHAMEDEN' and reported the bout would be held at Hampden. The *Evening Times*, in a page-long opinion column, wrote, 'British law clearly states jailed sex offenders like Tyson are barred from entering the UK. The fact that he is an accomplished sportsman is no reason to bend these rules'. The *Guardian, Scotsman, Independent* and *Sunday Herald* all took our side.

We were told Rangers had offered their stadium at Ibrox for the bout, and someone from Tyson's camp had looked it over. Celtic had at first shown an interest in staging the match, but withdrew when they realised this was hardly in keeping with their family values. In the end it was the newly refurbished Hampden, not long opened and seeking cash injections for this hugely expensive project, to be the venue as the *Daily Record* revealed.

Huge sales of tickets were claimed. In the event, come the night of June 24, Hampden was only a third full. The rain came on – even in June, there is no guarantee that there will not be rain in Glasgow – and the ringside seats became soaking wet. Those who had bought the dearest tickets at £500 a throw had to get under shelter much further back, and the poorer punters were being urged to take wet seats at the front for the look of the thing.

The event was shunned by Scottish celebrities, after a lot of hype about the big names that would be seen. Best of all, to my mind, was the reaction to the 70 or so women protesting outside Hampden. A number of scantily clad young women were also present, advertising a lap dancing club. When reporters, jumping to conclusions, asked them if they were against the women protesters, they vehemently stated that, on the contrary, they agreed with them. They were only there because they were getting wages for it.

After waiting and waiting, the audience, who must have been fairly out of patience by the time as it was nearly midnight, settled into their chairs. At last they would see what they had paid for. And they did – for all of 38 seconds. Tyson felled his opponent, and then in his haste to get at him again knocked down the referee, who hastily declared Tyson the winner. This was much to the disgust of several well-known boxers, who their views to the media in no uncertain terms.

Conclusions? We didn't prevent the match, but we did our bit to create a storm of protest. It was highly satisfying to see how widespread public opinion was on the issue: how often would such a spectrum of public opinion, in front page banner headlines, come together in support of women's rights?

CHAPTER FIFTEEN

Time to Go Home

1998–2001

IN JANUARY WE set to work on our Minimum Wage Bill. The Tories were in full-throated opposition, trying to filibuster it out, but our side kept doggedly on all through the night in the standing committee. In March we had the final vote. I was proud to be amongst the 200 or so Labour MPs who went through the night until 8.30am, defeating repeated Tory attempts to foil us. This was class war, and it felt great. The Scottish Nationalists played no part in securing the national minimum wage: a curious stance, for a party that represents itself as a social democratic alternative – nay, superior – to Labour. They chose to go home to their beds. I wish I could remember who it was that commented: 'Stand up for Scotland? They couldnae stay awake for Scotland.'

Plans were well in progress for the creation of the Scottish Parliament, and the Labour Party had begun the process of making a list of approved candidates. Constituency Labour Parties could then invite whoever they chose to form a shortlist for selection as their candidate for the forthcoming elections. We had decided on 'twinning' constituency parties, so that by choosing a man in one and a woman in the other we could ensure gender equality in the constituency seats at least. That was why the Parliament started off with such substantial representation of women, up there with the Scandinavian countries.

Being one of those most deeply involved in securing that aim, having spent several years representing Labour on the Scottish Constitutional Convention and been chair of the Scottish Group of Labour MPs, I now found myself in a farcical position.

When I bought my *Herald* on 5 March 1998, there was a front page banner headline: 'Blair to ban left wing Scots.' On reading further, I discovered that I was one of a small number who, it was asserted, would not be accepted if we applied to the panel for endorsement as candidates. Considering I had already stated on several occasions I intended to stay at Westminster, and not seek election to the Scottish Parliament, this came as even more of a surprise. So whoever the *Herald*'s source was, he or she was either not up to speed on their colleagues' intentions, or were just having a spiteful go anyway.

Although I had campaigned for the Scottish Parliament, and spent many years helping to bring it to fruition, I had realised all along that my own political interests were largely ones that would be reserved to Westminster. It was not a matter of 'Labour sending its big guns to Westminster', of which it is often accused – I had never seen myself as a 'big gun', and it was simply a decision based on which powers were to be reserved and which would be devolved.

Among those Members deemed unsuitable for the Scottish Parliament were Dennis Canavan and John McAllion. Both of them had been enthusiastic campaigners for the Scottish Parliament and had for several years been found suitable to be MPs. The article quoted an unnamed source as stating these two were' too nationalist' in their outlook. Well, no-one could deny they were somewhat Braveheartish for mainstream Labour tastes. And their Scotland United campaign had never succeeded in winning over more than a handful of Labour MPs and party members in Scotland. It was thought – not surprisingly – there was some danger of these two voting with the Nationalists on occasion.

But such was the anger felt in Falkirk at this rejection of the MP they had repeatedly sent to Westminster, Dennis went on to win his seat as an Independent with a very large majority. He travelled towards the Nationalists as the years went on, and supported them in the 2011 Scottish Parliament elections. He is now the chair of the Yes campaign. John did succeed in being approved by the interviewing panel, despite the assertions he would not. He was selected by his local party, and duly elected as an MSP. Then, after all that, sometime later he joined the Scottish Socialist Party, which calls for an independent Scottish state, and became one of their candidates.

But in that article in 1998, there were further names mentioned. Malcolm Chisholm and Norman Godman were rejected for the same reasons as me. All three of us had voted against the Government from time to time. We were not 'on message' with New Labour. Well now. John Smith had been feted when he defied the whip years ago over Europe, an action that advanced his career, but now it was a crime for an MP to dare to ever disagree.

I immediately phoned Donald Dewar, who had been appointed Secretary of State for Scotland the previous year. He told me he had certainly not authorised this. I complained by letter to Alan Howarth, the secretary of the Parliamentary Labour Party, pointing out that comments were to be found in the *Herald* article which breached one of the first rules in our code of conduct: namely, 'to refrain from personal attacks on colleagues orally or in writing'. These comments were all the more to be condemned, timed as they were for the eve of the Scottish party conference. Whoever provided these unattributed, malicious quotes created such widespread media interest that Donald had to issue an immediate rebuttal and Tony had to refer to the issue in his speech, when he affirmed there was no ideological bar. Their statements were of course very welcome, but the situation should never have arisen in the first place. It was not very smart of this anonymous loyalist to create a media distraction from the planned content of the Leader's speech. I closed my letter saying that:

> Whoever is responsible needs to be told that secret character assassinations can be, and predictably will be, countered by victims who believe they can guess who is attacking them. If they are allowed to continue, the infighting that will result can only do harm to the Party's interests.

On 3 June the PLP meeting discussed plans to change the Parliamentary selection procedure. A senior official, David Gardner, denied there was any skulduggery afoot, such as happened in Scotland.

In the event, some people who could have been a real asset failed to get through. Janet Andrews, a conscientious and hard working Glasgow councillor who had taught students at Jordanhill Training College, was deemed unsuitable. At her interview she told the panel she did not think elected members should always toe a line laid down by someone else. For example, she had been a member of CND for many years and she would not vote any other way. Interesting that she should have been rejected on that account. Tony Blair, when seeking selection as Labour's Parliamentary candidate in Sedgefield, wore a CND badge. Ian Davidson apparently turned up at his interview in informal dress and was thus held not to pay sufficient respect to the interviewing panel. Thus so trivially were years of work and commitment, not to mention ability, swept aside. Jim Mackechnie, a councillor of long experience and high regard, who committed to Labour values like the writing through a stick of rock, was turned down. Perhaps – and I am only speculating here – this was because, when much younger, he had the audacity to seek selection as Garscadden's Parliamentary candidate, which would have meant unseating Donald Dewar. Archie

Graham, one of the most capable and sensible men I have ever known, well liked throughout the party and who became deputy leader of Glasgow City Council, was turned down for no reason I can fathom. Rosina Macrae was also turned down, probably because she was too hard line a feminist, and Ann Henderson, as too left wing – but she was accepted the second time around when she applied again.

Some excellent people did get through the winnowing process and were subsequently elected. You did not, after all, have to be a Blairite, although it obviously helped. I was delighted to see Margaret Curran and Johann Lamont, my old chums who had been so loyal and supportive of me, making their way. They could hardly turn down Johann when she had been on the party's Scottish Executive for years and was its chair as well. These two would certainly be an asset. Malcolm Chisholm, a man of principle who had voted to support lone parents and had resigned from his front bench post, was forgiven his sins. Margaret is now Shadow Secretary of State for Scotland, and Johann is the first person to have been elected Leader of the party in Scotland.

When the Scottish Parliament was finally up and running, much of the Scottish media were so in love with the whole idea that they ignored Westminster and a fair amount of imbalance is still there. It became almost impossible for MPs to win any media attention. Some columnists even portrayed staying at Westminster as somehow not caring about Scotland. Not a criticism they levelled at Alex Salmond when he spent several years at Westminster. This, of course, is a particularly stupid criticism. Do they, or don't they, want the people of Scotland to have their share of a say in UK decisions? So, if we don't send MPs to Westminster, how do they expect to achieve that?

There is another idiocy that irritates me whenever I hear it repeated. When the Scottish Parliament met for the first time on 12 May 1999, the SNP's Winnie Ewing, as the eldest member elected, had the honour of acting as temporary presiding officer. As I sat with John Maxton up in the gallery, with jaw-dropping incredulity (both having taught history) we heard her assert that 'The Scottish Parliament, adjourned on the 25 day of March 1707, is hereby reconvened'. This is nonsensical, for a number of reasons. We have all heard of long adjournments, but three centuries is just silly. The English Parliament was also adjourned when it met for the last time. The reality that everyone in 1707 recognised was that both the Scottish and English Parliaments were no more. They had ceased to be.

They had become ex-parliaments. And just in case anyone was in any doubt, on 28 April the Scottish Parliament was dissolved by proclamation. There was now a Parliament of Great Britain.

The Scottish Parliament of that far-off time was elected by a tiny minority of wealthy men. The vast majority of men could neither elect it nor stand for it. Likewise for every woman in the land. Back then, women were still being burnt at the stake for less. Why would any of us want to associate our newly formed democratic Parliament, dealing with the issues of today's society, with an elite bunch of men whose sole qualification was their social position, and whose most heartfelt concerns were their lands and property, and whether the monarch would be a Catholic or a Protestant?

Fast-forward to more recent times. It is a plain fact that the first line of the Scotland Act 1998 says, 'There shall be a Scottish Parliament'. It does not say 'The Scottish Parliament shall be reconvened'. When I spent years in the Scottish Constitutional Convention, working towards achieving our Scottish Parliament, not once did anyone say this was about reconvening the Scottish Parliament of 300 years ago. We were all perfectly clear that this was about creating a new, democratic Parliament, not attempting to restore life to a body long since turned to dust.

Yet some continue to repeat this ludicrous statement unquestioningly, when a little research would show what a distortion of history this is.

But another aspect was the treatment of the new women MSPs. Many were making their mark as Ministers, chairs of committees and noteworthy back benchers. Yet they found themselves abused and derided by a press pack who disdained the accents of Glasgow and Lanarkshire – although they seemed happy to swallow any amount of Alex Salmond's kailyard vocabulary. They found fault with their dress size, their dress sense, and even in one case a Labour woman's choice of soft drink. I suspect that if a Nationalist had put a small bottle of Irn-Bru on her table – in preference to the bottle of water laid on – it would have been hailed as promoting the Scottish soft drinks industry. It was the media who failed, showing far more interest in such trivia than in debates on domestic violence or rape law, when the press benches would be empty. Women were making a difference, but the male-dominated media did not think such matters were the legitimate stuff of politics.

* * *

Deprivation in Glasgow had all along been one of my major concerns. In November 1987 I had taken issue with the newly published joblessness figures. In Maryhill alone 7,861 were out of work, a quarter of the local workforce. Maryhill was the constituency with the fifth highest numbers of unemployed in the country, and between the general elections of 1983 and 1987, the jobless total had increased by nine per cent. I pointed out that the horrific cost in foregone taxes and national insurance contributions took out £52 million from Maryhill alone.

In April 1998 I suggested that the Council and the housing associations could re-train jobless people to improve housing, and Ministers accepted the idea as one worth exploring. The previous year the Glasgow North regeneration area, which included Maryhill, had an unemployment rate of 22.4 per cent, compared with the city's 15.5 per cent and Scotland's 7.9 per cent. The country's top six jobless blackspots were in Glasgow constituencies: Provan, Springburn, Central, Garscadden, Govan and Maryhill. Glasgow North had the city's highest mortality rates. The uptake of free school meals in Scotland was 20 per cent, but the Glasgow average was double that. The uptake rate of clothing and footwear grants for school-children in Glasgow North was 80 per cent, and even higher elsewhere.

Things began to move with the Forth and Clyde Canal regeneration project, which provided over 4,000 jobs. Donald Dewar was instrumental in this. It would have collapsed without his instructing the Scottish Office to put a sum of over £7 million cash – not a loan – into the project, which had been languishing for lack of funds.

In September 1998 we were given information that really brought the scale of the problem home. Research commissioned by the Labour Government from the Department of Urban Studies at the University of Glasgow into the scale of deprivation showed that Glasgow had no less than 52 out of the worst 90 postcode sectors in the whole of Scotland. Some areas in my own constituency – North Maryhill, Wyndford, Botany and Garscube – were in the worst ten per cent in Scotland. Yet because Glasgow had even more highly deprived areas, these parts of Maryhill were not considered a priority for action.

In January of the following year I secured a debate on deprivation in Glasgow. I pointed out that the report showed that the level of urban regeneration needed in Glasgow far exceeded that of anywhere else in Scotland. However, Glasgow's share of urban programme resources was still lower than its share of deprivation. There had been a decline of £12

million in the urban programme in Glasgow outwith the Priority Partnership Areas in the past three years. Furthermore, deprived areas in Glasgow
which were not in a PPA or in a social inclusion partnership were among
the 20 per cent most deprived areas in Scotland. They did not receive any
other resources. I went on to say how unfair it was, that this population,
more impoverished than any other in Scotland by far, was the one carrying a range of subsidised metropolitan services: the Royal Concert Hall,
the Mitchell Library, theatres and museums. Too many of our people
could not afford to visit them, while others outside the Glasgow bound-
ary, in more prosperous areas, could benefit from them to their heart's
content. Calum Macdonald, then a junior minister in the Scottish Office,
replied and gave an account of what steps had been taken, and were being
planned, to improve matters in housing, health, education and job creation. Some useful steps had been taken. More than 900 Glasgow-based
companies signed up to the New Deal, pledging they would offer jobs to
the young and the long-term unemployed. By this time more than 600
young people in Glasgow were receiving a wage instead of jobseeker's
allowance. Better still, 15,000 new jobs would be created in Glasgow over
the next few years.

* * *

In October 1998 all our thoughts turned to the new patient at the London
Clinic, General Augusto Pinochet. The Government of Spain asked us for
his extradition on account of his record of torture, murder and terrorism
in Chile. Then the Home Office decided he could not be arrested or detained
by the police, as he had not committed offences under British law. Scotland
Yard advised Madrid that it required an arrest warrant, and soon afterwards the London Interpol Bureau received a formal notice requesting
Pinochet's arrest with a view to extradition. Receiving information he was
intending to leave Britain in a jet early the next day (apparently enjoying
a remarkably sudden recovery), they arrested Pinochet shortly before
midnight.

The matter came up at our Parliamentary Labour Party meeting. Peter
Mandelson, the Trade Secretary, commented it that would be 'gut-wrench-
ing' to see Pinochet granted diplomatic immunity. Tony Benn and 14 others,
including myself, signed a Commons motion paying tribute to Peter. At
our meeting, noting that Peter was absent, I moved we should send him a

message to congratulate him on his forthright condemnation, and request Tony Blair to pass on the message when he saw him.

The *Observer* ran a story on it, describing me as 'an incorrigible Bevanite', and recorded there was laughter and tumultuous applause for my motion from the assembled MPs. When Tony said some years before he would feel he had succeeded when the Labour Party learned to love Peter, he did not, I believe, mean this. He promised to pass on the message from the PLP, adding, 'Unfortunately Peter could not be with us because he is at a meeting of the Socialist Workers Party'. It was a joke, but why would a Labour leader seek to associate a perfectly normal left-of-centre, indeed simply democratic view, with the ultra left SWP? As if few but they would say something like that. The *Observer* commented that the joke had a cutting edge. A warning, it said, had gone out from Downing Street to every Minister that they were not to engage in any more free wheeling commentary about Pinochet. Robin Cook, the Foreign Secretary, had been enthusiastically supported when he made it clear there should be no refuge here for anyone accused of crimes against humanity, and there was plenty of evidence against Pinochet. Could this alleged ban be true? All this made me feel how right I had been to give up the front bench. I would not have found it easy to tolerate being told to say nothing about the likes of Pinochet. Only years later, when I read Chris Mullin's *A Walk-On Part*, did I learn that Jean Corston, who had recently been in Chile, reported to the Parliamentary committee two days after Peter's denunciation that the arrest of Pinochet was a problem for the left. Apparently the Christian Democrats, in a fragile coalition with the social democratic left, might be pushed back into the hands of the far Right. Therefore we should stick to the line that Pinochet's arrest was a judicial and not a political matter. But how do you expect to defeat in the court of public opinion the kind of vile abuses of human rights that Pinochet perpetrated, unless you speak out loud and clear? A sentence including the words 'trumpet' and 'uncertain note' comes to mind.

In December there was happier news. It was announced in the Queen's Speech that there would be a Bill to remove the right of hereditary peers to sit and vote in the House of Lords. I did not usually trot through to the Lords for the State Opening of Parliament. I resented the peers sitting in their seats while we, the elected representatives of the people, had to stand, but on that occasion I did. Just to gloat. We are still waiting for the final removal of people who take part in making our laws, just because some forebear gave service to the reigning monarch of his day. Not to mention the Church of England bishops, who ought to have been turfed out years ago from a Parliament with any pretentions to democracy.

The same month, academics at Hull University published the results of their analysis of votes in the Commons since Labour took office the previous May. They found that 78 Labour MPs, about 20 per cent of the total, had voted against the Government during the first session. Their evidence showed that, far from being meek and weak-willed, the current back benchers were one of the most rebellious groups of government MPs since the war. They produced a list of 20 such back benchers, which put Dennis Canavan and Jeremy Corbyn joint top (or bottom, from the whips' point of view). There were three other Scots: John McAllion, Tam Dalyell, and finally myself, barely making it onto the list.

The fact was, I just did not support 'The Project'. When I read in the papers that Tate and Lyle were now donating to the Labour Party, I sought a meeting with Tony in order tell to him that a lot of older Labour voters would remember the post-war years, when that company constantly paid for advertising in the newspapers under the name of 'Mr Cube', attacking the Labour Government. People loyal to Labour all these years would be unhappy and worried about how much the Party must have changed to actually win that lot's financial support. Tony replied, 'Won't they be happy that Tate and Lyle have changed?' He seemed completely oblivious to the fact that a large capitalist company looks after its own interests, first and foremost, and it had to be asked, why had they decided their best interests lay with *our* party?

On another day I was one of the small number of Labour MPs invited to Number 10 to meet Tony and discuss current issues with him. This was an innovation of Tony's – rank and file members were not used to having a face to face meeting with the Prime Minister in which they could raise anything they liked. This was my second such occasion – and last. As the meeting drew to a close, I had come to realise that this was not a two-way exchange of views leading sometimes to rethinking at the top. Tony simply told those who disagreed with him why they were wrong. So, as I was leaving the meeting, I asked Tony if he had ever changed *his* mind about anything as a result of these meetings. He looked at me, eyebrows raised in complete surprise at such a question. What left the memory with me was that it wasn't so much that the answer was no, it was his surprise that anyone should even ask it. Anyone who wants to be a politician must have some degree of self-assurance. That amount strikes me as too much.

January 1999

Things kicked off well at the beginning of the new year when the Labour Party announced it wanted a Parliament fit for the 21st century, not the 13th. A parliament based on merit, not inherited privilege. We were, of course, talking about Westminster: we already were going to have that in Holyrood.

On Burns Night I hurried away from a Burns Supper to vote in favour of equalising the age of consent for heterosexuals and homosexuals, provided it was not less than 16 for both.

Matters plodded on routinely until the summer, when Tony Banks, as Sports Minister, came to the rescue of Partick Thistle, our local football club. The club wanted to gain a work permit for a young Namibian player, Quinton Jacobs, and found itself up against the rules governing professional players from non-EU countries. The plain fact was that the Premier Division teams were treated more favourably than those lower down the pecking order, and obtained work permits easily when others were refused. The rules were changed, and I was at the first match when Quinton played for us, and Thistle fans delightedly flew the Namibian flag.

Irish affairs were, as ever, proving difficult. Kevin McNamara, John McDonnell and I launched a new organisation, The Friends of Ireland – Friends of the Good Friday Agreement. Our statement won the support of over 140 MPs, MEPs and members of the House of Lords, along with around a dozen trade union general secretaries, and Irish community, human rights and campaigning organisations. The initiative also won backing from 63 members of the United States Congress.

As a member of the British-Irish Inter-Parliamentary Body, I was involved in promoting the peace process. This was a group of British MPs and Irish TDs paving the way towards the Good Friday Agreement by building trust and letting the Irish members realise we were genuinely interested in the good of Ireland. No surprise that on the British side, many of us had Irish roots. Kevin McNamara had been Labour's opposition spokesperson, but Mo Mowlam was given his job and was subsequently appointed Secretary of State when Tony Blair became Prime Minister, because Kevin was considered too close to the Social Democratic and Labour Party (SDLP).

But there were problems with Mo. No-one realised it at the time, but Mo's brain tumour was having an unfortunate effect on her personality. I could see how her coarse language and eccentric behaviour affronted prim and proper David Trimble. He insisted on meeting Tony alone, even though Mo was supposed to be leading the talks, and this of course angered her. Somehow things did manage to move forward with the active involvement of Irish Taoiseach Bertie Ahern and US President Bill Clinton, and in late November the following year, we secured both Republican and Unionist support for the Good Friday Agreement.

I have in front of me a copy of the Hansard report for the debate on the Northern Ireland Bill on 13 July 1999, and it leaves no doubt that at that time Mo was entirely clear headed and able to cope with the questions being thrown at her. Note the month: Mo was able to congratulate all concerned on there being no violence during the marching season to date. The Bill covered contentious issues such as the timetable for decommissioning weapons, prisoner releases, and the creation of an inclusive Executive, exercising devolved powers. Yet, as a few interventions from Kevin McNamara show, she did not have – and could not reasonably be expected to have – the degree of knowledge of who said what when, which Kevin had built up over the several years he had been involved. I don't think he took any pleasure in having to correct her before the Unionists and the SDLP started jumping up and down. The Unionists were annoying enough already.

When it was my turn to speak, I invited intervention from anyone who would tell me why he thought, as they were alleging, that there was no real commitment to resolving matters and moving forward, considering the UK Government, the Irish Government and the former Prime Minister (John Major) had all publicly stated their intention to produce an agreement. Robert McCartney replied that it was terror and violence – especially that aimed at the city of London – that had driven the process from the very beginning. It was about conflict resolution between the British state and Sinn Fein-IRA. I went on to say that if the members of the Assembly were not committed to its success, it would fall apart in any event. The debate had concentrated entirely on the history of Nationalist violence, as if there had never been any on the Unionist side, so Members should be honest about it. At the end of all the point scoring, the vote was 312

Ayes for the Bill, and only 19 Noes. The Noes consisted of Unionists and a handful of Tories.

Later in 1999, Mo was replaced by Peter Mandelson.

The debate on 16 May 2000 on the rules for the flying of flags on public buildings in Northern Ireland was a good example of my patience being tried to destruction. We started at 10.26pm and finished at 11.55pm, most of us having been working since early morning. The issue was: would it be the Union flag alone, on all occasions, or might there be any specific instances when the Irish tricolour could be flown? Or any time at all, or never? The Sinn Fein argument was that if the Saltire could be flown in Scotland at the same time as the Union flag, then why not the tricolour in Northern Ireland? What had prompted Peter Mandelson to seek this debate was that two departments in the Northern Ireland Assembly, under the instruction of their ministers, had failed to fly any flag at all. They did not regard the Union flag as having anything to do with them. So he was forced because of Unionist indignation to bring forward this Order, to lay down that he would have a reserve power to set regulations on flag flying from Government buildings. He would use the reserve power only if it became clear that the Northern Ireland Executive was unable to agree a way forward and the issue was becoming a palpable source of division amongst its members. The vote finally supported the Order by 240 to eight. Everyone else, that is to say over 400 lucky MPs, had gone home to their beds. The eight had been given all the assurances they sought, but still voted against. And as usual, the Sinn Fein members were not even there. As I stood waiting and yawning in the taxi queue to get to my bed, I felt peeved at all this carry-on about flags. Bloody men and their flags! Had they nothing more important to worry about? I would seldom notice whether a public building was flying a flag, which one it was, or whether it was the right way up. Just as well I never had any ambitions in the ambassadorial line.

I think it was around this time that Ian Paisley devised a tactic which drove me up the wall. We were discussing a Bill that affected Northern Ireland, and only Northern Ireland. He moved amendments to each clause, one after another, to insert the words 'in Northern Ireland', and somehow got away with the Speaker letting them be called. In vain did everyone else point out that there was no point in this, as the Bill referred only to Northern Ireland anyway. These words were therefore superfluous. He would never give in, bellowing 'NO!' as only he could. After hours of this, it dawned on me that he was using this device to ensure he had his words down in Hansard in clause after clause. But my patience, never a quality I have ever been credited with having much of, was tried to the limit that night. I had to go out of the Chamber before I exploded. Looking back on it all, I remain amazed that he, of all people, could end up standing side by side, smiling with Martin McGuiness, for the benefit of the media.

My involvement in these matters included being elected secretary of the Agreed Ireland Forum (AIF). This organisation brought together politicians, from all quarters, who wanted peace in Ireland, and had been instrumental in helping to change hearts and minds in order to achieve the Good Friday Agreement. This threw up some odd circumstances, on occasion. At the Labour Conference in Blackpool, the AIF held a fringe meeting in one of the hotels, at which David Ervine, the leader of the Progressive Unionist Party, was one of the speakers. A working-class Unionist, he was opposed to the upper-class Unionist hegemony that used division between Catholic and Protestant to split workers and further their own economic gain. I wished there were more Unionists like him. After the meeting was over I went out for a short walk in the fresh air and returned to the same hotel, which happened to be the one I was staying in. David appraoched me and asked if I remembered what he had said. When I told him I did, he asked me to repeat the gist of it to him then and there. Why? Because the BBC's Northern Ireland news had been broadcasting a mistaken version of what he had said, indeed quite the opposite, and it would cause immense trouble for him if it was not put right. So I, a granddaughter of a fervent Irish Nationalist, willingly came to the rescue of a Northern Ireland Unionist, and the BBC changed its news bulletin accordingly. It was obvious that the Good Friday Agreement would be in needless difficulty – as if it needed any more – if we did not at least know what each other was really saying.

2000

In the doo-doo again. On 9 May we had a debate on the Transport Bill, which included a Government clause intended to make it possible to reduce the public sector holding in the National Air Traffic Control Service to 25 per cent, without having to seek further consent from Parliament. This was privatisation, not a partnership. I voted for three amendments, two that would have kept the service in non-profit hands, and a third to prevent it from being sold off before the Prestwick airport development was completed. Sandra Osborne was up against it, her constituency being highly marginal and with hundreds of air transport workers employed at Prestwick who simply did not believe the Government's assurances that this clause would not lead to outright privatisation. All three amendments were defeated.

We had opposed this move when we were in opposition. In the debate I asked John Prescott, who was speaking from the Despatch Box, why the change of mind? I had heard nothing all night to explain. I was not arguing we could never change our minds about anything, but there had to be an explanation which so far was not forthcoming. He did not explain, he merely said he considered this the best way forward. I quoted a letter from a pilot in that day's *Guardian*, explaining why he found this move worrying on safety grounds. The pilot seemed more convincing than our Deputy Leader, but I was basically opposed to any privatisation anyway.

Northern Ireland affairs rumbled on. There was a highly successful conference in London in support of the Good Friday Agreement, attended by a good mix of political leaderships and the women's movement from Northern Ireland. Peter Mandelson, to my surprise, turned out to be very willing to discuss circumstances as they changed with those back benchers who took an interest in Irish affairs, let us know his thinking, hear our views, and have a genuine discussion about the way forward.

One of my jobs was chairing Labour's departmental committee on International Development. The department was created in 1997 when Labour took office. Formerly its work was done by the Foreign Office, but a separate department was needed to ensure this work got the priority it deserved, and was seen as detached from our country's business interests. To show the Government meant business, the department got a far bigger increase in its budget than any other, because the Tory government had severely under-funded its work for years. When Clare Short, the Secretary of State for the new DFID, published a White Paper on tackling world poverty, it was the first in 20 years. People in Maryhill had shown a great deal of interest in campaigns like Jubilee 2000 for writing off the debt of poorer countries, and tackling disasters like the floods in Mozambique. Campaigning organisations had been successful in drawing attention to the fact that severe conditions attached to debt relief had been deeply damaging. In Ghana the introduction of school fees created a primary school dropout rate of 40 per cent. In Zambia the International Monetary Fund's structural adjustment programme created a fall in GNP of 16 per cent over a five year period. In Mozambique the introduction of fees for hospital visits meant a cost of $4 to see a doctor – the equivalent of 13 per cent of the minimum wage. Privatisation to achieve efficiency led to massive redundancies. With no social security available, families were pushed deeper into poverty. Our government was pointing that out it was not a question of conditions or no conditions, but what were fair and sensible conditions: conditions that would help to alleviate poverty, ignorance and ill health.

George Foulkes, in his ministerial role, visited Maryhill Co-operative with me to publicise Fair Trade products, which were something new on the shelves then. Most other supermarkets hadn't got any further than stocking Fair Trade tea and coffee, if even that.

And there was good news for Maryhill. The European Commission had agreed which areas of Britain would receive financial assistance for industry to create jobs, starting that year and running to 2006. Maryhill did well out of this funding, thanks to John Reid and Donald Dewar responding to my case for deprived areas in my constituency.

July 2000 provided one of the most farcical events I ever encountered. Betty Boothroyd announced her intention to retire, and so the election of a new Speaker was set in process. Usually there were only a few candidates, but this time there were no fewer than 12. So the Commons procedures committee decided that the way to carry out the election was to ask Edward Heath, as Father of the House, to preside. He was required to choose a proposer for Candidate A, and a proposer for Candidate B. The second candidate would become the amendment and MPs would troop through the lobbies to vote. When one of these two candidates lost, Mr Heath was to choose a third proposer for Candidate C, whereupon Members would troop through the lobbies again, and so on until a final vote when one of the candidates had more than 50 per cent of the votes. There was no explanation of why Mr Heath should have the power to decide the running order of candidates, which could affect the outcome.

Protests grew against this nonsense. I tabled an early day motion, with all-party support, to change the system to a secret ballot, in which Members would simply put a cross against the candidate of their choice. When Lorna Fitzsimmons, a member of the procedures committee, claimed there was no chance of the committee sitting to recommend any change before the election – which was strange coming from such a moderniser – Tam Dalyell appealed to Betty to postpone her departure. Betty declined to be helpful.

In the event, the thing went ahead with 84 year old Heath presiding over a series of votes that took over six hours of parliamentary time. Michael Martin was the leading candidate in each vote. I was pleased to see this, because it gave the answer to all the nasty jibes about 'Gorbals Mick'. As one born in The Gorbals myself (unlike Michael, who happened to be born in Anderston anyway – so much for respect for accuracy, quite apart from the snobbery), I wasn't going to forget that in a hurry.

At least a sensible system was used when John Bercow was elected Speaker. They used a secret ballot, eliminated the candidate with the fewest votes, and continued to vote until John won over 50 per cent of the votes cast.

* * *

In October 2000 I fell ill with some kind of post viral problem. Donald Dewar had died unexpectedly, and I had been at his funeral. I felt wretched at the loss of a good friend anyway, but I began to feel ill as I walked home from the reception through Kelvingrove Park. I had been feeling fluey and ignored it so as to carry out duties I thought I could not forego. Stupid of me, I know. Never having been unwell for more than a day or two in my life before, apart from that bug in Nicaragua, it now came as something of a shock to be in a condition where it was a struggle to walk around the block. I laid flat out in bed all day, feeling pain all over my body and having no energy to do anything. To eat, I could only manage to microwave ready meals. It still seems incredible that you can feel that ill and not be in hospital, but the fact is, there is nothing they can do for you, so there is no sense in taking up a hospital bed. I was terrified I might have ME, having made home visits to constituents with that affliction and seen how low it laid them, and how long it went on.

This may seem bordering on superstition, but every night before I fell asleep, I said to myself: *tomorrow you will wake up feeling better*. I forced myself to walk to the corner and back, and then take longer walks, bit by bit, until I could manage ten minutes. Then 12. And so on, a few minutes more at a time, until I eventually recovered months later.

There was a night when I dreamt my husband Jim, who had died 14 years before, was standing up in a small rowing boat in darkness at the foot of a flight of stone steps, with a river flowing gently behind him. I was standing on the top step. He looked up and said to me, 'Not yet.' I do not believe in communication between the dead and the living. But I did think of this as my subconscious mind determining to recover. Then one morning in December I woke up thinking, *I could go some sausages, eggs, black pudding and ham.* My son Stephen drove me to the supermarket where he helped me buy the wherewithal, and from then on I began to mend. My brother Joe and his partner Anna Dyer constantly monitored me and enticed me into looking at lunch menus, even when I could hardly eat a bite.

But I still felt so weak I could not go down to London to attend Parliament. I tried one day in December, and got no further than Glasgow airport. When it came to Hogmanay, I was determined to keep to my lifelong practice of putting out my bin bag before midnight so as to have no rubbish in the house. Even that took a real effort, but it made me feel I was more in charge of my own body. I was worried about being unable for so long to carry out my work, although my staff and local party members were exceptionally helpful.

I was also worried about the General Election: that might not be long away. It would simply be impossible to campaign as I ought, if I was still in this condition.

There was another complicating factor: MPs aren't allowed to be ill. I had learned that through the bitter experience of Tom Clarke, when I was one of his underlings and he was off sick for a few months. Instead of leaving the man in peace to get well, he was constantly backstabbed by people who should have given him loyalty, and who were strongly hinting that he was only ill because he was not up to the job.

I began to think over how could I lighten my load. My problem was, the jobs I loved doing most were the ones I would have to give up if I pared down my work to the essentials.

And there was another consideration bothering me. I thought, I'm a granny who loves her granddaughter Catriona, now a toddler, and I don't get enough opportunity to see her because her parents live in Oxfordshire. What with long hours in Parliament and being at home in Glasgow at weekends for local meetings and surgeries, it was beginning to seem ridiculous that I had to search my diary for weeks for a date when I was free.

I had always thought, in any case, that I would retire at whatever General Election fell between my 60th and 65th birthdays. So if I were going to go, now was the time to tell my constituency party. I would not under any circumstances do to them what some of my colleagues had shamefully done, leaving their resignation to the last moment before a General Election so that the Blairites could impose a candidate on them with the excuse that there was no time to select one themselves. Maryhill party members had been completely loyal to me over the 14 years I had been in Parliament, and the least they deserved was a similar loyalty back.

2001

I returned to Parliament in March, keen to take part in the Second Reading debate on the International Development Bill. I had spent several years as chair of Labour's back bench committee on that subject. Now here at last, under a Labour Government, was what I had long hoped for: establishing in legislation the reduction of poverty as the aim of UK development assistance, and ensuring it was spent for that reason alone. For years aid had been linked to our commercial interests, often resulting in no net benefit for the country concerned. Now here was Gary Streeter, the Tory Shadow Minister, giving an undertaking that a future Conservative Government would not re-link aid to trade. This was truly remarkable. The previous Tory Government had taken so little interest in the subject over nearly 20 years in power they had published not even one White Paper on the matter. So I was glad when he agreed to let me intervene on his speech. I then said:

> To enable the House to gauge the sincerity of Opposition attitudes on this matter, will the Hon. Gentleman remind us of how many White Papers on International Development were published between 1979 and 1997?

Streeter replied, 'I was going to welcome the Hon. Lady back after her recent illness, but now I am not so sure.' He then confessed that he did not know. In summing up, Chris Mullin revealed that the answer was none. He went on to note that the Shadow Minister had the good grace to blush when I asked that question. The 10 April was the day of my last contribution on this matter. We had the Third Reading debate that day, and I took the chance to draw attention to women not having any say in the government of their countries. I wanted praise for Clare Short's substantial achievements over the past four years to be on the record. She had developed literacy and numeracy programmes, and that alone was a key element in offering populations the opportunity to challenge, to think for themselves, to argue, to campaign, to speak truth to power, and to get things done.

At the end of the debate I was struggling to hold back the tears as a number of Members, even Bowen Wells for the Tories, said kind things about me.

My last chance to say anything in the Chamber was in Scottish Questions. The 2001 General Election had been called. The first question was Ian Davidson's, about employment in Scotland. Helen Liddell, Secretary of State for Scotland, was able to answer that we now had the lowest level of unemployment since 1976, and the highest employment since 1960. Since the 1997 election, employment was up by 105,000, long-term unemployment was down by 60 per cent and youth unemployment down by 2,000. When I was called I mentioned that no Conservative Member had even tried to speak on unemployment on this occasion. Could that be because the Conservatives are embarrassed by the fact that the last time the unemployment figures were as low as this, Labour was in government?

Why do I remember these last two brief contributions, out of so many over the 14 years I spent in Parliament? I suppose it must be because they related to two of my chief interests: tackling world poverty, and pulling my own constituency out of the hell of widespread, long-term unemployment. I could never say anything about unemployment without thinking of my own father, cast aside for four years during the 1930s Depression.

The commentariat are fond of quoting Enoch Powell's dictum that all political careers end in failure. They also harbour a belief that every MP wants to be the Prime Minister, regardless of evidence to the contrary. I had done what I wanted to do. And that had never included being PM. As I sat in my taxi taking me to Euston, heading back home to Glasgow, I looked back at the House of Commons and wondered if I had done the right thing. Would I regret my decision? I can only say, as it turned out, I didn't. Retirement did not mean hibernation. Well, maybe sometimes when it was cold and wet.

Being a Labour MP was the biggest thing in my life for a long time. I had been immensely lucky and highly privileged. But now it was time to move on.

CHAPTER SIXTEEN

Ding Dong

THAT VOICE. We lost count of the number of times we heard it say, 'There is no alternative'. TINA became a catchword. Who will ever forget 'The lady's not for turning'? But why applaud pig-headedness? Nigel Molesworth might well have observed, 'As any fule kno, if you're going the wrong way you *need* to u- turn.' And now, from 8 April 2013, that voice would speak no longer.

We have been grandly assured we are all Thatcher's children. Well, if you want to be, it's a free country. Me, I'm one of Attlee's children. Most of us are. Inheritors of a National Health Service brought in by an English Prime Minister and created by a Welshman. The inheritors of a welfare state that has lasted for decades but is now under threat. The beneficiaries of an education system that opened doors to working class youngsters.

As an MP seeing her in action during the remains of her reign, Mrs Thatcher seemed to me an increasingly bizarre figure. Remember 'We are a grandmother'? Yes, a grandmother that wouldn't support a crèche in the Commons for other women's benefit, when she as the wife of a millionaire had all the help she could ever want.

John Major's task was to think up another system of paying for local government, or he'd be out on his ear too. Having ditched her flagship Poll Tax policy, few would call him one of her children.

Then along came Tony Blair. Why did he not do more with his massive majorities? Compare the modesty of his defence of historic Labour achievements, to the destruction wielded by the present coalition, which only has the power to do so because the Tories, lacking a majority, found the Lib Dems willing accomplices. And don't think today's austerity is because of the size of the national debt. The 1945 Labour Government faced a far higher proportion of debt to GDP. No international body, no credit rating company, no bank was telling them to rein in. Why was that? Because people had spent six years in a bloody war that cost the lives of millions, and they were not in the mood to put up with going back to the unemployment, poor housing and health inequalities they knew all too well from the past.

When Clement Attlee died, Harold Wilson commented:

Fainter hearts than his would have used the nation's economic difficulties as a reason for postponing social advance. He felt, on the contrary, that the greater the economic difficulties, the greater the need for social justice.

Then we got a huge Labour majority once more in 1997, but the Party had undergone a change Tony Blair argued it needed to get elected. So, no tackling the fundamentals of wealth and power. No tackling the shackles put on trade unions by the Thatcher Government. In fact, Blair boasted that Britain's labour laws were the most restrictive in Europe. Far from all this being popular, New Labour managed to lose four million votes by 2005.

Yet there were good things that New Labour Government achieved, and it is unfair and dishonest to deny it. The Good Friday Agreement. Record investment in schools and hospitals. Devolution for Scotland and Wales. Sure Start. Debt relief in developing countries, not tied to our commercial interests. The National Minimum Wage.

But they were so reluctant to claim credit for these reforms. They were doing good by stealth, in case the *Daily Mail* noticed. I remember being quite appalled to learn from a young mothers' meeting in my constituency that they thought the substantial rise in Child Benefit was something the local civil servants had provided, and did not realise it had anything to do with a political decision by the Labour Government.

Nowadays, too many people believe that when the country is in trouble, we all have to make sacrifices. Don't they notice that Google, Amazon and Starbucks are doing quite the opposite? And are allowed to get away with it because they are not breaking any law? So if you think this state of affairs needs to be sorted, without delay, you need to consider what you are prepared to do to bring such a change about. Just moaning at the news on the telly isn't going to cut it.

But the real children of Thatcher are not the earnest souls who think it is their duty to accept cuts, when profiteering, tax-dodging and bonuses for non-achievement have never been more blatant. No, displaying an effrontery unequalled in any other modern state, they are to be found on the Tory-Lib Dem front bench.

That has been the most significant change in the past 12 years, the coming to power of this Tory-led coalition. Then getting away with a crime sheet that has put many another ruling caste in prison, if they were lucky. You think I am exaggerating?

Let me introduce Ha-Joon Chang, in case you have not heard of him before. This man is so brilliant, he has won a prize for advancing the frontiers of economic thought. He writes in words you and I understand, and he's on our side. In March 2013, he and numerous colleagues called for a people's assembly against austerity, to bring together campaigns against cuts and privatisation with trade unionists in a movement for social justice.

In 2010 Professor Chang (presently Reader in the Political Economy of Development at Cambridge University) was pointing out that the 2008 global economic crisis was the second largest in history. It was not some force of nature that caused it. Free market economists have deliberately taken advantage of people's justified fear of hyperinflation in order to push for excessive anti-inflation policies, which do more harm than good. Increased job insecurity (euphemistically called greater labour market flexibility) is a direct consequence of free market policies.

But to be fair, Ha-Joon Chang goes on to point out that governments that espoused upward income redistribution have ruled most of the time since the 1980s. Even some so-called left wing parties, he writes, such as Britain's New Labour under Tony Blair, openly advocated such a strategy. And a memory comes back to me of Peter Mandelson saying, 'I am intensely relaxed about people getting filthy rich as long as they pay their taxes.' Only their tax burden didn't sit particularly hard on their shoulders, and it's been lightened even more under the present government.

Professor Chang blames the economists, who, over the past three decades, played an important role in creating the conditions for the 2008 crisis. They provided theoretical justification for financial deregulation and the unrestrained pursuit of short-term profits. They advocated theories that justified the policies that have led to slower growth, higher inequality, heightened job insecurity and more frequent financial crises.

All of that is true. But it wasn't a case of right-wing politicians not knowing what to think until Milton Friedman and his like told them. No, he gave them the ammunition for the war they wanted to fight anyway. Now they are closer to unravelling much of the Welfare State than they have ever been, and they have even managed to convince a large proportion of the population that none of this is the fault of free market enthusiasts governing over us. Oh dear me, no. It was the New Labour Government, falling into old left wing bad habits, squandering money on stopping the rain running down classroom walls, and cutting hospital waiting lists. This is just a lie. It is simply not true that Gordon Brown crashed the global economy. As has been pithily said by others, Lehman

Brothers in the USA didn't collapse because Brown splurged the budget in Britain. Bear in mind, too, that at the time of the crash, our national debt was less than New Labour inherited from John Major in 1997.

Things are not on the mend. According to IMF figures, if George Osborne gets his way, Britain is going to end up with a smaller public sector than any other major developed nation. We have just seen the Royal Mail sold off, something that even Margaret Thatcher would not do. This is a nation where there are people depending on food banks. Where disabled people are evicted from their homes because of the 'bedroom tax' that has been proved to waste money, not save it. Where families and old people living on their own are faced with ever-rising energy bills. Both in Scotland and in England, we have an education system that is failing working-class children, because of a failure to recognise that many pre-fives have needs that are not being met.

The war in Afghanistan began in 2001, the year I left Parliament. I remember telling my brother, Jim, who had become an American citizen, that no foreign force had ever managed to subdue their fierce tribesmen in the hills. He thought that record might change. No doubt a lot of people in the Pentagon and amongst our own top brass thought so too.

We were told we were going to protect women's rights to education and medical treatment, concepts regarded as ungodly by the Taliban. Well, that was a great success, wasn't it? Today we hear from women in Afghanistan that they fear things will be little better, if at all, when the British troops pull out. The Taliban's successors may be an improvement in some respects, but their attitude to women is no better. Women are still at risk of murder if they dare to run a secret school for girls. The Ministry of Justice has been drawing up a draft revision of the country's penal code, to bring back public stoning – banned in many Muslim-majority countries – as a punishment for sex outside marriage. The Parliament has already cut the number of seats set aside for women on provincial councils. It drew up a criminal code that will make it almost impossible to convict anyone for domestic violence.

There was talk of ending the farming of poppies for opium, and encouraging farmers to grow other crops. And certainly there were attempts to do so, but now we learn that there are huge poppy fields, not just poor farmers scratching a living, and they get away with it because they have friends in high places.

Our troops have been out there, in a hideous climate, constantly in danger of losing their lives to these fanatics, and a lot of the time not even equipped to the best of our ability. This, at a time when the Navy has more admirals than ships. Many, indeed, probably a large majority of these soldiers, realise winning hearts and minds is what they are required to do. Therefore, one might imagine that any soldier convicted of child molestation would be booted out the army and sent back home. At the time of writing, this has not yet happened. Is it too much to ask that our words are backed by deeds? Don't senior officers realise that this puts every decent soldier in yet more danger, while the Taliban no doubt cannot believe their luck at this propaganda coup?

Then the Iraq war began in 2003. It still seems stupefying to me that a *Labour* Prime Minister stood side by side with one of the most right wing Presidents in USA history. Remember, Gordon Brown in his role as Chancellor had already paid off our debt from the Second World War to the USA, so the perennial wisdom in politics that you must try not to upset your creditors was no longer relevant. Tony spent a lot of time persuading Bush that he ought to promote a 'road map' to peace in the Middle East, in order to persuade the Arab countries to join the coalition of the willing. Does that ring any bells? It did with me. Precisely the same carrot was dangled during the first Gulf War, and by now the Arabs were incandescent over the failure to make progress in all that time, while Israel continued to flout UN resolutions. The Middle East is now in an even worse state than it was then. Israel has built thousands of settlers' homes on Palestinian territories. Since this land is necessary for a Palestinian state, the likelihood of a two-state solution is lessened with every foundation that is dug. So, while we lost patience with Iraq, no such impatience was shown towards Israel.

Did Tony Blair really believe there were Iraqi weapons of mass destruction aimed at us? Not only that, but ready to be fired against us at any moment? Would that explain why Hans Blix was refused time to carry out further searches? No, I think the real answer is this: Blix was called off because he would soon be able to confirm there were no WMDs, and where would that leave those who had every intention of attacking Iraq, WMDs or none.

The other reason for going to war was, of course, regime change. Those of us who marched against the war were offended, but not surprised, at the establishment claim that we were supporting Saddam Hussein. I don't remember anyone saying that killing 3,000 Kurds in one day was fine by us. There were huge anti-war demonstrations in 60 countries. In London it was a million-strong, the largest in British history. Had all these people suddenly become fans of this brutal dictator?

The obvious question was put back: are the British people to be expected to fight wars against every dictator in the world? Or if some, but not others, on what criteria? In Burma the military junta were massacring its own population. But seeing China was their ally, not much ever got done about that. The United States itself had quite a record of upholding deeply unpleasant regimes. Seemingly it was ok to throw dissidents out of aeroplanes or have people 'disappear', provided it was done by governments that were friendly to the USA.

I agreed with Tony Blair when he said you cannot expect the USA to be attacked as they were on 11 September 2001 and not retaliate. I just assumed that meant against those who did it. But the Twin Towers massacre was not planned and executed by the Iraqi Government. In fact, Saddam Hussein was a secularist opposed to Islamic extremism.

I can do no better, as a summary of the argument that persuaded me in 2003, than to quote from Robin Cook's resignation speech:

> The reality is that Britain is being asked to embark on a war without agreement in any of the international bodies of which we are a leading partner – not NATO, not the European Union, and now, not the Security Council... Our interests are best protected not by unilateral action but by a multilateral agreement and a world order governed by rules... What has come to trouble me most over the past weeks is the suspicion that if the hanging chads in Florida had gone the other way and Al Gore had been elected, we would not now be about to commit British troops.

MPs stood up to clap and cheer, brushing aside the long-standing convention that approval should only be indicated by a decorous tapping of the bench in front, or a 'hear, hear'. It has never happened before, or since.

A majority voted to support the war, but not all who did were simply sucking up to the Yanks. Some thought a lasting Middle East settlement might come out of it. If you read Alastair Campbell's memoirs, you will grasp that Tony Blair put in stupendous efforts to try to influence Bush, particularly over the Middle East and the importance of the second resolution at the UN. At one point Bush told Blair he didn't need to join the coalition for war against Iraq if that made things too tough at home. The USA could manage without Britain. But in the end, Blair was so convinced he had to support Bush he would rather step down as Labour Prime

Minister than give in to the building opposition within his own Party. In the course of the run up to the invasion, in the view of Sir Christopher Myer, our Ambassador to the United States at the time, Tony 'became an honorary member of the Bush inner group of neo-conservative hawks while moderates such as US Secretary of State Colin Powell were relegated to the outer fringe'. Judging by events as they unrolled, there seems no reason to doubt it.

I find that degree of involvement extraordinary, and quite the opposite of what I would expect from a Labour Prime Minister of this country. Yet there were plenty of others who had no inside knowledge, no engagement with the negotiations, but who simply believed it was our duty to save Iraqi citizens from this monster. I think they were mistaken, but it was an honourable mistake.

If anyone could have foreseen that ten years on, Iraq would be riven by Sunni and Shia fighting, with 180,000 dead as result of the violence, I wonder if they would have thought that a price worth paying to get a pro-western prime minister.

As a Glaswegian, of course, I took pride in our city's answer to the attempted firebombing of our airport in 2007 by a two-man Islamic extremist bomb squad. Who turned out, incredibly to most people, to be doctors. Good grief, doctors! People who you believe are devoted to saving lives. They may or may not have seen themselves as martyrs. But when they were tackled by John Smeaton and the other guys, it certainly was suicidal. His quote – 'Glasgow doesnae accept this. If you come tae Glasgow we'll set aboot ye' – went around the world and was even to be seen printed on t-shirts in California. And incidentally, Smeaton never claimed he was the sole or main hero. He was simply around for the newshounds, seeing he was at his work, while the others who had tackled the terrorists had left the scene to board planes or gone home. One was taken to hospital in an ambulance.

Thinking about weapons of mass destruction brings up the question of Trident. On 27 May 2013 Hans Blix, the former UN weapons inspector, urged Britain should give up our own WMDs. He pointed out that Germany and Japan had no such weapons, and they suffered no loss of respect. The British military are not keen on it. Even Michael Portillo opposes it. He pointed out, 'It is neither independent, nor is it any kind of deterrent. It is a tremendous waste of money and is done entirely for reasons of national prestige.' He is right.

Yet, for as long as anyone can remember, it has been thought the British public would not vote for unilateral nuclear disarmament. Tony Blair writes in his memoirs that in 2007 he hesitated over the renewal of Trident. There was a case either way. The missiles were hugely costly, a declining deterrence and would never be used. To give them up, however, would mark a downgrading of the UK, and, he thought, a defence risk. So he renewed.

So, how do we set about getting rid of it? For years now the SNP has promised it would get rid of Trident from the Clyde come Independence. The White Paper says the 'aim and intention' is to remove Trident from Faslane 'with a view' to achieving this by 2020. I don't know whether they really believe this themselves, but they argue that when an independent Scotland does that, they will have done the rest of the UK a favour, as the submarines cannot be berthed anywhere else around the British coastline on account of the inordinate expense of creating a new home for them. This is drivel. No-one would spend umpteen billions on a weapons system that could only be parked in one place. Yes, it would be hugely expensive to bring some other port up to scratch, but can anyone really doubt the British State would do it if they continued to see a need for it? There are a number of ports worth considering in such an event. The MP for Barrow-in-Furness, for one, would love to have the jobs for his constituency.

But a fresh angle on the subject was raised when Alex Salmond announced in 2013 that a SNP Government of an independent Scotland would wish to remain in NATO. Not only that, the USA could have army camps here too. To what purpose was not explained. Does he think the USA needs them, when they have umpteen already dotted throughout Europe? Presumably, if they had any such desire, they would have already mentioned it to their ever-willing ally. Now we learn from the White Paper that an independent Scotland would allow submarines and warships armed with nuclear weapons from the USA and other NATO countries to dock in its ports 'without confirming or denying whether they carry nuclear weapons'. Many a long-standing Nationalist, who sat down against Polaris at the Holy Loch, must be sadly saying: if this is an independent, nuclear-free Scotland, they can keep it.

There is no shortcut to getting rid of Trident. No hey presto solution. We will do so when enough of the British public want rid of it. At a cost of £100 billion for its renewal, and considering the deepening austerity to be imposed on us if George Osborne gets his way, who knows how soon this may happen.

* * *

As we grind our way towards Referendum Day, I look back on the past 13 years in Scottish politics. The Scottish Parliament had barely begun its work when I left Westminster in 2001, but it had started to make its presence felt. It soon became clear that it could, and would, do things differently from Westminster. Each could learn from the other. The outstanding difference was how it looked. Here was a Parliament with a large number of women, Labour having ensured that its own ranks contained equal numbers of women and men.

The Parliament having been run for eight years by a Lib-Lab coalition, the SNP won a minority government in 2007, and spent the next four years getting their budgets approved with the backing of the Tories. Then, having won a majority in 2011, they now have the gall to present themselves as the true upholders of social democratic values against, er, the Tories.

When they are challenged about inadequacies on numerous fronts, who is to blame? The Tories. Never themselves. I wish I had a pound for every time I have heard a Nat say nothing can be done until we gain independence. They want the Tories to continue pursuing their austerity programme, because that may steer many a voter, suffering hardship and seeing no end in sight, towards voting Yes in the referendum.

This 'nothing can be done until we are independent' line is particularly deplorable, because that is *not* what they said when seeking votes in 2011. They repeated again and again that this was not a vote for independence. They were simply asking for a vote of confidence in the capability they had shown as a minority government. Then, when they won, they immediately claimed 'Scots want Independence'. Now there would be a referendum in due course. The cry was 'What do we want? FREEEE...DOM!!! When do we want it? Er, not yet. What's the hurry?'

Then a few years ago my old chum Johann Lamont was elected as Scottish Labour Leader. She is tackling Alex Salmond so incisively people are beginning to feel sorry for him. What she has successfully nailed, more than any of her predecessors in the Scottish Parliament, is that the SNP has spent years campaigning for independence, but has not thought through the nuts and bolts of the many issues that arise from separating ourselves from the rest of the UK. Nor do they pay sufficient attention to the matters they can deal with now, with the powers they presently have, while they spend our money planning how to win the referendum.

A few years ago Salmond came out with a statement that is so economically illiterate it seems surprising that he studied economics at all at St. Andrew's University. He argued that Scotland objected to Margaret Thatcher's social policies, but not to her economic policies. But a huge range of social policies flow from economic policies. What do you tax? How much do you tax? Large state or small state? What are your spending priorities?

If there is one policy Alex Salmond is absolutely clear about it, it is that he intends to set corporation tax 3p lower than whatever an English chancellor sets it at. It has already been reducing since 1999, when Gordon Brown reduced it from 33 per cent to 28 per cent. But that is considerably higher than the current 23 per cent, due to fall to 20 per cent under the present Westminster Government. Which means 17 per cent under Salmond's plan for Scotland. Our great social democrat wants to tax big business less than the Tory Chancellor.

Reduction to this level is neither social democratic nor a smart move. They want to draw jobs and business opportunities away from England. At the same time, they expect England to agree to all sorts of favourable outcomes for Scotland in the negotiations over the breakup of our shared institutions. What is to stop England undercutting Scotland in turn? Brigadoon was more realistic than this.

In May 2013 Jim McColl called for this size of cut in corporation tax, and just for good measure he added he'd like no capital gains tax as well. Alex Salmond not only agreed to the first demand, he claimed it would gain Scotland 27,000 jobs. There is no evidence whatsoever that cutting corporation tax creates more jobs in the country where the tax is levied. Capital is international and big corporations look for other advantages that are more important, such as lower wage costs and cheaper transport of raw materials and finished products. It can be so unscrupulous that sweatshop workers die in a fire in a building the workforce complained was unsafe. Here at home a health and safety rep on a building site can be secretly blacklisted, and kept out of work for decades. Ricky Tomlinson has recently pointed out that 49 construction workers were killed at work in 2011–2012. So, having run an Anti-Blacklisting Campaign in my own time in Parliament, I am glad to see Ian Davidson MP and his colleagues on the Scottish select committee take up this issue so strongly, and hope they succeed where previous efforts have failed to finally put a stop to this blot on our democracy. It is mildly surprising to hear David Cameron state he is against blacklisting. John Major's view was that employers had a right to know whether anyone was a 'troublemaker'.

* * *

Parties of the left who support the Yes campaign are, of course, opposed to cuts in corporation tax, joining NATO, and keeping the Queen. What they hope is that Scotland will be a land in which their views will prevail. So far, the record is not promising. They have not succeeded in getting a single candidate elected to the Scottish Parliament since Tommy Sheridan came to grief. Nor have they persuaded the SNP to drop their commitment to NATO. They don't seem to realise that if Scotland votes Yes, the White Paper is what we will get, not the wish list they didn't try all that hard to win.

But another difficulty the ultra-left nationalists are so far failing to see is this. Over four-fifths of large corporations in Scotland are externally owned. Nearly all the biggest employers in Scotland are UK-owned and controlled, quoted on the London Stock Exchange, or dependent on the £60 million UK market. None of us need reminding of the power that the City exerts. It has been able so far to fend off all efforts to make it come to heel. Does anyone really believe that a newly-independent small nation could enforce its will on the financial sector more successfully?

Then again, they act as if the Con-Dem Government's attacks on the welfare state are going to go on for ever. But the next General Election has to be in 2015, only months after the Referendum.

These small vanguard parties have never shown much interest in women's rights. The Trotskyist view was that first the revolution had to be won, and women's equality would follow after. To pursue such matters was a bourgeois distraction from the class war.

Nationalist movements generally aren't noticeably better. Here at home we only have to look at the record. Nicola Sturgeon creates a new policy group to look at the welfare state, without one woman being appointed until this was brought to her attention. Six hundred hours of care for three and four year olds was promised by Salmond in 2007. In the closing months of 2013, we were still waiting for it. Then we get told in the White Paper that a full programme that benefits the disadvantaged, and all children from one year upwards, will be delivered following a vote for independence. So, why not get on with it now? Because, we are told, the Income Taxes paid by mothers newly in work, plus those of the nursery workers, needed to pay for it all, would go to the UK Treasury. By that logic, he should not bother travelling abroad to bring jobs to Scotland, as their income taxes, too, would presently go into what he termed 'George Osborne's back pocket'.

* * *

It is impossible to review the last 13 years without considering the loss of the public's trust in politicians. Good, honest and hardworking MPs continue to feel tarnished. There have been endless stories in the media about cash for questions, and expenses claims that were so outrageous they had the nation laughing in disbelief. It never seems to end. That kind of thing brings the miscreant's party and parliament itself into disrepute, and ought to result in expulsion and loss of their seat. But it's not right that people should be led to believe that 'they're all at it'. It is disheartening for those who are trying to serve their constituency and their country and meet doubt and hostility when there are no grounds for it. Worse than that, it is dangerous for our democracy. For if we don't believe we can elect an honest person to represent us in our Parliament, where do we end up?

If it had not been for the Hacked Off campaign, and campaigning journalists, we would not have known about the poor moral standards in some sections of the press, when the hacking scandal was revealed. We had all known about the Murdoch empire's power over politicians, but Hillsborough and the Millie Dowler scandals were the last straws for most of us. So it was particularly gratifying to see Ed Miliband and Tom Watson stand up to Murdoch. I hope yet to see controls that prevent the press from lying about ordinary people who have done no harm to anyone, while not dismantling in any way the ability of investigative journalists to expose bad things going on.

Conclusion

We are living through a bad period, but there is no need for despair. TINA isn't true. If enough of us care enough about our welfare state to defend it then we will win through. But how to do it?

I think it is time we revised our notion of how to do politics. On the left we tend to think we have achieved something when we have written a motion that was supported at a conference of like-minded people. We are far too fond of thinking we have done something when all we have done is tell our leaders what to do.

Contrast that with how Mary Barbour did her politics. She led the Glasgow tenants to victory against the private landlords who had been hiking up their rents during the First World War. She secured a change in the law that benefited the whole of Britain. When she became one of the first few women councillors in Glasgow in 1920, two years after women first won the right to vote in national elections, she campaigned for children's play parks, wash houses, municipal baths, free milk for schoolchildren, and organised the first family planning clinic in Glasgow. Again and again she faced down opposition and won. She didn't say, nothing can be done until we've got a Labour Government. With none of the technology we have today at our disposal – they were far too poor to have telephones – Mrs Barbour's Army, backed by the men in the shipyards and munitions factories, won. If these women, who left school at 14, and had to struggle against dirt and disease in their slum tenements, could do all that, what is stopping us?

CHAPTER SEVENTEEN

Where Do We Go From Here?

WE ARE IN THE worst economic depression in nearly a century, but the problems we face are not solved by putting a border between England and Scotland. Quite the reverse. Ownership and control of Scottish industry would still predominantly rest outside Scotland. What makes anyone think a small country of five million would be more successful in dealing with corporate power than a country of 60 million?

Considering, too, that the SNP is committed to living with UK monetary policy and financial regulation, this makes 'independence' seem hardly worth the upheaval. Alex Salmond assures us all would be well. We would have a seat on the Bank of England's monetary policy committee. Has he sought their agreement? No. Has he asked himself why should they, when we have just turned ourselves into a foreign country? No.

But, the cry goes up, if the country votes 'No', we will be left with the status quo. It is claimed that Westminster will see no reason to accommodate the popular desire for further powers for the Scottish Parliament.

Could this expression of public opinion be simply an attempt to compromise between outright separation and sticking with the status quo – a middle road in which we would not get run over? The more realistic Nationalists will see more powers as getting the best they can, seeing it looks unlikely they will win the referendum. At least it would be a stepping stone on the way.

When pollsters asked people what they would like to see added to the Scottish Parliament's powers, quite a few named powers it already has. Not surprising, really, when the present SNP Government would rather concentrate attention on the referendum than use all of its current powers to good effect. But then, if they did, that would not help their argument that they need powers that only independence can give.

The argument that we would be lumbered with the status quo for years to come in the event of a 'No' vote is easily refuted. First, don't forget who delivered the Scottish Parliament. It was the 1997 Labour Government, losing no time in responding, in John Smith's words, to 'the settled will' of the Scottish people. This was no knee-jerk response to seats won by the SNP. It had the wholehearted commitment of John Smith and

Donald Dewar. It was the culmination of the years of work put in by the wide spread of civic society involved in the Scottish Constitutional Convention – in which the SNP played no part whatsoever. I know. I was part of it, chairing a working group on achieving equal representation.

UK Labour naturally wants to keep Scottish votes. It has learned the hard way that great success at General Elections for the House of Commons does not mean similar results will follow for Holyrood. Right wing Labour for many years argued that the left had nowhere else to go, while the message of SNP by-election successes was staring them in the face from the 1967 Hamilton by-election onwards. But people were not voting to break up Britain, as poll after poll has shown for decades. They were using their votes as a protest. Or just to give the other lot a shot.

The Tories and Lib Dems are facing huge unpopularity. If they don't know what to do to turn things round, it is not for me to advise them. Perhaps I could just mention that leaving things unchanged will not win them many votes. While some of the Tory backwoodsmen want rid of Scotland, it bothers the majority that they have so little success in Scotland, Wales and the North of England, because they genuinely believe in the United Kingdom. As for the Lib Dems, their very existence depends on votes around the Celtic fringes. If they cannot regain trust, they will be in no position to affect anything.

We have spent a long time being asked to choose between Devo Max and Devo Plus. The political parties are asked if they will commit themselves to either, in the event of the Yes campaign failing to win the referendum. Devo Max, as defined by the SNP, would mean all revenues were raised in Scotland, with payments made to Westminster for our share of reserved matters. That would mean at least two undesirable consequences. We would lose out on the substantial redistribution of wealth that has existed in the UK for decades. We would still be part of the UK, but have cut ourselves off from such help whenever we have the need. An even worse consequence would be the intention of an SNP Government to cut corporation tax so as to encourage business to come to Scotland, away from England. This could only encourage a race to the bottom, and who pays when the big corporations don't? The rest of us, either in higher taxes or cuts in public services.

Devo Plus has so many interpretations it is impossible to summarise in one short pithy description. But it, too, carries implications that suit business interests more than the rest of us. When the Scottish public says, in answer to polls, that it would like the Scottish Parliament to have more powers, I am certain that few mean giving greater powers to Donald Trump and Rupert Murdoch. Or giving tax breaks to ex-pat millionaires who proclaim their devotion from a safe, tax-avoiding distance.

So, what do we need to do? Start by squaring up to our problems. When Churchill told the nation in 1940 he had nothing to offer but 'blood, toil, tears and sweat' he was right, and when we defeated the forces of Fascism and defended our country, it was one of the proudest times in our history. It's one reason I am happy to call myself British as well as Scottish.

I would offer some suggestions that are, happily, a lot more palatable in our current difficulties.

First, let us make the criterion for any extra powers for Holyrood, or indeed any other elected body, a simple one. Which is in the best interests of our people? Possibly local government, possibly Holyrood, possibly Westminster. Local government is badly in need of reform. The clue is in the name. It should be local *government, not an arm of the central state.* Council tax needs to be reformed so that everyone pays their fair share. It is simply unjust that people living in the highest- banded properties pay a far lower proportion of their income than those living in the bottom-banded ones. And a continued freeze on council tax means the better off benefit even more. So if you're happy with your council tax freeze, just remember it is paid for by the loss of decent home care for the elderly and infirm, libraries, school equipment and road repairs.

But why not go further? When people become teachers, nurses or join the police service they want to do a useful job, not tick boxes designed by people who have never done the job. Can we think of ways to give them a say in the running of their services?

And shouldn't those who are the recipients of these services also get back some of the say they have lost? You do not have to be much of a cynic to regard official consultation as a joke. Again and again, people sourly comment that it's a waste of time, as 'they' will do what they want anyway. We need to rebuild trust in the methods of seeking consent. I myself always found that when you told people the facts, and listened to what they had to say, you could rely on the good sense of most. Even if we disagreed, it was still possible to maintain mutual respect. A dialogue is what is needed, not people being misled, patronised or ignored. We might do better at this if appointments to quangos and health boards were seen to be people with something to offer, rather than rewards to those who will do the bidding of the government of the day, or are too meek to make waves.

Take, for example, the issue of what kind of hospitals people want and need. The first consideration must surely be the welfare of the patient, and at its most basic, the best chance of survival. Which means concentration of expertise in well-equipped units. Who would not rather be operated on by a surgeon who knew the way around that part of your innards, than someone of much more limited experience?

This choice may well result in difficult and expensive journeys for some patients' visitors, but people who drive BMWs to the board room should not be allowed to airily dismiss the inconvenience of those who wait in the rain for a bus, to visit granny in hospital and ensure she is getting decent care. Is it too much to ask that health bosses should do, and be seen to be doing, all that they can to convince public transport operators to co-operate, not shrug and leave it to market forces to determine whether it ever happens. Maybe Government, at appropriate level, could use powers to ensure it happens? And while we're at it, shouldn't bus companies be told to provide adequate services, or get out and leave it to those who can?

We need to rebuild trust in our banking system. Let's never forget it was greed and incompetence at the highest levels in our banks that got us into this mess, not benefits claimants, lone parents or the disabled. Trusting souls that we were, we believed that banks were careful to prevent money laundering. Then we learned that some actually provided that handy service to drug barons and despots. The guilty must be punished. But we need, urgently, to get the country back on its feet, and having a banking system that serves our economic needs is an essential part of the solution. Happily, we can simply vote for it when we have the opportunity. All we have to do is post the ballot paper or make it to the polling station before it closes. We are more likely to succeed in reforming the banking system if they have to answer to a British, rather than a Scottish, government. What success can we think is likely for a small, newly independent nation, in getting banks to behave themselves?

But we also need to defend our fellow citizens who are under attack with cuts not seen in living memory, by a Government that is dismantling the welfare state and using the national debt as their excuse.

We need to recognise that we cannot have Scandinavian social services on Irish taxes. But that's not the whole story. We lose out on tax fraud, bankers' bonuses, and from the failure to implement the Tobin tax. Millionaires get a tax reduction, while social services get cut even more. The poorest should not have to pay for the tax breaks of the rich.

It is particularly scandalous that child poverty is so widespread. There are moves that can be made now, in opening educational opportunity, health, housing and fair pay. It's not England that's the problem, it's the Tories.

The inequalities of class are staring us in the face, and women lose out in many ways. In the debate so far between the Yes and the Better Together campaigns, it is striking that there has been hardly a word about what either prospect holds for women.

Women are less keen on a Scottish breakaway than men. But so far, all I have seen in our media is speculation as to why that might be, and precious little evidence offered. Women more cautious, men more adventurous? Perhaps. Women's recognition of an empty promise when they hear one? Could be. The White Paper did not have a lot to offer women. Not surprising, when we consider that there is not a single improvement in women's lives, voted for in either Holyrood or Westminster, in which the SNP led the way.

National Minimum Wage – voted in by Labour MPs through the night while the Nationalists were tucked up in bed.

Living Wage – put in place by Labour councils from Glasgow to London before the SNP made a move. And a number of people on the Yes campaign board come from sectors where the pay levels are notoriously low.

Equal Pay – only warm words for years. Then no direct help, just permission for councils to borrow money, when they are already in deep difficulties finding money to run services.

Abortion Rights – their health minister would weaken, and the voting record of Alex Salmond at Westminster speaks for itself.

Equal Representation – the Scottish Parliament began life with a substantial number of women MSPs. We were up there with the Scandinavians. Now we have fallen back, because the Nationalists won a majority of seats, but didn't care about their activist women taking their fair share.

And why does all this matter? It is a matter of justice. But not only that. Tackling inequality is also essential for returning to growth. The lack of demand, through people not having enough money to spend, means makers and sellers of goods shut down. Those who own great wealth spend much less of their income than those at the bottom or in the middle.

And women are over-represented at the poor end. So, who do we believe are more likely to tackle inequalities? Those with a record behind them, or those whose record is thin to non-existent? Who is more likely to successfully negotiate agreements to make recalcitrant employers stump up – a British trade union movement, the majority of whose members are now women, or a movement fractured into separate organisations for separate countries with different laws?

Throughout Britain, we who think of ourselves as democratic socialists have ties that bind. The shared history of the Labour movement: the fight for shorter hours and better pay, the right to vote, equal rights for all. The rent strike against greedy landlords in Glasgow during the First World War, that made the Government deliver rent control throughout Britain. The creation of the Welfare State, particularly the NHS, described at the time of the Olympics as Britain's religion. Our internationalism. The statue of Dolores Ibarruri (La Pasionaria) stands in Glasgow at the side of the Clyde, a reminder of those who fought Fascism in Spain, and the millions who died stopping Hitler.

I think back on our history, because we ought to learn from it. If we don't know it, or have a distorted view, we are less likely to form a desirable future. As Aneurin Bevan famously said, 'You don't need a crystal ball when you can read the book'. And I don't mean kings and queens, I mean the history of our being the first industrial nation, the advances gained by struggle, and the warning things can go backwards as well as forwards.

There are people alive in Scotland today who consider themselves oppressed by England. I would recommend they read some history of the past century or two, and realise proud Edward's army stopped marching many centuries ago.